Secret Beaches

of Southern Vancouver Island

QUALICUM *TO THE* MALAHAT

THEO DOMBROWSKI

H
HERITAGE

VANCOUVER · VICTORIA · CALGARY

Heritage House Publishing Company Ltd.
www.heritagehouse.ca

LIBRARY AND ARCHIVES CANADA CATALOGUING IN PUBLICATION

Dombrowski, Theo, 1947–
    Secret beaches of southern Vancouver Island: Qualicum to the Malahat /
Theo Dombrowski.

Includes index.
ISBN 978-1-894974-97-4

    1. Beaches—British Columbia—Vancouver Island—Guidebooks.
2. Recreation areas—British Columbia—Vancouver Island—Guidebooks.
3. Qualicum Beach Region (B.C.)—Guidebooks. 4. Malahat Region
(B.C.)—Guidebooks. 5. Vancouver Island (B.C.)—Guidebooks. I. Title.

FC3844.4.D64 2010   796.5'3097112   C2009-906914-8

editor: Lenore Hietkamp
proofreader: Karla Decker
designer: Jacqui Thomas
maps, artwork and photos: Theo Dombrowski

Printed in Canada

This book was printed with FSC-certified, acid-free paper,
processed chlorine free and printed with vegetable-based inks.

Heritage House acknowledges the financial support for its publishing program from
the Government of Canada through the Canada Book Fund (CBF), Canada Council
for the Arts and the province of British Columbia through the British Columbia Arts
Council and the Book Publishing Tax Credit.

BRITISH COLUMBIA
ARTS COUNCIL

CONTENTS

INTRODUCTION

Imagine suddenly discovering your house has rooms you never knew existed. The discovery is magical, even breathtaking. Who would have thought that the familiar old place had more and yet more wonderful places hidden within it?

Then imagine yourself in the outdoors, making the parallel discovery of hidden, wonderful beaches that you never dreamed existed. For, in fact, the eastern shoreline of mid-to-southern Vancouver Island—the scope of this volume—is full of magic doors that open on hidden or little known beaches. These beaches differ enormously from each other, both in their physical features and in the way they are administered. Some are community parks, large tracts of land, often the size of several waterfront lots. A few others are provincial parks, municipal parks, regional parks or simply raw chunks of undeveloped land.

THE VANCOUVER ISLAND BEACH

The word "beach" is used here in the way most people who live on Vancouver Island would use the word—loosely. For us, a "beach" is simply a shorefront. It can be covered with sand, pebbles, boulders or even slabs of rock. Now, we all know that some people, usually from southern climes, become (politely) superior when they consider our use of the word "beach." To them, unless it is an unbroken expanse of golden sand bashed by surf, it is not a beach at all. In fact, there is a true story about a wealthy woman from Australia who came on holiday to central Vancouver Island to experience, among other things, the beaches. After staring disapprovingly at the *grey* sand beaches of Parksville and Qualicum, she went straight to a local travel agent and first implored, then insisted, that she be flown somewhere, *any* place, where she could spend her beach holiday on *golden* sand. One wonders if she noticed that the beaches of the interior lakes of the Okanagan—for this is where she was flown—had no tides and no surf. Let such people betake themselves elsewhere. The rest of us know what a beach is, and we love our beaches!

Finding these beaches is not always easy, but that is part of their charm. The technical maps used by regional district or municipal offices can be misleading. You can waste many hours combing back roads looking for what appears on a map to be a perfectly viable access to the waterfront but turns out to be something altogether different. Sometimes it will be an impassable tangle of blackberry vines blocking a steep descent through heavy brush to a cliff face—not the most enticing approach to waterfront bliss. Sometimes it will look for all the world like part of someone's manicured property, giving you the distinct impression that you will be trespassing if you take a single step in the direction of the shore. On the other hand, it may also be an enticing, well-beaten path, winding through arbutus and oaks to a magnificent view and a perfect picnic spot on a polished pebble beach.

PUBLIC ACCESS

Most of the "public access" routes to the beaches in this book are government-owned land lying between private waterfront lots. These routes lead to shoreline that is free for public use. However, the conscientious beachgoer should know a few further facts. The term "foreshore" is used by the government to describe the beach area between low tide and high tide. Even when the land above the foreshore is private, the public generally has the privilege of using the foreshore and the water beyond it, though not the right to do so. When this area has been granted special status, such as a lease for farming oysters, the public does not have access. Often signs are posted if the public is restricted from using the foreshore.

We have the privilege of enjoying the beaches in this book, a privilege that entails responsibility. This book was written with two key beliefs:

- In keeping with the ideals of the community of which we are all a part, everyone who lives on Vancouver Island (and, indeed, visitors to our paradise) should be able to enjoy waterfront that is, after all, public property.

- The kind of person who will make a point of seeking out a little-known beach will be the kind of person who values quiet beauty and undamaged natural settings.

This introduction explains not only how to use this book to discover the many wonders of Vancouver Island's secret beaches, but also how to behave as a conscientious beachgoer.

BEACH ACCESS WARNING

Quite understandably, many waterfront property owners and other locals want to keep their secret beaches *secret*. Who, after all, doesn't enjoy seclusion by the waterfront (other than, perhaps, those who have been working hard at the gym to build the perfect Beach Body)? More important, what property owners welcome cars blocking driveways and high-decibel midnight parties, not to mention rotting litter, aromatic dog excrement, gutted berry patches, depleted clam and oyster beds or ugly firepits? No one finds such abuse acceptable, neither waterfront owner nor visitor. On the other hand, the more people who visit the shorefront, the more beachgoers there will be to encourage its preservation. Everyone who loves our shores will doubtless find in the pleasures and peace of the "secret beach" the inspiration to act on behalf of these and all other areas of natural beauty.

BEACHES IN THIS BOOK

Only about half of the public access spots in the mid-to-southern area of the Island are fully described in this book, and there is little point in writing about the others. Those who are determined to get to *all* such places can get an appropriate map from a regional district or municipal office and follow it to their heart's content. They will find that nearly all

Mariner Way

of the spots excluded from this book exist only in terms of legal status. There are several spots in the Dolphin Beach and Beachcomber areas or around Cedar, for example, where anyone determined to get to the shore will have to be very, very determined. Such a determined person will have to come with surveying equipment and the bushwhacking skills of Indiana Jones. Other spots are omitted because they are close to similar but more appealing spots. Such preferable spots may offer better parking, for example, or an easier path.

In contrast, a few places have been included even though they are not, by most people's standards, very attractive. They might, for example, bring you to an estuary rich in bird life. Or they might be a convenient place to launch a kayak. Others have an idiosyncratic character. They are the kind of place you might like to visit once every few years, more out of interest than anything else. There is no reason you should trust the value judgements that lard this book—they arise from irrepressible enthusiasm or from mild distaste, not from a desire to warp visitors' reactions to their beach experience!

THE GREAT BEACH EXPERIENCE

Armed with this book, then, and sensitive to the possible impact of their beach-going on local residents and the beaches themselves, the adventurous can head out with camera, sunscreen and picnic basket. To be sure that you have a wonderful beach experience, however, consider the following.

Weather The first question that anyone with an iota of West Coast experience will ask before going to the beach is, "What will the weather be like?" Even a sunny day does not guarantee a pleasant experience. As any *real* West Coaster will tell you, your beach experience is affected by not just the cloud cover and precipitation, which you can find out from basic weather forecasts, but also the *wind*. Use this book to identify which beaches are partially or fully exposed to which winds. Unfortunately, most radio or newspaper weather forecasters will tell you little or nothing about the wind, except for tossing in the occasional phrase "windy near the water."

Enter the *marine forecast*. This kind of forecast is readily available by telephone as a recording (250-245-8899) or on the Web as printed script at http://www.weatheroffice.gc.ca/. To find the online forecast, simply type "marine forecast Nanaimo," for example, in your search window and you will soon be looking at a prediction something like "Strait of Georgia, winds light in the morning, rising to northwest 20 knots late morning and dropping this evening." In fact, a version of this particular forecast is the one you are most likely to find during the summer (when, let's face it, most of us head to the beach). Almost every warm, sunny day with settled conditions on the east coast of central Vancouver Island begins with barely a breeze. Before long, however, the first ripples spread across the mirror-like surface, and before breakfast is long over the first whitecaps appear. For the next several hours the Strait is alive with the brisk, deep-blue charge of waves that makes for an intoxicatingly beautiful summer day on the water.

These conditions, however, make for some pretty chilly sunbathing or sandcastle building. This is where your handy book is so important. Except on the warmest days, and unless you enjoy the exhilaration of beachcombing with wind in your hair, you will have to make some decisions: wait until late morning, when northwest winds may have subsided; bring a sweater; or *look for beaches that are not exposed to northwest winds.*

But don't get cocky. This particular daily pattern is common, but in some conditions, and especially during very warm weather, the northwest wind can blow all day long and all night. If, for example, you head off late afternoon to Madrona Point (south of Parksville) with your canoe, expecting a dinner picnic and a paddle over silken seas beneath a radiant sunset outlining Mount Arrowsmith, you might just have to change your plans. Check the forecast or be prepared to be flexible with your plans.

Don't always expect northwest winds in sunny weather. Although these winds dominate during the summer, they aren't inevitable. In fact, it is entirely possible to have sunny skies and winds from the southeast, the other most common wind direction. It is true, nevertheless, that southeast winds often mean the weather is becoming a little iffy. This kind of southeast wind seems most often to arise in the afternoon and fade in the evening. During bad weather, you can (almost) guarantee any winds will be from the southeast. Unlike northwest winds, southeast winds near the water tend to feel cold. Still, if you use this book properly, you can find delightful beaches either fully or partially protected from a southeast wind and enjoy a blissful bask. Before trusting too fully in a wind forecast, though, remember that in the southern area of the coast covered by this book the winds can be fluky. Once winds funnel through the Gulf Islands, as they often do, their direction and strength are unpredictable.

Beware the Qualicum winds. These winds, though rare, can be a little dangerous, particularly for people planning an evening paddle and, as the name suggests, particularly in the Qualicum area and extending to Nanoose Bay in the south and Bowser in the north. Watch out for these winds, because they can arise suddenly, can be intensely gusty, and in most places are "offshore"; that is, they will tend to blow the weak paddler away from the shore.

But don't avoid all blustery days. You might, in fact, particularly enjoy a strong wind. In a storm, for example, it can be thrilling to drive to the end of Cottam Point and watch the giant waves crash around you. Likewise, kite flying can be a great diversion on a windy day—if you choose a long flat beach and arrive at low tide when it is not underwater! Then, too, there are those (few) stiflingly hot days we have each summer when a windy section of shore feels delightful while everywhere inland feels the opposite.

And don't avoid foul, rainy weather. In even the worst weather, you can, by consulting this book, find some great spots to park your car in full view of the shore and enjoy a cozy car picnic while simultaneously feeding your soul on the splendours of the wind, waves and gulls. In fact, winter, when we are treated to most of the foul weather, is also the best time for spotting sea lions and many species of waterfowl that spend their summers in the far north. Be careful, though, if you venture onto the shore, since rocks are often more slippery in winter than in summer.

Sun direction Do you want to sunbathe on a baking bit of shore or picnic in a patch of cool shade? Use this book to select just the right beach. We tend to think of beaches as being permanently in sun on a sunny day. Because the coast of Vancouver Island has many large trees and many steep shores, however, a particular piece of shore can be deeply in shadow for part of the day. Use this book to consider the right time of day for finding sun or shade on your beach.

You will find that, on this part of Vancouver Island, the morning is most often the sunniest time of day, at least for the upper shore. This pattern arises—think about it—because the coastline in most places faces northeast. There are many exceptions to this pattern, however. You will find in this book some spots that get afternoon sun and a few (a very few) that allow you to picnic in the full sweep of evening sun. Don't forget the seasons, though. Both the length of shadows and the time of day at which they appear on a beach or disappear from it will significantly vary between even June and September, let alone in December.

Tides Beaches can, of course, change character completely between high and low tide. This is particularly the case where tides go out a long way. The same beach that is a tempting swimming spot with turquoise waters over sun-dappled pebbles can, at low tide, be a broad swath of oysters, barnacle-covered boulders and tidal pools. Panting for a swim, you might arrive at a beach to find a nice sandy shore, yes—but *far too much* of this nice sandy shore between you and the water. Conversely, and especially in winter, you might arrive shod and snack-laden for a favourite shore tromp—only to find that the shore is under water. You cannot use this book to predict tides, except in a very general way. You can, however, use it in combination with your tide tables to decide the best time of day or best day of the week to go to your chosen spot.

Learn about tidal patterns. As all Islanders know, we have two high tides each day and, it follows, two low tides. All Islanders also know

Madrona Point

that the sequence moves forward about an hour each day, so that if, for example, the tide is high at 4:30 p.m. on Tuesday, it will be high at approximately 5:30 on Wednesday. Not all Islanders, however, are familiar with other patterns. In the summer the tides tend to follow one pattern, and in the winter the reverse.

This seasonal shift should help you in your planning once you realize that tides are generally *in* during the day in winter and generally *out* during the day in summer. That general effect is created because in mid-summer, any high tide during the middle of the day will not be very high; in fact, it will often seem like a half tide. Similarly, any low tide in late afternoon or evening will not be very low; it, too, will seem like a half tide. You can launch your kayak easily in late morning and come back to the shore a few hours later without discovering you now have to carry it over a hundred metres of rocks. In contrast, if the low tide occurs mid morning, it is likely to be very low, and its companion high tide in mid-to-late afternoon is likely to be very high. On wide expanses of beach, this water comes rushing in over the warmed pebbles or sand. These tides often produce the warmest swimming, though the warmth can be a little patchy as the newly warmed surface water is still "floating" over the comparatively colder water.

This, then, is the pattern of mid-summer. In early and late summer, the pattern is a little different. If you're looking for days with extreme tides in early summer, expect an afternoon low tide to be extremely low; in late summer, expect a morning low tide to be equally low. Confused? Simply search out one of the dozens of websites that provide tide tables. The most official one is through Fisheries and Oceans Canada (http://www.waterlevels.gc.ca/).

Children We all associate the seaside with children and sandcastles. Public access routes can certainly lead you to many wonderful spots with sand and warm tidal pools. The few large expanses of sand have, thankfully, been snapped up for the big public parks: Qualicum, Parksville, Rathtrevor and Bamberton. If, however, you are using this book primarily as a way of finding places for your children to build sandcastles, you will be restricted.

Nevertheless, one strategy for finding beaches for children away from the big parks is to recognize that even a small area of sand can afford lots of entertainment. Almost half of the spots in this book offer this kind of beach-going experience. Another strategy is to break the stereotypes. Children can play for hours in rocky tidal pools attempting—fruitlessly— to catch "bullheads" (actually sculpins), or building magical little kingdoms of seaweed, rocks and seashells for their shore-crab citizens. Likewise, and particularly with adults leading the way, children can discover wonderful creatures under boulders at low tide—the frantically wiggling eel-like "blennies," for example, or the porcelain crab with the single giant claw, or the deliciously slimy leather star.

Some beaches, too, are magical with polished pebbles. Even adults can spend hours sifting through the multicoloured little gems looking for favourites. Other beaches, particularly if made of sandstone, have great skipping stones, or great stones for making not sandcastles but rock castles. And don't forget the hours of play that can be had on the shores with fantastic rock formations just begging to be climbed over, conquered or converted into fantasylands.

Because there is nothing much on our beaches that will hurt children, life is made comparatively easy for protective parents. Perhaps the greatest threat is the oyster or barnacle, those sharp-edged creatures whose wounds constitute the rite-of-passage for all Vancouver Island children.

Jack Road

Despite the relative safety of our beaches, remember that antibiotic cream and some colourful Band-Aids, along with the sunscreen, can be useful items in the beach bag.

Not all of the beaches in this book are suitable for children, though. Adults will enjoy a steep path through broken rocks and arbutus to a bluff with a magnificent view of the Winchelsea Islands and the Coast Mountains. They will enjoy sipping their favourite drink, pulling out their watercolour set or juicy novel and finding a nest amidst amazing rock formations. They will not, however, enjoy watching a toddler teeter toward the edge of a cliff or wail as she attempts to struggle through a maze of weed-covered giant boulders, crashing and slithering to a bloody-handed halt.

So read the descriptions and advice in this book carefully. If you have a high panic threshold and nimble, adventurous children, you can have a wonderful time at some of the lumpier beaches. Do, however, consider what you will be facing and what decisions you will have to make once you get there. Be prepared to move on if a beach isn't suitable for your children. One of the delights of this area is that beaches even a hundred metres apart can be wildly different in character.

Signs Glorious confusion and amazing inconsistency reigns in the world of beach signs. Some beach access spots are heavily burdened with signs. Many have none. Some have one kind, some another. In some places you will find two access spots a hundred metres apart, one of them carefully signposted, the other with only a half-hidden path to guide your way. As you hunt down a remote beach, you will want to have some knowledge of what signs to expect. Signs will help you know you're not lost. At several locations, in fact, the only indication that you have come to a public access trail is a single sign warning against fires or collecting shellfish. Signs will also help you plan. If you know that you must leave a shore at 10 p.m., there's no point selecting the spot for stargazing in the summer. Likewise, if you're planning a wiener roast, you will want to know where fires are not allowed. Fire restrictions often increase in the summer, but at some spots fires are not allowed any time of year. Dog walkers will want to know where Cuddles must stay on a leash or is not allowed at all. Similarly, if you're hunting for ingredients for your paella, there's no point coming to a beach with a shellfish warning sign.

Signs can change quickly, though, so don't treat everything you read in this book as gospel. Below are the signs you are most likely to encounter.

Public access (or beach access or public beach access) In the Parksville area, these are often small blue rectangles atop a bevelled post. Throughout the area, signs also appear on low cubes of concrete. Near Ladysmith, they are mounted on monumental rock cairns, while around Mill Bay, signs are vertical, about 30 cm long, and attached to a waist-high post or road sign. And so on. These are the friendly, welcoming assurances that you are at the right spot and belong here. Many plots of public access land do not have them, however. At a few places, original signs have been carefully crafted, carved or painted out of a whole range of materials. They make you feel welcome, but their source is tantalizingly mysterious. In the Nanaimo area, dynamic—but often faded—red-and-white signs are sometimes used, posted on a main road (like Stephenson Point Road) where they actually seem to encourage beachgoers to leave the beaten track.

Park In fact, some parks are merely designated areas, completely undeveloped; others are beautifully managed parks with benches, picnic tables and washrooms. The largest and, generally, most beautiful parts of shorefront you will find in this book are community parks, "nature parks," regional parks, municipal parks or even provincial parks. Don't limit yourself to parks, though, or you will miss some real gems.

Danger/Shellfish area closed Some of these signs have been in place for decades and are so faded that one wonders about them. One particularly wonders about those that are posted where beaches are also oyster leases. Some recent versions of these signs have a prominent skull and crossbones to give a ghoulish panache to the message. Unless you make some rigorous inquiries, it is best to heed the warning of these signs, even the very old, nearly illegible ones.

Do not dump refuse Ironically, at many access spots this is the clearest—and only—indication that you have found the right location. In fact, at a few of these spots, locals have evidently decided to ignore the sign and gleefully used them to dump their grass clippings or other garden waste.

Dead-end road/No turnaround These are the yellow and black road signs at the beginning of a cul-de-sac that make you feel really, really unwelcome. It is tempting to speculate how these signs found their way to the beginning of some dead-end roads and not others. Occasionally, just occasionally, one wonders about the enthusiasm locals feel for having *outsiders* in their neighbourhood. The alternative NO THRU ROAD, after all, conveys the same information but less threateningly. Not surprisingly, the NO TURNAROUND signs are misleading. Unless you are driving a semi-trailer or some large Winnebago-beast, you will find yourself perfectly capable of turning around at the end of these roads— you are not condemned to remain, as they suggest, forever jammed at the end of the road in question. In one particularly striking case in the Fairwinds area, while a sign declares very vehemently that there is no turnaround, in fact there is a very *large* turnaround with a garden in the centre.

No overnight parking Again, this is sometimes the only indication that you have found a public access spot. Presumably there have been bad experiences with Winnebago juggernauts blocking such spots or even using the landscape as a toilet. Otherwise, one wonders what is the harm in a camper dozing away for a few hours on a secluded spot on a secluded road. Still, the sign should be heeded, even if you are hoping to use this book as a source of get-away-overnight information. Often the hours are posted, again with intriguing diversity. Usually they are 10 or 11 p.m. to

6 or 7 a.m. But stargazers feeling thwarted in the freewheeling mid-Island area, take heart. In more southerly places around Victoria, between 9 p.m. and 7 a.m., no one is allowed on the beach at all—or even to park on adjoining streets.

Tsunami warning A few beaches are posted with signs that show a dramatic wave washing ashore. These signs warn beachgoers to move to higher ground in the case of an earthquake. This is a good warning, but one wonders why you will see this sign at one beach and not at a beach a hundred metres away with an equally exposed and low foreshore.

No fires (or fire ban or no open fires) Sometimes conveyed through words, sometimes through symbols, these are, perhaps of all the signs, the most important to heed.

Dog or pet signs One assumes the "pets" in question are dogs. It is hard to imagine what else these might mean. Sometimes the signs tell you to keep your pet on a leash, but more often they are concerned with your pet's excrement. Particularly charming are the signs with the diagram of a squatting dog slashed through with a red line. At some access points, plastic bags are provided. In fact, the creativity and enthusiasm of locals in creating signs for dog owners could make a special study! Waggish exclamations about "pooper scoopers" and invitations to "Paws here,

Rover" are probably trumped by the Osborne Bay sign written in Doggy Talk. You have to see it!

Wildlife management area At many access points in the Parksville–Qualicum area, attractive blue diamond-shaped signs will tell you YOU ARE ENTERING PARKSVILLE–QUALICUM BEACH WILDLIFE MANAGEMENT AREA. Lest you feel that you mustn't enter, they pleasantly add "WELCOME" in large letters. There is a brown variation of this sign with a First Nations design in the centre and *without* the word "welcome." Presumably these signs do not suggest that visitors *shouldn't* set foot on the beach.

Brants In the Parksville–Qualicum area, wherever access is to a flat beach, you may see an additional large sign with two pictures, one of a beach covered with the migrating brant geese, another with a dog running along the beach. DO NOT DISTURB! and WHOA! make their points loudly and clearly—and all the more so when you are told that a hefty fine awaits you if you let your dog loose among the geese.

Parking Whether or not your access spot is along a through road or at the end of a cul-de-sac, you might find parking is not great. Almost invariably, there is no problem finding parking for two or three cars, even on the shoulder of the road. While in general the smaller public access spots in this book are not suitable for groups—avoid taking your 64-member family reunion to anywhere other than a large public beach—there are some spots where half a dozen cars can park comfortably. You should, of course, be sensitive about blocking driveways. Unless you are going beaching by yourself, therefore, or with one other family, use this book to select a beach spot that fits your parking needs.

Facilities Few of these spots have public toilets. Keep that fact in mind when you plan your outing. The last thing locals or other beachgoers want to face is the unpleasant sight of toilet paper festooning wild rose bushes.

Remember that the same applies to your toy poodle or your Irish wolfhound—even if there is no "pet" sign. Even worse than festoons of toilet paper is a mound of dog excrement. If you are going to take Fang or Fifi to the beach, bring a pooper scooper.

Boat launching Use this book to find suitable canoe- and kayak-launching spots. Only a couple of the spots in this book are suitable for launching boats of any weight—say a dinghy with a small outboard—and even in these cases, such launching is easily done, but only at high tide. Many more spots are suitable for launching kayaks and canoes, though you should check the information about the length of the trail and the trail's steepness, width and roughness. Parallel information on the extent to which the tide goes out will also be relevant to your planning. The best spots for launching kayaks are listed in the final chapter, but other spots can be used, depending on your tides and your determination.

Cyclists Some of the most nature-loving free spirits are cyclists, who will want to use this book to find charming hidden spots and to identify challenging beach approaches. Any truly motivated cyclist will have no difficulty gaining access to any of these spots, but will probably want to bring a lock in order to leave a cycle on the road, particularly where the path to the shore is long and difficult. For a few access spots, however, this book includes information specifically for cyclists. After all, this is Vancouver Island. Vancouver Island can be very, very hilly. Those who don't enjoy a little hearty puffing won't, for example, want to plan a bicycle trip that ends with the public access at the end of Garry Oak Drive.

Beach fires Don't even think about having a beach fire during fire season, even when you crave s'mores. Enjoy the tranquility and freedom from lungfuls of smoke. Even when beach fires are permitted, be considerate to others and build your fire well below the high-tide line. Nothing ruins the pristine pleasures of a shiny pebble beach more than an ugly firepit with ashes smeared into the stones, or adjoining logs scarred with burnt areas. In addition, rocks that have been overheated turn an ugly orange-brown, permanently blemishing the beach.

Beachcombing Do you most like to use a public access spot as the beginning of an exploration of a piece of shoreline? Whether you enjoy poking through tidal pools or striding along with the wind in your hair, many of these access points will allow you considerable opportunity for uplifting waterfront walks. There are a few things to remember, though, before you set off along the beach. First, land below the high-water mark cannot technically be privately owned, so don't be intimidated if your walk takes you embarrassingly close to someone's front yard. Do, however, respect private property and, as much as possible, keep your distance. Also, be prepared for the heavy development that sometimes affects this section of coast.

And don't forget to consider tides. Some carefree rambles can, at high-tide, turn into awkward scrambles over bluffs or steep rocks. At the same time, you needn't worry overly much about tides. It is true that at many points on the Island's *west* coast, being trapped at high tide can lead you into dangerous situations. In this area, there are no spots where you will be endangered by high tide approaching—though you might be inconvenienced. Finally, consider the season. Many rocky beaches, easy to stroll along in summer, can be dangerously slimy in winter. Tread carefully when you return in winter to a beach you explored in summer without difficulty.

Seclusion You may feel motivated to hunt down a small, remote beach to get away from the madding crowds that throng the big public beaches. If so, you might be unhappy that about two-thirds of the beaches in this book lie between private houses. Take heart! At some of these places you can expect to sit for hours at a time contemplating, undisturbed, the play of light on the waves and the cry of the gulls (or how you are going to tell your partner that she snores.)

This book will alert you when an area possesses one of the four key factors that provide that sense of seclusion. First, a few spots border on undeveloped or otherwise "wild" land, such as that belonging to National Defence or a First Nations reserve. Second, at some spots you can walk more than half a kilometre out to the low-tide line, far away from everyone. Third, some access points are rarely if ever used, even by local residents. Last, you will learn from this book that neighbouring houses are sometimes built well back from the bank or behind a high hedge or screen of trees. Indeed, some spots are configured in such a way that rock bluffs, cliffs or the like will keep you invisible from all waterfront houses.

Compass directions Compasses? Don't be alarmed; you don't need a compass for any of these spots. The point is simply this: all *real* Islanders use the terms "north" and "south" with the very misled, and misleading, implication that Victoria is at the south end of the Island and the rest of the Island is to the north of it. In fact, as Islanders point out to each other at regular intervals, the "northern" tip of the Island is actually northwest of its "southern" tip. Thus, for example, visitors can observe the interesting phenomenon that as they drive "north" from Victoria, they pass the clearly marked forty-ninth parallel in Ladysmith. Continuing "north" to Parksville, they then turn "west" to head out toward Pacific Rim Park—only to find themselves crossing the forty-ninth parallel again as they approach the park! They have really been driving more west than north in going to Parksville and driving more south than west in driving toward Pacific Rim Park. Still, because we all participate in the tradition, let's continue to do so. When you read that there is, say, a sandy patch at the "north" end of a beach, understand that simply to mean "away from Victoria"!

Mountain views Something that Islanders take for granted, or don't really think about, is that the east coast of Vancouver Island offers a kind of view that is extremely rare on a world scale. For most people on planet Earth, a "sea view" means perhaps an odd promontory or two, maybe some islands, but beyond that, the horizon—the blank, unadorned horizon. To get such views on Vancouver Island, of course, you need to go to the west coast. For Islanders on the east coast, north of Nanaimo, a view means promontories and islands, yes—but it also means mountains, and in most cases the Coast Mountains. South of Nanaimo, the view is equally unusual on a world scale. In this area it is the Gulf Islands that provide a welter of land contours.

From certain perspectives—from, say, Pipers Lagoon looking south, or the south Qualicum beaches looking north—a small section of

Pipers Lagoon

Mount Moriarty overlooking Madrona Point

horizon appears completely open. In both cases that is an illusion. In both cases, just below the lip of the horizon lie islands, hills and— mountains. And, since most views in this central bit of the Island are thick with mountains, those who would most enjoy the view will look at the mountains, *really* look at the mountains, and grow to appreciate them. Such connoisseurship is made all the more piquant because all the best mountains are not visible from any one spot. Each area along this part of the coast offers different craggy pleasures.

Don't assume that the familiar misty blue silhouettes of the Coast Mountains are the best views of the mountains you can get. If you like the mountains, make a point of coming to a favourite viewing spot in the evening, near sunset, and on a clear day, and you will see the mountains jump out of their background, thrown into relief by the low shadows. And don't forget the rather obvious point that it is in the winter, when they are covered with snow, that they are at their (photogenic) best.

Among the clutter of peaks, even the beginner will quickly grow to distinguish a few of the most remarkable:

Mount Baker Mount Baker, located in Washington State, is the only (almost extinct) volcano visible. Everyone is familiar with the permanently white pyramid that on a clear day rises mystically straight out of the sea. What most don't think about, though, is that they are not actually looking at very much of Mount Baker. Instead, they are looking at the *peak* of the mountain, the bulk of which is actually below the horizon. Cherry Point and the spots adjoining are those to choose for the most stunning views of this stunning mountain—bring your zoom lens for some astounding pictures!

Howe Sound mountains This is the jumbled array of left-tilted peaks, The Lions among them, above the grey-blue shadow of Bowen Island. Next time you take the ferry to Horseshoe Bay, watch these mountains come more closely into focus so that you can pick out individual peaks once you are back in heaven—on Vancouver Island.

Mount Tantalus Mount Tantalus can be seen along this whole stretch of coast, but it is most striking in the area around Parksville. From this angle, the entire vast glacier that covers most of the mountain is clearly visible. On a baking-hot beach day, when the heat waves are shimmering off the sands, that icy white wall in the distance is particularly compelling.

Mount Churchill This spectacularly shark-toothed pinnacle on the north shore of Jervis Inlet is best seen from the Dolphin Beach and Fairwinds areas. Farther north it is hidden behind the flank of Texada; farther south and it fades into the distance. It is not named after Sir Winston, but an explorer.

Jervis Inlet peaks This distinctive combination of three peaks stands out from the surrounding, more rounded mountains. Best seen from Beachcomber to Fairwinds, they have given rise to various anthropomorphizing interpretations of their shapes. Can you make out the profile of a fat man lying on his back?

Tetrahedron and Panther peaks These aren't as striking as some of the other mountains, or as high. Rising straight from the shore on the Sechelt Peninsula, they nevertheless are fun to pick out because of the absolute appropriateness of their names.

Mount Arrowsmith This is central Vancouver Island's most prominent and beloved peak (or, actually, series of peaks). Wonderful views of Mount Arrowsmith are to be had from a few of the spots identified in this book—in fact, much better views than you can generally get. Even better, because you will be viewing its north face, it will appear snow-adorned later than many of the Coast Mountains. Mount Arrowsmith, named after a family of 18th-century cartographers, is the highest mountain south of Strathcona Park.

Mount Washington Mount Washington, as far as peaks go, is dull to view. Those who spend their winters (and a sizable part of their income) skiing on its slopes, though, should be interested to know that, from Beachcomber, and various spots on Columbia and Qualicum beaches, it is dimly visible as the last bit of Island mountainscape to the "north." It was not George but Rear Admiral John, of the Royal Navy, who kindly lent his name to the mountain.

Mount Moriarty Just as Mount Arrowsmith is the highest mountain south of Strathcona Park, Mount Moriarty is the highest mountain south of Mount Arrowsmith. If you find one of the spots in this book where you can see Mount Arrowsmith, you will almost inevitably let your eyes swing south to the only other significant, and usually snowy, peak against the skyline.

Maps I've provided sketch maps to help you find your way, but you will want to use printed street maps as well. The numbered beaches start at Qualicum and move south to the Malahat. Unnumbered beaches are described only briefly, in "Also nearby" sections at the end of entries and shown on the sketch map with an asterisk (*). When there is more than one beach in an "Also nearby" section, each spot is also given a capital letter to distinguish it (*A, *B and so on). In almost all cases, you'll find these places on the sketch maps to the south of the numbered beach to which they apply.

QUALICUM
PARKSVILLE
LANTZVILLE
PART 1
NANAIMO
LADYSMITH
PART 2
CHEMAINUS
DUNCAN
MILL BAY
PART 3 MALAHAT
GOLDSTREAM

PART 1 Qualicum to Lantzville

covered in this book, the area between Qualicum and Lantzville provides the highest density of beaches. As you move south through this region, you will discover that, except for a large piece of military land around Nanoose Bay, almost all of this coast is residential—and presents all the attendant advantages and disadvantages. For beach-hunters, the advantage is that with development can come paths through otherwise impenetrable bush and stairways down otherwise dangerously steep banks. Note the choice of words "can come," though—such paths *can come* with development, not *do come*. Sadly, developers do not always consider public access when they are building along a coast. In this section of coast, most of it under the care of Regional District of Nanaimo (but not covering all of the RDN), you may find yourself barred from a long section of coast for two reasons. First, as development policies have varied with time and values, so have the provisions for public access. Look at the maps and you will see Lantzville and Beachcomber peninsula, for example, thick with provisions for public access. Look at maps of Cedar and Yellow Point and you will see very few such provisions. Second, even when land has been set aside for public access, the effort put into clearing paths or building stairs varies enormously. Within this area, it is only the city of Nanaimo, not the RDN, that deserves kudos for narrowing the gap between maps and reality—but not closing it completely. The Cowichan Valley Regional District is a little better than the Regional District of Nanaimo, but best of all are most of the municipalities around Victoria. See *Secret Beaches of Greater Victoria* for this area.

Geographically, this area has in common an exposure to the elements in their most unmuted form. North of the protective barrier of the Gulf Islands, the waves are allowed as much play as the Strait of Georgia will permit. The result for beachgoers is that in the most exposed places at least, the sand is fine and hard, the rocks smoothed and the upper shore extensive. The other main geographical feature affecting these beaches is that the land between Nanoose Bay and Madrona Point is a sequence of rocky peninsulas made up of granite, basalt or sandstone. Most of this shore is solid rock interspersed with pebbly bays. Both north and south of it, expect some pebbly or boulder-strewn shores, but also many stretches of sand.

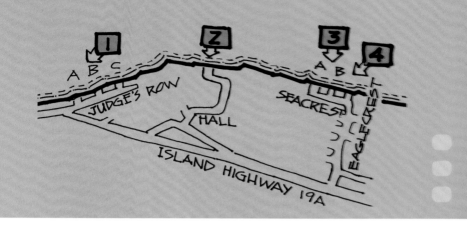

1

JUDGE'S ROW A, B AND C

A southern continuation of the sandy beaches of central Qualicum Beach

These three access points are grouped together because they are all within a very short distance of each other along the same road and are similar to each other. All three are great alternatives to the main part of the extensive Qualicum Beach strip, particularly because they are more sheltered from the rush of cars along Highway 19A. In some cases, too, they actually provide better beaches than at the main public strip—and particularly better than the beach area immediately to the north. What they lack, of course, is ice cream and washrooms!

Location, signs and parking At the bottom of the hill at the south end of Qualicum Beach turn onto Judge's Row. Various signs warn against parking overnight, not collecting shellfish and keeping dogs on leashes. All three spots allow several cars to park next to the shore. Be warned, however: all three of these spots are quite well known and can be busy on a sunny summer's afternoon.

Path All three paths will have you onto the beach within a few steps from your car. You can come laden with all of the spades, buckets, kites and Frisbees you like, or leave them in the car for easy retrieval. The third access point in the sequence has a few huge boulders at the end of the parking lot, but still allows quick access.

Beach This is Qualicum Beach at its best. In fact, this beach is different from such similar ones as Rathtrevor and Parksville beaches in three chief ways. First, there is not much eelgrass near the low-tide mark, so even when the tide is mostly out, squeamish swimmers or those who love the turquoise sparkle of water over sand can swim with pleasure. Second, because the tide doesn't go out nearly as far here as at the other big beaches, it is easier to reach the water's edge—though, of course, it is harder to find huge expanses of sand for, say, kite flying. And third, kite flying wouldn't be great anyway, because there is probably no other big beach on the east coast of the Island where winds are so light.

Suitability for children The predictable strip of golf-ball-sized rocks at the upper edge of the beach creates a barrier to the sand for tender little feet. Flip-flops or beach shoes are the stock-in-trade of all beach-going parents on Vancouver Island, however, so children will see the rocky strip as no real difficulty. With its tidal pools, sandy expanses and warm water, this beach is almost perfect for most kinds of beach play. Bring sunscreen or beach umbrellas, though; there is no shade any time of day.

Suitability for groups If you come with a large group, there is no real point in stopping at these comparatively confined areas. You would be better off going a few hundred metres to the main part of the beach, where there is lots of parking, a strip of lawn, picnic tables and public washrooms. Leave the Judge's Row access points for families or very small groups.

View Because Qualicum Beach itself forms a shallow, broad bay, beach-goers here will be facing slightly north up the Strait, where the islands are below the horizon. Thus they will find their view even more expansive than the views offered by similar access spots slightly farther south.

Winds, sun and shade You need a pretty hefty blow out on the Strait to find much wind on these beaches, even though there is no obvious reason for the phenomenon. The bay is shallow, and no lumps of geography impede any wind that is determined to blow into the bay. There isn't any shade. Be prepared to make your own.

Beachcombing You can walk in either direction for many, many kilometres. Be prepared, however, to deal with changing tides and a beach surface that, while primarily sand at low tide, will throw up a few surprises in the way of tidal pools and barnacle-covered rocks.

Seclusion There isn't any. This being said, note that the beach B approach has high hedges on either side. Likewise, beach A has a strip of manicured grass (not lawn) on the right, giving beachgoers less feeling here than at B and C that they are wedging in between waterfront houses. In addition, those who go beach walking long distances south will find increasing seclusion as the foreshore rises higher and higher above them, the houses become more and more remote, and the shorefront trees more and more plentiful.

2
HALL ROAD
A relatively obscure access to a southerly continuation of the Qualicum sands

Location, signs and parking Finding Hall Road off the highway at the top of the hill just south of the main Qualicum beach might seem a breeze. Following it to the end isn't. Unless you realize that Hall Road is roughly shaped like a giant question mark (appropriately enough), you might well end up on Knightly Terrace. Once you have wound your way to the end of the question-mark road, look for the paved parking spot between two giant hedges. About four cars can park at an angle.

A sign will tell you that your dog should be on a leash. Respect this sign. You will also see a sign that, oddly, is posted only on this beach and no other on this entire section of coast. This is a notice from the Department of Fisheries alerting visitors to the regulations on collecting crabs, both rock crabs and the much more treasured Dungeness crabs.

Path Only a few steps separate you from the shore end of the lot and the shore.

Beach Like many other access spots on this section of coast, this one is clearly used as a convenient spot to arrange drainage from the surrounding land. Here, as at some other places, you will find a less-than-pretty circular concrete object planted firmly in the gravel at the top of the beach. Though some will want to stay on this pebbly, drier upper edge of the beach if they are planning one of the more languorous ways of spending their time, most will no doubt make a beeline over the narrow strip of gravel for the fine sandy beach beyond.

Suitability for children This beach is great for those beach-going activities of childhood. Sand and tidal pools should make for some very happy children. Beach shoes of some sort will be handy for getting your child over the section of gravel, however.

Suitability for groups Groups will find lots of space to spread out on the sands if they come at low tide. At high tide the beach is not very suitable. In fact, any group this close to the main public beach will be happiest going there for its facilities.

View In general, the view here seems open and expansive, unornamented by small islands or sharp peaks. You will see that to the south the shoreline is steep and high—the reason, in fact, you will find no access spots along this stretch.

Winds, sun and shade This beach receives even less wind from either direction than the beaches immediately to the south, except when winter storms rage. Like the other beaches that are part of the Qualicum strand, this one gets lots of late afternoon and evening sun—a rarity in the area covered by this book.

Beachcombing Whether sauntering, striding or running, you will find the expanses of fine sand great for stretching your legs.

Seclusion Although this is a busy beach, the actual point of access is reasonably secluded from the houses on either side. It would, however, be misleading to use the word "secluded" of any beach on this highly developed section of coastline. As you head south on the beach you will get to a section where the houses are high above on a wooded bank—far enough away that you can steal a quick smooch with your honey.

3

SEACREST PLACE A AND B
Well maintained, with park
benches and easy access to
large areas of low-tide sand

Location, signs and parking These two access spots are similar to "Seacrest Place C" (entry 4). They are easily grouped because they are close to each other and very much alike. Both offer wide, level parking areas for several cars off the road, and require only a few steps down onto the pebbly upper shore. The easier one to find of the pair is at the very end of the road. The other access is through the gap between houses and the parking area toward the northern end of Seacrest Place. Count one house past the house number 1039. It is difficult to read the number of the house immediately before the access. Both accesses have enough signs about wildlife viewing areas, overnight parking and the overseeing eyes of the Eaglecrest residents to reassure you that you are, indeed, at public access spots.

Path A few steps take you from the parking areas, past park benches and to the pebbly upper shore amidst clusters of beach logs.

Beach Both beaches, like all of those in the area, begin with a band of pebbles and rocks and merge into areas of sand interspersed with gravel. Similarly, both extend a considerable distance out to low-tide water. The more northerly of these two particular spots has a large tidal pool immediately at the beginning of the sandy area. In fact, if you are looking for the spot with the largest area of sand, you will probably prefer the more southerly spot.

Suitability for children You can't do much better for sand-and-water-loving children than to bring them for a low-tide romp and splash at this beach. You will have to warn them, of course, of the patches of barnacles and exposure to sun.

Suitability for groups All three spots along Seacrest Place can be busy on warm days. If you are going to bring a group here, obviously you will want to limit the number of cars you are bringing and choose the parking area with the most space. Otherwise, expect a good deal of space for a picnic and even more space for wandering and wading along the kilometres of pools and sandbars.

View Like all the other spots in this area, these primarily offer a view of open expanses of the Strait between Vancouver Island and Lasqueti and Texada islands.

Winds, sun and shade Neither spot is sheltered from wind, though at both spots a southeast wind is felt more directly than an equally fresh northwest wind. At both places, too, the upper shore is considerably warmer than the low-tide shore. If you are nursing a sunburn, or want to avoid having to nurse a sunburn, don't expect to find much protection from the sun's burning rays at either of these spots.

Beachcombing Properly shod and properly prepared with tide tables, you can step out (or trot out) for many kilometres in either direction.

Seclusion All of these spots are well used during the warm summer months, though none is often crowded. The shorefront is lined with houses, but if you want seclusion, you need only take a long, low-tide walk to the north, and soon the sand lovers will be far behind you and the scattered shorefront houses far above you among the trees.

Seadog Road

4

SEACREST PLACE C

A large parking area and well-maintained access to some fine stretches of low-tide sand

Location, signs and parking Descend below Eaglecrest golf course to the beginning of Seacrest Place. (If you use a GPS or Google Maps, beware being sent to Seacrest Road in the Nanoose area.) There is parking on the side of the road for three or four cars. A large PUBLIC ACCESS sign accompanies a battery of far too many signs to list here. Of particular interest to those planning to give Fido a salty romp, though, is that this is one of the few spots to insist that *no* dogs are welcome on the beach. Remarkable, too, is the sign reminding visitors to "be sun smart." This colourful sign provides a good deal of information issued by the Canadian Dermatology Association. This sense of nurturing is echoed in a notice that the spot is patrolled by volunteers of the Eaglecrest Residents Association. Predictably, too, there is a sign forbidding overnight parking (and, by implication, late-night carousing).

Path This is one of those access spots where it is extremely easy to reach the shore. Ten new concrete steps lead through a shallow bank of broken rock, evidently put into place to prevent erosion and stabilize the bank. On a hot day you are likely to appreciate the fine big maple and the park bench. Also potentially useful is a litter barrel for your post-picnic scraps and wraps.

Beach After a narrow band of pebbles (suitable for sunning or lunching), the beach offers another narrow band of larger, ostrich-egg rocks and then lots of sand interspersed with occasional patches of barnacles and gravel. At low tide, expect almost 100 m of sandy shore between you and the turquoise wavelets. On an incoming tide, indeed, the sand is exposed here longer than at the beach off Johnstone Road, immediately to the south. Be aware that if you (or your child) swim over this sandy area when the tide is in, you might swim into one of the big barnacle-covered rocks hidden at high tide—with unhappy results.

Suitability for children With all the information you have about the need to protect yourself and your children from sun, and with such easy access to the shore and its sand, you would be making a family-friendly decision in choosing this beach for a sandy afternoon. The ease of getting to the beach or retrieving Frisbees and water bottles from the car is also a clear asset.

Suitability for groups Only a small group of friends or like-minded enthusiasts should come to what is very much a neighbourhood beach. If the group intends to spread out and walk away from the actual point of entry, large groups would probably be happy here.

View Although the view is characteristic of this stretch of coast, the slightly convex curve of the shoreline here amplifies the effect of expansiveness.

Winds, sun and shade Kite-fliers be warned: only on the windiest days will you find enough air for your sport. On the other hand, the winds pass the shore at enough of an angle that your kite will generally stay over the beach rather than crash into the roof of one of the waterfront houses. As for shade on those warm sunny days, the advice to be "sun smart" is more than appropriate for a beach like this one, where there is scant shade to be found.

Beachcombing Kick off your shoes at low tide and walk for kilometres on the sand that extends more or less unbroken as far as Qualicum. At high tide you can also walk a long distance, but your pace, and what you spot on the shore, will be very different.

Seclusion Even on hot summer afternoons, it is rare to find anyone here. If you walk south, in fact, you will soon be away not only from people but also from houses. On the other hand, as you settle down on your beach blanket with your ugly sun hat, be aware that you will be in full view of some houses.

5

MALLARD ROAD

A quiet, easily reached section of shore leading to large areas of low-tide sand

Location, signs and parking The sequence of roads from the highway is easy enough: first onto Johnstone and then, before its end, left onto Mallard *Drive*. Press on, because Mallard Drive turns into Mallard *Road*. And, to add to the merriment, note that there is a Mallard *Place* in the Fairwinds area of Nanoose and Mallard Way Road just north of Lantzville. Just before the end of the road, you will see an apparently empty lot of generally groomed (but unwatered) grass dotted with a few small evergreens and a shorefront park bench. A row of huge Lombardy poplars lines a gravel drive that leads to the water's edge. The only three signs here are the familiar warning not to park overnight, the encouragement to feel welcome because you are entering the wildlife management area, and the spooky skull-and-crossbones-adorned warning against collecting shellfish. Several cars can be comfortably parked along this gravel drive, but drivers will have to be careful not to block each other.

Path With the gravel road approaching the shore so closely, there is no path to negotiate. Heavy objects, like kayaks, could be easily managed here—but you would want to launch only at high tide.

Mallard Road

Beach Like so many other beaches in this area, this one has an upper margin of beach grasses, then a strip of fine grey gravel that gradually gives way to larger barnacle-covered rocks and, at low tide, lots and lots of sand—mostly in bands parallel to the shore and interspersed with tidal pools. There are two large, shallow ones immediately in front of the access strips. A few very large rocks stick well above the general surface of the beach, some of them covered by only high tides. Since a broad band of sand spreads to the left from here, it would be surprising if most visitors didn't head in this direction.

Suitability for children Safe and level, the beach is without dangers for little ones, except, of course, for the nearly inevitable barnacle-covered rocks that lurk below the high-tide line. Like the access from Seacrest Place, this one, too, makes trips to and from the car easy. Come prepared for full exposure to the sun.

Suitability for groups Large groups should avoid this spot, though they would be less intrusive here than at many access points, because there is no house immediately behind the beach for about 100 m to the north.

View Those who love a horizon with lots of islands will be less pleased than those who like the open expanses of the Strait of Georgia at its widest and least embellished stretch.

Winds, sun and shade Although the northwest and southeast winds do come ashore here, the winds are generally not as strong in this area as farther south. There is a little shade available in the afternoon, but otherwise the whole shore is mostly in sun.

Beachcombing This is a continuation of the stretch of level shore where beachgoers stroll for considerable distances without having to worry about impediments or challenges. You will enjoy walking most, however, if you bring water shoes and come at low tide.

Seclusion Because of the empty grassy area immediately to the left, this beach is a good choice for those who really don't like being wedged between waterfront houses. Because the shore is low in either direction, however, beachcombers will be walking past the "front yards" of most of the local houses. A stroll of half a kilometre toward the north will bring the beach walker to a long stretch where the shore rises higher and higher and where the houses are, as a consequence, more and more removed. This is where, in all senses of the expression, you can let down your hair.

✳ **Also nearby** The very end of **Johnstone Road** (which you will pass on your way to Mallard Road) is clearly marked with a green and white pointer to the public access at the end of the paved turnaround area. Here, however, the shore is less attractive because of a water drainage structure and because of the shortage of sand nearby. Few beachgoers will want to stop here rather than carry on to Mallard Road, though they will find plenty of room for parking, only a few steps to the upper shore, and at low tide, a broad swath of sand on the opposite side of a barnacle-and-rock strip.

6

ADMIRAL TRYON BOULEVARD

A large public area of logs and rounded rocks, occasionally used by surfers

Location, signs and parking This is Columbia Beach by any other name, signposted as such from the highway. The size of several lots, this large, open, public area dominates the road. It really is one of those places where the claim "You can't miss it" happens to be true. An unusual homegrown sign invites the visitor to "Enjoy your community wild flower garden," though flowers seem to be scarce, even in summer. It is possible to drive right onto this land along the gravel road roughly configured as a figure eight. More significantly, it is possible to park immediately behind the row of beach logs that separates this low stretch of grassy and sandy land from the beach itself.

Path There is no path to speak of, because it is possible to park virtually on the beach. You will, however, have to climb over low logs to get onto the beach so, if you have a lot of elaborate equipment, choose your spot appropriately.

Beach The upper beach is in three distinct bands—first coarse sand, then golf-ball-sized pebbles, and last, ostrich-egg rocks. One of the distinct (though temporary) features of this pleasant, open beach is a huge driftwood stump with a set of wooden steps cobbled onto it. One can imagine diversion for clambering children or perching spots for a family wanting a carefully posed group photograph. The spot is perfect, too, for unusual wedding photographs.

Suitability for children Although the beach lacks sand even at low tide, it does have an expansive, open feeling and scope for roaming. Many children will be happy here doing what children do best—turning every object on a beach to imaginative use. Water-loving children will be happiest at high tide or, in the company of parents, at the low-tide mark.

Suitability for groups The space is open enough to accommodate even a dozen or so people. The beach area is flat enough that beach chairs, beach umbrellas, beach blankets and the other paraphernalia of beaching could be arranged. Still, this is a local community beach and a much larger group would be intrusive.

View Lacking the views of mountains that give the beaches farther south their particular appeal, this stretch of coast, and this beach typical among them, nevertheless opens onto intriguing vistas of the north end of Lasqueti Island and, behind it, Texada. Farther north rise the grey-blue outlines of Denman and Hornby islands. Since the islands even farther north, like Quadra and Cortes, are below the horizon, one feels that the Strait is much more open than it actually is.

Winds, sun and shade The beach is exposed to the (sometimes deliciously) cooling effects of both northwest and southeast winds. Because the shore faces more to the east than the section of shore between here and Qualicum, it catches both the southeast winds and, in a good blow, the accompanying waves. In fact, choose a southeast storm to visit the spot, and don't be surprised if you see a few surfers catching the waves. The beach even has a live webcam, which you can find, along with weather statistics fed from Ballenas Island Lighthouse, at http://www.bigwavedave.ca/ColumbiaWS.htm.

Sun lovers, rejoice. With no bank and no trees behind, there isn't a square centimetre of shade to be found. Others might want to invest in a beach umbrella.

Beachcombing Plans exist for a walking route beginning here and heading north. It is possible to wander the beach for a long distance, especially at low tide, and especially to the north. To the south you will run into French Creek before long.

Seclusion The land provided for the access is big and open enough that you won't feel in the lap of neighbours. You will feel, though, that you are in but a gap in what is otherwise wall-to-wall shorefront suburbia.

7
FRENCH CREEK ESTUARY
An interesting viewpoint on the estuary and marina, good for birdwatching

Location, signs and parking Drive to the end of Admiral Tryon Boulevard as it curves away from the open coast and grinds to a halt in a large dirt turnaround area lined with dune grass and broom. This dirt area can accommodate seven to ten cars easily, though if there ever were a larger number coming to this spot, they could wedge themselves into adjoining spots.

Path A very short dirt track leads through the brush straight onto the gravel shore and the banks of the northernmost branch of French Creek.

Beach The term "beach" is stretched almost as far as it will go here. Particularly at high tide there is only a small strip of gravelly shore where the creek forms a deep channel directly in front. This does not, however, mean that the spot is limiting in other ways. Like most estuaries, this is a great area for birdwatchers or those who want an unusual spot to sit and read in wind-sheltered day-long sun.

Suitability for children Some children will enjoy a short time here, possibly skipping rocks (when there are no birds around) or exploring up and down the shore. Most, however, will find the area limited and confining.

Suitability for groups Birdwatchers, yes. Sketchers, yes. Otherwise it is not obvious what a large group would do here.

View Although limited, the view, particularly on a sunny, windy day, is interesting and varied. Upstream you will see the various branches of French Creek leading into woods. Across the creek you will see the busy amenities of French Creek itself and, extending beyond the parking

French Creek Estuary

lot, the long finger of the boulder breakwater behind which the masts and superstructures of crowded fishing boats criss-cross picturesquely. Downstream on your side of the creek, the shore curves out to a slight gravel promontory, but the phalanx of cheek-by-jowl houses starts within a short distance.

Winds, sun and shade The relative protection from all winds means that the spot can be warm on a cool day, hot on a warm day. Bring your sun hat and sunglasses.

Beachcombing At low tide it is possible to follow the gravel shore all the way down the creek and around the corner onto the open coast (though the plans for walking routes in the area do not include this section of shore).

Seclusion You will rarely find many other people here. In addition, you need not fear scrutiny from houses around you. Still, with the marina opposite and the subdivision clustered on one side, you will hardly feel immersed in nature.

⁎ Also nearby Turn toward the water at the traffic light on the south side of the French Creek bridge for the well-signposted entry to **French Creek Marina** (see map below). Besides the picturesque fishing boats, you will find a picnic table, bench, public washrooms and a footpath along the breakwater. Also of interest are the pub, restaurant and seafood store. For a great wave-viewing spot in a southeasterly storm, drive to the south end of the parking lot. From here, through a chain-link fence you will see a sandy beach. To reach this beach, go to Breakwater Road (next entry).

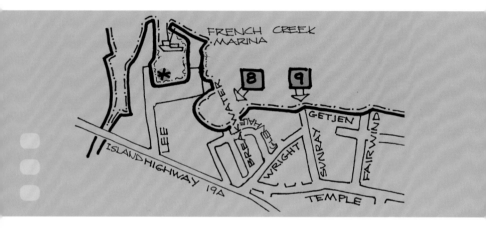

8
BREAKWATER ROAD
A varied shore with a sandy-beach walk to French Creek Marina

Location, signs and parking Although some maps still show Breakwater Road leaving the highway, you must approach it via Wright Road and Glendale Crescent. Look for mailboxes and the house numbered 906. You will see an overgrown patch of bushes. Three signs will tell you, variously, that the beach access is unstable (and you must use it at your risk), that there is danger in collecting shellfish, and that you are entering the wildlife management area—to which, be glad, you are "welcome." There is room for one car on the gravel path straight ahead. If that spot is taken, you will have to find a spot along the shoulder of the road.

Path The bank is about 15 m high here. A broad, somewhat slippery dirt track leads some 50 m to the shore. Be careful of the heavy ruts in one section of the path.

Beach The beach here is, arguably, considerably more interesting than similar beaches farther south in this section of coast. Directly in front and farther to the north are sandstone shelves. The upper beach is composed largely of granite dinosaur-egg-like boulders. Lower down the shore, large boulders stretch to a low-tide line more than 50 m away. The breakwater of French Creek Marina (remember the name of the road you drove down to get here?) largely encloses the shore. You can walk toward the marina on the large swath of low-tide sand.

Suitability for children Of the various access spots in the immediate area, this may be the one most suitable for children. The comparative ease of access and the variety of the shore can provide the well-shod child some diversion. Most, though, will want to head toward the sandy bay a few minutes' walk to the left. Still, it is unlikely that any but adventurous children would single out this spot as a favourite beach. Even getting to the beach down the steep path can be something of an adventure for children!

Suitability for groups Parking isn't great for groups, and picnic spots aren't great either. Looking for a beach spot to photograph your wedding party? Don't even think about this spot unless you want some very, very funny pictures. It is conceivable, however, that a birdwatching group or smattering of shore strollers would enjoy coming here.

View Depending on your aesthetic sense, the view to the north is either restricted by—or enhanced by—the broken-rock breakwater of French Creek Marina. To the south, however, you will see an expanse of sea between you and Lasqueti Island.

Winds, sun and shade Northwest winds are deflected because this spot is, in effect, in an east-facing bay. Southeast winds are not. Even though this is a north-facing shore, the bank is not as steep or heavily wooded as at some other spots.

Beachcombing French Creek Marina, a few hundred metres to the north, is an obvious destination for a beach walk, though at low tide you may get wet feet if you cut across the bay.

Seclusion Turn south and you will find considerable seclusion. Turn north and you will find yourself among the low-key bustle of the marina. In neither direction, however, will you find many others using the shore.

9

SUNRAY ROAD

A steep access to a little-used section of shore with unusually shiny boulders

Location, signs and parking Many routes lead through the suburban labyrinth to what appears to be the end of Sunray Road—but only if you are approaching from Temple Street. If you are approaching from Wright Road, the spot you are looking for is at the corner of the two forks in Sunray. Permit yourself to feel a little confused—and look at the map! You will see a 30 m wide access strip behind a yellow barrier gate. Park on the shoulder of an adjoining road. In addition to the sign identified below, you will see a faded shellfish warning sign and a spanking new purple wildlife protection sign.

Path Oddly, this is one of two similar access banks in the area with a sign warning UNSTABLE BEACH ACCESS. USE AT OWN RISK. While there is no doubt that the sign is both appropriate and informative, this bank is not as unstable or risky as some others without such a warning. In fact, a kind soul has installed steps made from planks held in place with rebar pegs and topped with gravel. There is even a bit of rope to aid in negotiating the 15-m drop to the shoreline. The path ends amidst alders beside a splashy and somewhat ditchy-feeling little creek.

Beach It is possible to picnic, pause or ponder at the uppermost beach among the pebbles and logs. The large, polished-looking boulders extend to a tide line some 70 or 80 m out. High tide is the time to come for a swim, if that is on your mind.

Suitability for children Choose another spot to take your toddlers. If you really want to see this spot, however, and have an older, nimble child, don't be too intimidated by the warning sign.

Suitability for groups As with similar spots in the area, the difficulty of access and the bouldery nature of the beach do not make this an obvious choice for a group. It would, in addition, not be kind to the anonymous step builder to put very much wear and tear on the stairs.

View The view is pleasant but unremarkable, looking as it does almost directly across the Strait. To the north, however, you can see the promontory on which French Creek Marina is situated.

Winds, sun and shade Expect to feel both northwest and southeast winds here, though the latter will hit the shore somewhat obliquely. Don't worry about bringing the sunscreen if you're just going to picnic on the upper beach. From mid morning on, you will be in shade.

Beachcombing Not an obvious spot for walking on the beach, Sunray Road nevertheless can offer a sense of being off the beaten track and can

Sunray Road

be appealing to those who would like a destination—in this case, French Creek Marina—for their walk.

Seclusion You will not see many others or be seen by them, so feel free to wear your most comfortable and ugliest beach clothes.

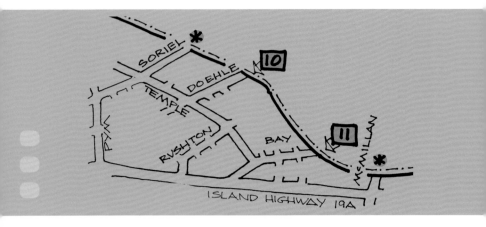

10
DOEHLE AVENUE
A well-developed access down a high bank to the north end of Parksville Bay

Location, signs and parking Although there are many ways you can thread through the network of suburban roads to this spot, it is easiest to turn off the highway at Pym Street and, after one long block, take the first right on Doehle and follow it to its end several blocks away. You will immediately recognize the spot by the ranks of benches and the signs warning you against overnight parking, collecting shellfish and lighting fires. You will also be blinded by the glare from a high-tech, stainless steel litter bin. A bicycle rack completes the fine array of facilities here. Since no special parking area exists for this otherwise highly developed access spot, you will have to make do by parking on the shoulder of an adjoining street. Because of the configurations of the adjacent yards, you will find parking easiest if you turn around first and then pull over. Expect the ranks of benches to be full during a fireworks show, but otherwise allow yourself to feel surprised at how many there are!

Path A spanking new, and slightly daunting, set of 112 metal-and-concrete stairs arranged in several flights will take you to the shore far below.

Beach This spot is close enough to the huge area of sand that is Parksville Beach that upon reaching the store most visitors will immediately turn right to head toward it. Those who don't will find that poking through the large boulders on the comparatively narrow shoreline will yield very different creatures from those to be found on the sands. Those visitors, too, who want to picnic in pebbles rather than experience grit in their potato salad, or those who would like a shady spot to nurse a sunburn, might want to linger here.

Suitability for children As long as your children aren't yearning for the distant sands of Parksville Beach, they could enjoy playing around among the barnacle-covered rocks, exploring the tidal pools and splashing in the sea itself. Of course, tender feet should be very well shod. Most children, like most adults, will make a beeline for the sand. The formidable flight of stairs is an obvious consideration.

Suitability for groups If your (small) group can find suitable parking, it can be easily accommodated both on the benches at the top of the stairs and on the empty expanses of beach. Brant-viewing season in spring is an attraction of the area.

View Like some other spots along this section of coast, this one offers a double view. From the cluster of benches at the top of the bank, the view is wonderfully airy. Framed by some beautiful large Douglas-firs, this essentially south-facing view overlooks the curve of Parksville Bay and extends to the Ballenas Islands in the middle distance. Beyond these, the southern Strait and Howe Sound mountains can be seen as blue shadows in the distance. The view from the shore itself is wider, but it too is essentially directed south and, of course, lacks the depth of the view from the top.

Winds, sun and shade Winds are largely irrelevant from the upper viewing spot, though a southeast wind, especially in winter, can pack quite a punch. The shore itself is reasonably protected from a northwest wind, though the farther you go toward the low-tide line, the more wind you (and your kite) will feel. By early afternoon, some shade from the high, wooded bank will start to spread across the upper shore, increasing as the afternoon progresses.

Beachcombing If your shoes are sturdy and your determination is high, you can walk for a long, long way in either direction on this essentially flat, gravelly beach.

Seclusion The highly developed and kempt nature of the view spot and the access stairs suggest that many come to this spot. However, expect to be alone—until you are drawn toward sand lovers at the main beach. The high, wooded bank assures you of considerable privacy from the houses behind you. Make the most of it!

✻ **Also nearby Soriel Road** ends in a somewhat informal little park. From the edge of this area you have a pleasant bird's-eye view over San Pareil Island and, beyond, the Ballenas Islands.

11
BAY AVENUE
A quiet, suburban approach to the main Parksville Beach

Location, signs and parking Beware! Bay *Road*, another access spot (see entry 18), is within a few kilometres. Bay Avenue leaves Highway 19A on the entrance to Parksville. Follow it as it turns slightly and brings you to a high bank overlooking the south end of Parksville Beach. You will feel less than welcomed by a sign that tells you, grimly, NO ON ROAD PARKING. In spite of the sign, it is possible to find parking along the shoulder, though this can be a bit of a trick for more than a very few cars. A sign warning of the dangers of gathering shellfish is the telltale indication that the shore is accessible from this airy spot.

Path The path is considerably more welcoming than the parking facilities. In fact, 31 spanking new concrete steps and terraced gardens (not always maintained) bring you down to the shore. Allow yourself to feel put off by the giant metal structure at the bottom of the steps and the *eau de sewage* that your nose might detect. Press on for the pleasures of the beach.

Beach The shore directly at the bottom of the steps is not Parksville Beach at its most attractive, but it does have some qualities to recommend it. A considerable breadth of fist-sized rocks, bristling with barnacles, stretches away from the upper beach, acting as something of a barricade between you and the stretches of sand and sandy tidal pools. Take heart: some helpful sand lovers have cleared a sandy track through the rocks a few metres to the left of the access spot. If you wish to picnic at this spot before moving on, you will find a few beach logs and soft pebbly sand to nestle in.

Suitability for children It goes without saying that Parksville Beach is great for the wee folk and, because of the cleared path through the barnacles, they can be got out to the sandy area with little difficulty. Be aware, nevertheless, that beach shoes or flip-flops are a good idea and that the 31 steps back up can seem more of an impediment after an hour on the beach than before it. Public washrooms and fountains are available at the public park at the opposite end of the beach.

Suitability for groups Parking is a big issue here. There is no obvious reason to choose this spot for a group over the main park access at the south end of the beach—unless, for example, the brants in spring are more collected at this end of the beach or unless you are looking for some shade in which to sit while enjoying the beach.

View Because this spot is at the north end of a significant bay, you will find your line of vision steered toward the curve of the main bay, the gravelly point at the south of the beach, and the Strait to the south. The mainland mountains, and especially the icefields of Mount Tantalus, look magnificent from here.

Winds, sun and shade This spot has some advantages over the main beach on a day when the northwest wind is a little cooler than you want. The bank to the north gives considerable protection from this wind, though not when the wind is from the southeast. The upper shore (where sunbathing or meditating can be pleasantly accomplished) provides patches of sun and shade throughout the morning and afternoon.

Beachcombing This is Parksville Beach that beckons you. Of course you will want to walk out along the sandy flats at low tide. Be aware, though, that you can't walk much beyond the sandy part of the beach before you hit Englishman River. If you are determined to Get Away From It All, however, you can check the sturdiness of your walking shoes and head off—for some kilometres, in fact, along the flat rocky shore to the north.

Seclusion The access spot itself is very quiet, and the area to the north is quiet as well. Parksville Beach, in contrast, is about as crowded as a sea beach you are ever going to find on Vancouver Island (which is not, in fact, very crowded by world standards).

✳ **Also nearby McMillan Street** provides a handy access directly onto Parksville Beach from the centre of town. In fact, it is often easier to park right beside the beach here than at the public park farther south. McMillan Street crosses Highway 19A at the first traffic light north of the junction with the highway to Port Alberni. While most public access spots are embellished with two or three out of the possible range of some 10 signs, often with fascinating arbitrariness, this spot has almost all of them. All of the prohibitions about collecting shellfish, lighting fires, letting dogs off leash, parking overnight and so on are complemented by warnings against tsunamis. In addition, you will see the more cheerful signs welcoming you to the wildlife area and telling you about brants.

About 20 cars can park in this rectangular paved area. A few steps will take you through sand and beach grass to a loose gravel area and some beach logs. This spot gives you such easy access to your watery and sandy pleasures that it is clearly the spot to choose if you have ornery little ones or mounds of beach clutter.

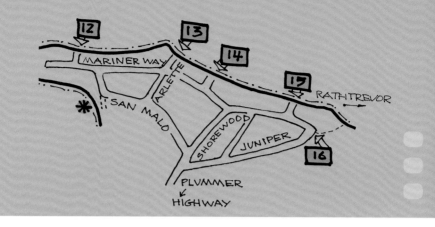

12

MARINER WAY A
A level approach to an unusual combination of sandy area and large tidal pools

Location, signs and parking This is the northernmost of four very similar access points in the San Pareil area. In case you are puzzled by the name "San Pareil," take solace in the fact that you are not alone. It seems as if some waggish developer decided to combine the French expression *sans pareil*—meaning "without parallel" (and therefore "extraordinary")—with the Spanish word *san*, meaning "saint" (as in San Francisco, equivalent to St. Francis). The result is bizarre.

In any case, this whole area, a little like Columbia Beach to the north of French Creek, has a strong beachy feeling. The whole area is a low-lying, sandy promontory covered with several streets' worth of houses and backed by the complex network of streams and sub-streams that make up the Englishman River estuary.

For this access point, once you have entered San Pareil Drive toward the cul-de-sac at the north end of Mariner Way, you will notice the striking geography, particularly as you pass the lagoon-like part of the Englishman River estuary on your left. Look for the gap between the houses second and third from the end. You will know that you are at the right spot by the usual array of signs concerning wildlife refugees, shellfish dangers, overnight parking and so on. Because there are no houses on the lagoon side of the road, you can park there easily, but otherwise simply pull into the sizable dirt-and-gravel area, where there is plenty of space for eight or ten cars.

Path Of all of the beaches along this strip, this one is the easiest to reach from the car. In fact, you can drive right to the end of the spot—making this a good place for car-picnicking when the rain and wind are too much to handle but your soul needs an injection of ocean spirit. On the other hand, those with extreme difficulty with walking will find obstacles in the uneven surface and logs.

Beach At this point the shore has curved out significantly, as if in preparation for the final thrust it is about to make toward Englishman River. A significant patch of coarse sand among the logs makes sunbathing and picnicking an easy and attractive option, though you should choose Mariner Way B if you want the protection of midday shade and easy access to sand. The beach is curiously configured at low tide. Immediately in front of the access spot, low tide reveals a large, circular break in the rocks. The front half of this "oasis" is a pretty sand-patch; the other is a large, shallow tidal pool.

Suitability for children The beach, like all other beaches in the area, is child-friendly, but the rocky parts can be hard on little feet. For a certain kind of child, the beach could be ideal at low tide. Plunk a normally wandering child on the large patch of sand, and that child will be effectively "babysat" by the surrounding perimeter of barnacles! The tide pool, too, is deep enough that a small child, properly shod, will find that the unusually warm water is a great source of splashy fun.

Suitability for groups Of the various options along this road, this one, perhaps, is the best for planning a group picnic, since there is little traffic at this end of the road. Likewise, the spot provides lots of room to spread out in both directions without crowding in on the local residents.

View The view, of course, is more or less the same as for the other beaches on this stretch, but the curve of the beach is such that you will find your eyes drawn a little more to the north.

Winds, sun and shade On a windy day, a northwest wind can be more than a little fresh here, but its effect is considerably diminished if you lie low among the logs. A southeast wind, too, will assert itself here, though at an oblique angle. Boon or bane, there is no shade, though the sun will be coming over your shoulder and from behind in the afternoon.

Beachcombing Although you can walk easily in both directions, don't be misled into thinking you can walk very far to the north. You will soon be facing the considerable depth of Englishman River as it cuts across the shore separating you from Parksville Beach.

Seclusion The arrangement of houses and the flatness of the foreshore are such that you will feel little or no seclusion. Nevertheless, you will be able to spread out a little without feeling you're in a neighbour's front yard—particularly if you go about 50 m to your left, where no houses back the shore for a considerable distance.

✱ **Also nearby** Walkers and nature lovers will want to take advantage of the close proximity that Mariner Way A provides to the southern shore of the **Englishman River** estuary. Designed as a "wildlife" viewing area (birds, in this case!), the boardwalk extends more than 100 m along the edge of the water and includes a raised platform, all the better to see the mergansers and harlequins. The path, in fact, extends beyond this river area and becomes a wide and level gravel walk that carries on an equivalent distance to the corner of Plummer Road and Shorewood Drive. You can go up yet farther and enter the trail network that cuts through the cedar forest that lines the shores of the river. Emerging onto the road again, you can enjoy several gravel side loops (one with a bench) from the main road along the shore of the river all the way to the highway.

High tide is the most attractive time to visit the estuary. When the mud is covered with water, the various ducks are best able to carry on with their watery life. Even if you decide that estuary walking isn't for you, it would nevertheless be criminal for you not to glance across this area and drink in the view of the grasslands and bushes in the foreground and Mount Arrowsmith in the background.

13
MARINER WAY B
A level, sandy spot with little seclusion but lots of low-tide play area

Location, signs and parking Drive along Mariner Way until you see Arlette Road. On the shore side of the road, you will see a considerable opening between houses with lots of signs telling you that you mustn't camp, collect shellfish, or let your dog off its leash. In an extended dry spell (which tends to include most of the summer), avoid the centre of the parking area unless you like the challenge of driving through loose sand or are driving an ATV. Otherwise, choose any one of the many easy parking spots near the beginning of the open area.

Path There is no path to speak of to get from the parking area to the shore. On the other hand, once you are on the shore you are not really *on* the shore, since you have to traverse a broad expanse of low dunes, logs and dune plants before you reach the high-tide line. Take a sharp right as you come toward the shore if you want to avoid this area. If you're toting unwieldy beach paraphernalia, be prepared for a little staggering—or choose Mariner Way A.

Beach The beach here has two great advantages over the two access spots immediately to the south: lots of foreshore, even at high tide, and full sun the entire day (if, indeed, that is what you want). Access to the sand isn't as quick and easy, though the sandbars start nearby if you turn to the right. The low-tide line here is about 60 m away, so it's not difficult even at low tide to get to a spot for splashy fun.

Suitability for children If the lack of shade isn't a concern, this spot, with its extensive foreshore and easy approach from the familymobile, can be great for toddlers. For quick access to low-tide sand, though, or for mid-tide swimming, you might prefer the other spots immediately to the south.

Suitability for groups This is a good spot for a group picnic, because parking is adequate for several cars and the broad foreshore allows you plenty of space to get away from the residents. Be aware, though, that there are no toilet facilities.

View One of the prettiest views is from the back of the sandy area, where you can look at the expanses of sea, islands and mountains through a lattice of beach grass and old logs. From the shore itself, your view will be a little more extensive than from the similar spots in the San Pareil area, because the shore is largely convex here.

Winds, sun and shade If it's windy out there, then it's windy in here—though not quite so windy in a northwest wind as it would be at Mariner Way C. There is almost no shade, except a very little right near the parking lot. Come prepared.

Beachcombing To the north, beachcombing is limited, though you will be able to walk a few hundred metres to the point where Englishman River cuts across the gravel promontory. To the south, however, you can go, literally, for kilometres—at least if you're prepared for walking over loose sand, gravel or wet sand. At high tide, be warned: the walkable strip can get very narrow.

Seclusion You will, of course, be in full view of the stretch of houses on either side so will want to minimize behaviour of questionable taste. On the other hand, you can get far enough away from these houses that, to a large extent, you can Be Yourself (whatever that might be). Likewise, to the north, the dune area can provide a considerable buffer between you and Watching Eyes. In fact, one of the most secluded spots is right near the parking lot, where a bench is placed in a nest of short, bushy firs.

14

MARINER WAY C

Good for foul-weather car-picnicking or good-weather sunbathing

Location, signs and parking Instead of turning right onto Shorewood Drive, turn left onto Mariner Way and, in a short distance, you will see an obvious, large area with mailboxes and a view of the sea through some firs. There is plenty of room for several cars here. In fact, one of the advantages of this parking spot is that on a hot day you can find a place for your car in the shade. Signs telling you not to park overnight (nor, presumably, carouse late into it) and welcoming you to the wildlife area further indicate that you've come to a public access.

Path From the end of the parking area, a few steps will lead you directly through pebbles and logs onto the pebbly upper shore. At high tide a kayak could be easily launched here—but be aware that if the tide is going out when you launch, you could be faced with a broad strip of beach when you return.

Beach Because this access spot is so close to that on Shorewood Drive, it shares much the same beach features—a strip of gravel on the upper shore, and, at low tide, some broad bands of sand. Unlike its neighbour to the south, however, this spot retains some foreshore even at high tide, plenty for sitting among the logs and staring out to sea or drinking a mug of coffee. In foul weather this is a good place to come for a car picnic—indeed, it is one of the best spots between Wall Beach (entry 24) and Parksville to park with a good view of the beach. Swimming is good for adults at high tide, since the bank shelves off quickly enough to give you easy access to deep water.

Suitability for children In some ways this is a better spot to bring children than the neighbouring Shorewood Drive access, if only because you can get onto the beach here without struggling over the boulders. In addition, there is more room at high tide for very little ones to investigate the pebbles and to attempt to ingest as many as possible. Otherwise, access to the sand stretches of low tide is probably a little easier from Shorewood Drive. In either case, don't forget that tender tootsies need to be got over the many metres of gravel before you get to the sand.

Suitability for groups This isn't a bad spot to bring two or three cars' worth of beach buddies or family members. The area in front of the access road is wide enough that you can spread out your picnic baskets without daunting the neighbours, and the beach—at low tide—is expansive enough to allow considerable wandering and wading.

View In some ways the view is prettiest as you approach the end of the parking lot, because from this point you will see the Strait framed by some fine Douglas-firs. From any point, however, the view is wide and amply larded with the mountains, peninsulas and islands that characterize this part of the coast. To the north you will see the shore curving gracefully out to the gravel- and low-dune promontory that is the distinctive feature of the beach access there.

Winds, sun and shade Both northwest and southeast winds make themselves felt here, but both obliquely, making this area at low tide a good spot for a bit of kite flying. You can come any time of day if it's sun you're after. If, however, if you want some shade, you should come in the afternoon and be prepared to move along the shore as the dappled shadows of the shorefront firs creep across the beach.

Beachcombing Long-distance walkers will head south toward Rathtrevor. Beach explorers will don water shoes or flip-flops and search out the low-tide line, tidal pools and sand bars.

Seclusion Because the access spot is quite wide, you won't feel like an intruder—but neither will you experience any lonely communion with the spirit of the sea. The houses on either side are set somewhat back from the shore, but on neither side is there a high fence or hedge to screen you from them—or them from you.

15

SHOREWOOD DRIVE (PARKSVILLE)

A short distance from your car to a fine sandy beach

Location, signs and parking Although the upper beach is less appealing than at some of the other nearby spots, this access is nevertheless attractive and a good alternative if the other spots are crowded. You will see the gap between houses opposite the house numbered 920. One sign will tell you that it is dangerous for you to collect shellfish. Others, forbidding overnight parking and identifying the spot as a Wildlife Management Area, mark the spot. Like all of the other access spots along here, this one, too, is identifiable by a bank of mailboxes. There is room for six or seven cars in this gap between houses, and room for more on the nearby shoulders on the off chance that this spot is crowded.

Path It is easy to get onto the beach. Unlike the other three access points of the San Pareil strip, though, this path passes through a foreshore-stabilizing bank of broken boulders.

Beach This part of the beach has very little foreshore, particularly at high tide. Indeed, at high tide this is by far the least appealing of the four similar access spots in the area. However, at low and mid tide— when some look forward to swimming over a sandy bottom— the sand is glorious. Of all the access spots in the San Pareil area, this one leads most quickly and readily at low tide onto a considerable expanse of fine sand. Be warned, though: if you come at high tide for a swim, don't expect to find sand underfoot unless you are very, very tall.

Suitability for children If your children can clamber over the jagged rocks without coming a cropper, they should have a wonderfully beachy day or afternoon at this spot, primarily because of the proximity of the expanse of sand. At low tide they will be able to build castles and plaster each other with sand pies to their hearts' content. On an incoming tide, they will be able to splash and squeal with equal abandon. At high tide you would be better off choosing one of the spots to the north. Note the observations on wind and sun below, too, before you come to this spot.

Suitability for groups The comparative lack of foreshore and the proximity of the neighbours don't make this a great spot for groups. Choose the nearby Juniper Road on the next page instead.

View Like all the spots along this stretch, this one gives you a slightly modified version of the classic Parksville view—lots of open sea (or, at least, as much as you're going to get on the east coast of Vancouver Island), yet embellished with Texada Island, Tetrahedron Mountain, Panther Mountain, and, best of all, Mount Tantalus across the Strait. In addition, to the south you will see the middle horizon dotted with both the Ballenas and Mistaken islands.

Winds, sun and shade A northwest wind can become quite enthusiastic here, so, if the weather is only marginally warm, come prepared. A southeast wind strikes the shore obliquely but can nevertheless be quite strong when "she's a-blowin'." The first half of the day provides no shade. During the second half of the day, shadows from adjoining firs will crawl in patches across the shore, making it easy to find sun or shade, depending on your druthers.

Beachcombing From this spot, if you don't mind a little slipping and sliding among pebbles, you can choose to do long-distance striding along the upper beach in either direction. At low tide, you can also walk long distances in either direction (particularly to the south), but you will have to be shod for a mixture of rocks, water and sand.

Seclusion You are, in effect, in the middle of a suburb. The houses on either side are set slightly back and are partly hidden behind high fences and hedges, but even so, don't expect any sense of seclusion.

16

JUNIPER ROAD
The "back door" to Rathtrevor
Beach Park

Location, signs and parking Once you've found your way into the San Pareil area, follow Shorewood Drive as it curves right and takes a sharp turn onto Juniper under a stand of large firs. You will see a chain-link fence, a gate and a sign telling you not to park overnight. There is space for several cars along the shoulder on either side of the road. Beyond the immediate vicinity of the gate, though, signs will inform you that you are not welcome to park—presumably because local residents do not want their front lawns and drives crowded with cars.

Path A gate—closed overnight—gives you direct access to the network of shoreline paths that intersect for the next several hundred metres through the beautiful old-growth fir forest at the north end of Rathtrevor Provincial Park. The widest paths will keep you going all the way through the park. The narrow paths that lead toward the shore a few metres away all come to halt on the shore itself. The path is horizontal the whole way, but a few roots would provide obstacles for anyone with extreme walking difficulties.

Beach This is the end of Rathtrevor Park to come to if your real interest is in walking through the forest and enjoying a few hundred metres of quiet beach. It is not a quick access to the vast expanses of sand that most visitors expect from Rathtrevor Beach. Along this stretch, the tide retreats a fraction of the distance it does on the main beach. In addition, the upper beach is made up almost entirely of bars of golf-ball- and ostrich-egg-sized gravel and rock. Wait for low tide if you are after sand—or head for the main beach. Picnickers and novel readers take note, though: the upper shore has many patches of coarse sand and pebbles if nestling among the logs is what you're after.

Suitability for children When the weather is too cold for water play, children might happily accompany their parents here, particularly for a winter walk, when the tide is high during the day and the waves can splash around close at hand. Otherwise, this is not the best choice of spot for a summer-and-sand trip: head for one of the spots immediately to the north or the main public beach.

Suitability for groups If parking can be managed, then a group could easily bring themselves to this spot for a picnic or shore walk without fear of crowding out the neighbourhood. None of the picnic tables (or washrooms) available at the main park are available here, but the area has plenty of logs on which to perch and much space to enjoy.

View The view is much more open here than at the main part of Rathtrevor because you are no longer partly behind Arbutus Point. To the south you will see not just Arbutus Point, but, immediately behind it, Mistaken Island and Cottam (Beachcomber) Point. From this far north, too, you will get almost the same glorious view of the glaciered flanks of Mount Tantalus that you see farther north along the coast. On the other hand, by this far north the peaks of Jervis Inlet are tucked behind the landmark mound of south Texada Island.

Winds, sun and shade You will feel a northwest wind and all of its either refreshing or cooling strength here. A southeast wind is likewise unhampered here, though it hits the shore at an oblique angle. Morning is the time of day to come if you want sun; afternoon is the time to come if you want shade. Of course, for shade, any time of day will do if you walk under the trees.

Beachcombing Although the easiest walking is done in the forest immediately behind the shore, it is easy enough to walk along the upper shore, even in winter. In fact, if you are after a long walk, you can choose either direction. One will take you to the main Rathtrevor park, and the other along the nearly flat stretches of pebbles and sand in front of San Pareil (at least as far as Englishman River, just over a kilometre distant).

Seclusion You will find others, particularly walkers, passing up and down the shore here. Very few people seem to choose this spot to settle down with munchables or drinkables. The large forested area immediately behind, and the relative quiet of spring, winter and autumn make this a great area to saunter in if you find yourself intoning that threadbare line from John Masefield's poem "Sea Fever": "I must go down to the seas again, to the lonely sea and the sky."

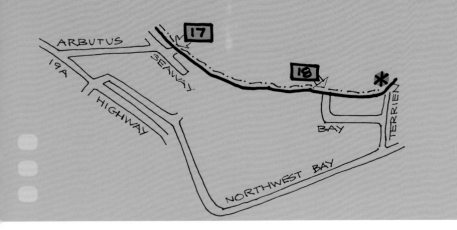

17
ARBUTUS ROAD
Easy and pleasant access to the southern end of Rathtrevor Beach

Location, signs and parking Arbutus Road leads diagonally off Highway 19A past the stretch of big resorts and descends the hill onto the flat part of the shore. Slow down when you come level with the water. As soon as you turn onto Seaway, keep your eyes open for a 15 m gap between houses. Too many signs bristle on posts to list here, but they will make obvious what you will already have guessed by now—this, indeed, is public access. The signs you might want most to take note of are an unusual version of a restriction on dogs and the alarming tsunami warning sign. There is room for a couple of cars in the gap between the houses. If this spot happens to be full, you can fairly easily find parking on the shoulder.

Path Parents and picnickers take note: a short, almost level track leads you directly onto the pebbles and sand amidst the logs of the upper beach.

Beach This access spot brings you closer than the two previous spots to the main Rathtrevor beach. You will see some large patches of eelgrass and the giant, eelgrass-filled tidal pool that divides the north part of the beach from the south part. Adults coming to this beach for a swim in the justly renowned warm water will be frustrated unless they come at a genuinely high tide. The shore slopes so gradually that, under most tide conditions, swimmers have to be very, very determined indeed to reach water deep enough to swim. Instead, choose this spot for throwing Frisbees or sauntering through sandy tidal pools with tiny flatfish tickling your feet.

Suitability for children This is the best access spot to choose if your primary aim in coming to the beach is to take your children out onto the sand with kites, spades and sunscreen. Don't overlook the fact, however, that at a very low-tide, the water is a long way off and that far out on the beach, it is often much breezier than it is closer in. Buried shards of seashell can pose some hazard for little scampering feet. Experienced parents will also be alert to the fact that on an incoming tide, a child standing in knee-deep water atop a sandbar might have to negotiate much deeper water in the attempt to reach shore. That being said, do choose an incoming tide if you want the warmest water. The top few inches of a flood tide can become bathtub warm.

Suitability for groups The access itself is too limited to bring more than two or three cars' worth of friends or family. Likewise, the gap between houses is too limited for a group if your plan is to have several picnic blankets festooned across the logs and sand. Needless to say, however, a group could use the spot as an access to the stretches of sand that lie before them. And then there are always those (small) wedding parties that want an unusual place for photo ops.

View The view from this spot is very much the classic Rathtrevor view. You will see Arbutus/Madrona Point directly in front, and, beyond that, Texada and a glimpse of the Jervis Inlet mountains on the mainland.

Winds, sun and shade The northwest wind is largely reduced here because it blows slightly offshore at this point. Out on the sand, however, it can be felt enough to fly a fine kite or raise goosebumps on a bare arm. A southeast wind is likewise partly screened here, but on a blowy day will assert itself a little. Expect as much sun as the sky offers. During the first half of the day, the sun will be most direct on the upper beach. In the afternoon, it will swing behind you. A few trees along the shore will provide shade if the sun is a-blazing.

Beachcombing Although you can walk in either direction, you will probably want to head north to the main Rathtrevor beach and, if you're ambitious, to the paths through the old-growth forest at the north end of the park. Though you will have the impression that you can head out across the sand and keep your feet dry if you avoid the tidal pools, you will soon discover that this is a false impression. Plan your footwear accordingly. You may wish to avoid the crowds and head to the south end of the bay, but be aware that the sand starts to become very soft, even unpleasantly so, at the extreme end of the bay. Some visitors also proceed with the misguided impression that they can walk all the way to Madrona/Arbutus Point at a low tide. They are wrong. They can walk within 100 m, but then will have to do some deep-water swimming if they really want to reach the point!

Seclusion Close to you is a public beach and one of the most popular parks on the coast. It is also one of the beach areas most densely lined with condos and hotels. Nevertheless, amazingly, you can walk to the low-tide line almost a kilometre from shore and be virtually alone except on the hottest days of mid-summer.

18

BAY ROAD

Unusual access to the sheltered south end of Rathtrevor Beach

Location, signs and parking Be warned! Similarly named Bay *Avenue* is on the north side of Parksville Beach. Take Terrien Road off Northwest Bay Road and then the first road left. Follow it to its end as it curves to the right and brings you to a gravelly dead end just a few metres from the shore. A cluster of signs will greet you with the information that you have, indeed, found a public access, but will warn you of the dangers of collecting shellfish and of the undesirability of you (and your poodle) alarming brants during the spring migration. It is fairly easy to park at various spots along the shoulder.

Path A 10 m long path about 1 m wide leads almost horizontally through high dune grass. You really don't want to bring your kayak here, though, unless you plan a short paddle at high tide.

Beach If you reach the spot at high tide, you will see a sloping shore of sand and gravel and, in hot weather, will feel enticed to swim—as well you should, for some of the warmest swimming waters on the coast are to be found at this and nearby beaches. At low tide the whole vast spread of sand and eelgrass flats is before you. From this angle, however, you will notice a striking feature of the Craig Bay (or its sand flats) are not on the map. The bay does not completely empty at low tide. Instead, a huge, fairly deep "inlet" separates the north end of the flats from the much smaller south end. If it is bare sand you're after, you will want to head north along the shore and then turn out onto the sand, noticing that the farther you go toward Rathtrevor, the less prevalent the eelgrass becomes. If, however, you're interested in seashore life, consider wading and even snorkelling in the "inlet" in search of some fascinating creatures.

Suitability for children Lots of sun, lots of sand, easy access—all of these can add up to a real "beachy" day for a child. Be aware, though, that many children will be squeamish about the amount of eelgrass on the lower beach and that sometimes sharp bits of shell can be buried in the sand or half-hidden by the eelgrass.

Suitability for groups This is a good spot to bring a group. You can park many cars without having an impact on neighbouring houses, and you can even bustle fairly noisily from your cars and onto the beach without disturbing anyone. In fact, because this access road borders on the sprawling and meticulously groomed insta-community of Craig Bay Estates, you will find that instead of houses to your north, you have a huge empty field of beach grass acting as a kind of community park for the Craig Bay Estate residents. Once on the beach, you and your in-laws can settle yourselves among the logs and sand without worry about overwhelming neighbours.

View This is not, of course, a wide-open view, but with most of the tourist and condo development spread along the shore to your left, you will want to look out to sea past Madrona Point opposite and Texada Island, with even a glimpse of the Jervis Inlet mountains beyond.

Winds, sun and shade You will feel a somewhat muffled version of a northwest wind from this spot. This is a great spot to come when a southeast wind is cooling the rest of the beach because you are sheltered here. A few firs will offer some occasional patches of shade, but most of the day you will be in the sun.

Beachcombing Needless to say, this is a great place to begin walks either along the foreshore or out onto the flats. You may, however, want to plan footgear appropriate to where you want to walk. You will be guaranteed to get wet feet if you head for the sand flats. On the other hand—or foot—you won't want to wear flip-flops if you head to your right, where the sand becomes very soft and can pull loose shoes off your feet.

Seclusion Although it would be a stretch to call the spot "secluded," it is surprisingly quiet—partly because of the cluster of trees by the access spot and partly because the houses on either side are set so far back.

✳ **Also nearby** Look for public access at the very end of **Terrien Road** (off which you turned to get to Bay Road.) Most will prefer to come to the nearby Bay Road access, however. In the first place, the sand is less muddy near the Bay Road access. In addition, you will feel a little intrusive crossing the grass adjacent to the house at the end of Terrien Road before entering the path beneath the trees.

Hungry gulls and the Ballenas Islands

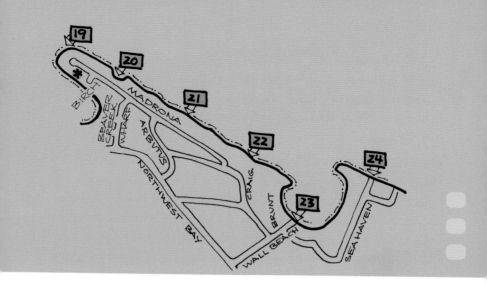

19

MADRONA POINT COMMUNITY PARK
Sandstone formations, evening sun and pebble pocket beaches

Location, signs and parking To reach this beautiful little park, turn left onto Madrona Drive from Beaver Creek Wharf Road. Drive to the end of Madrona Drive while cheerfully ignoring the sign that tells you that there is "no turnaround" to be had. Another sign will tell you that you may not park overnight. Several driveways lead directly into the small cul-de-sac, so parking can be a bit of a trick—and all the more so since scuba divers (understandably) love this spot. If worse comes, as it sometimes does, to worst, park farther down the road and be prepared to walk to the park. You won't regret that you did.

Path There is really more than one path, though the main, well-used path descends gradually over 15 or 20 m to a pebble foreshore. An equally wide trail branches off to the left, but, after a short distance, is intercepted with a large sign nailed to a tree informing visitors that the land beyond is private property. (It is a little puzzling that the path continues obliviously past this sign with no indication that visitors respect the sign.) Also from the main trail, however, another branch takes you an additional 20 m parallel to and slightly back from the shore to a wooded bluff with some gnarled and picturesque trees. Here you will find a bench donated by a local resident.

Beach The beach is a curious and complex arrangement of shelving sandstone, pebbly patches, bluffs and large, bulbous bumps. Since the sandstone strata extend away from the main upper beach, they form pockets where pebbles collect. Once you walk around the point to the right, however, you reach an area where the sandstone shelf is dramatically and colourfully embellished with a few large sandstone boulders and bizarre protrusions. At any tide, this is a great place for snorkelling and scuba diving, as well as picnicking, sunbathing or simply staring out to sea in one of the many different directions open to you. Unfortunately, one of the pebble beaches has been scarred with the remains of a beach fire.

Suitability for children If the tide is in and your children want to play in the water, they would probably be happiest at the first beach you come to before the point. However, if it's shore play they're after and they have energy and imagination, they should be kept happy for a long time exploring the nooks and crannies, rock castles, tidal pools and so on.

Suitability for groups If you can carpool so that you don't enrage the locals with congesting the road approach, you could bring several friends or family members here. The fact that the area is quite large and has many little coves and knolls means that you should be able to take your gaggle to a spot without overwhelming the whole park. Don't be misled by the term "park," however. Like many small local parks, this one has no washrooms or picnic tables.

View The views are enormously varied, since this is a point. By walking all the way around the shore you can experience something like a 300-degree series of views. If you walk around the point to the left, you will see, probably with little delight, the entire residential and tourist network of condominiums and hotels that covers the Rathtrevor strip. More interestingly, you will have great views of Mount Moriarty and Mount Arrowsmith (particularly in the morning before they are silhouetted by the afternoon sun). Looking directly out from the point you will see the old-growth forest at the north end of Rathtrevor merging

Madrona Point Community Park

into the residential area of San Pareil. Now, if you walk around the shore to the right you will see Mistaken Island, Beachcomber peninsula and a tiny fragment of the Ballenas. With the mainland mountains, and especially the glaciers of Mount Tantalus behind, your palette of scenic splendours should be complete.

Winds, sun and shade If there is any wind, from any direction, you will either be able to find spots fully exposed to it or spots completely sheltered. Complete shelter from a northwest wind is a little more difficult to find than shelter from a southeast wind, but even with this wind, you can tuck yourself with your novel and sunscreen into a spot facing the mainland. As the sun moves through the day, so do the areas of sun and shade. At any time of day, you will find both. That being said, you might note that this is one of the few spots along the entire section of coast from Nanaimo to Qualicum where you can enjoy an evening picnic while, on a cool day, experiencing the full warmth of the evening sun.

Beachcombing Because this spot has so much variety, you will probably want to spend your time poking around here. You may, at a glance, think you can cross over the very short distance to the low-tide line of Rathtrevor Beach. This is an illusion. You can't. You could swim over, perhaps, but you cannot walk. On the other hand, you can head south along the sandstone and conglomerate shelf all the way to Wall Beach if you want to get some kilometres under your belt. At high tide, though, the shelf can be narrow, and in winter it can be slippery.

Seclusion The spot is understandably a popular one, but the shoreline is irregular enough that you can always find a place in which to nestle and let down your hair. And you will not be under inspection from locals anywhere.

٭ Also nearby Birch Place is a short dead-end road that leads from your left as you approach Madrona Point. Technically a public access, it is worth visiting only for a pleasant stroll through the arbutus and for a view from the clifftop toward the Island's mountains. Unless you have a rope and harness, don't expect to get down to the water!

20

MADRONA POINT ROAD A

A gradually sloping pebble beach with views toward Mistaken Island

Location, signs and parking Turn onto Beaver Creek Wharf Road from Northwest Bay Road and left at the T-junction onto Madrona Drive. You won't see any signs, but find the house numbered 1407, and opposite it you will see a paved area with room for five or six cars.

Path The path to the beach begins at the left end of the parking area. The 1 m wide path, beginning in a forest of blackberry vines, descends only slightly for 20 m or so before opening onto the beach. If you need a spot in the area to launch a kayak, this would be the easiest path to choose, though Madrona Point Community Park is another possibility. Partway to the beach, a sign reminds you that you are approaching a public beach and requests you to do what, one hopes, it would be unthinkable not to do—clean up after your "pet" (though it's hard to think what such a pet might be other than a dog).

Beach The beach is the only significant break in the sandstone-conglomerate shelf that extends from Wall Beach to the tip of the point. The beach is about 100 m long and curves into a gentle bay that dries at low tide. The upper beach is made up of polished little pebbles, perfect for sifting through in pursuit of the world's most beautiful and unusual specimens. The rocks remain fairly small all the way to the low-tide line, but you wouldn't want to attempt the lower beach with bare feet. At the lowest tide, the sandstone points actually connect to form a complete ring. The beach, in fact, is probably at its best at high tide, when the graceful curve is particularly beautiful and the water is best for swimming.

Suitability for children This is a great swimming beach for children at high tide, since the shore slopes gradually enough that you don't need to worry about suddenly losing your child into the depths, yet slopes steeply enough that your child doesn't have to wade out for miles in search of knee-deep water. The small pebbly upper beach, too, is kind on little feet. At low tide, when the somewhat sharper and rougher stones are exposed, the chief attraction could well be a large tidal pool—a favourite fishing spot for great blue herons.

Suitability for groups The problem with bringing more than a small group here is really that the beach curves in such a way and the houses are so arranged that you really feel that you have come into a neighbourhood. That neighbourhood may be friendly and generous to visitors, but it can hardly be thrilled with the Munster Family Reunion crowding and clamouring in what is really a fairly limited space. Two or three couples, a family or two—such is the size of groups that would be most appropriate here.

View The view is charming in all directions. It is framed by the elegantly curving bay, yet is open enough to give you a varied view of the mainland islands across the Strait, the Jervis Inlet mountains beyond and Mistaken Island slightly south.

Winds, sun and shade Though gale-force winds batter the beach, any lesser wind is considerably reduced. A northwest wind tends to slide by the mouth of the bay, and a southeast wind, though a little more intrusive, likewise hits the bay at an oblique angle. Morning floods the entire bay with sun. If you need shade, you will be forced into the trees at the back of the beach. By early afternoon, though, shade spreads across the southern part of the beach (immediately in front of the point of access.). If, however, you like to swim in the full sun, the north end of the beach (which is in front of private houses) remains in sun well into the late afternoon.

Seclusion Needless to say, there is no seclusion to be had here, except perhaps if you come at an odd time of day or odd time of year. At the same time, the houses are set well back on (largely treeless) lawns and at angles to the shore rather than straight on, so you won't feel—quite—in someone's front yard.

21
MADRONA POINT ROAD B
A level, conglomerate stone shelf with close access to the low-tide line

Location, signs and parking You won't see any signs here, but as you drive from Craig Road, you will see a set of mailboxes and a wide, paved shoulder area. An alternate approach is via Arbutus Drive off Northwest Bay Road. Turn right at the T-junction onto Madrona Drive. You can park near the mailboxes, but it would be less than considerate to block access for locals who wish to scream up in their Miatas and snatch their mail. It is also possible to park along the shoulder.

Path Make your way through a thick forest of blackberries down a well-used path that descends some 4 or 5 m as it covers the 30 m distance through thick woods.

Beach Unlike the other spots along here, this one offers no patch of pebbles and sand at the entrance to the shore. In fact, at high tide there is little foreshore. At low tide, however, you will find yourself on the characteristic sandstone and conglomerate shelf that defines this whole side of Madrona Point. Mid tide is the time to choose if you want to snorkel. High tide, in contrast, will give you the warmest and most accessible swimming waters.

Suitability for children This may be a less obvious spot to bring your children than the other spots along this point, though access to the shore is easy enough, and the shore itself is free of obstacles or dangers. Be aware that at low tide, it is difficult to scramble down the comparatively steep rock to the water since, of course, the ubiquitous rock weed can make life a little…slippery.

Suitability for groups Parking is better here than at the similar spot immediately to the south, and the area of foreshore between houses is considerably wider, so it is possible to be largely unobtrusive. Sketching, photography, birdwatching and walking are good activities for a group here.

View Because this spot is slightly farther north than the previous beach access, the view from here feels a little less enclosed. From here you will see Mistaken Island and Beachcomber peninsula to your right, and, past Texada, the open waters to the north. The curve of shore is such that your view north will be contained by the tip of Madrona Point itself, so you won't have a distant perspective on Rathtrevor and Parksville.

Winds, sun and shade Though a northwest wind can become quite bumptious at this point, generally it runs parallel to the shore. The shore is exposed to a southeast wind but it, too, is roughly parallel to the shore. It is only the first half of the day that will give you a lot of sun on the upper shore. Since, however, there is not much place to lounge on the upper shore, sun or shade should not be much of an issue. Even in the afternoon, when shadow covers most of the beach, you will find some patches of both sun and shade.

Beachcombing The advantage of coming to this spot to begin your wanders is that you can venture in either direction and still enjoy the easy walking on the sandstone and conglomerate shelf. The disadvantage for those who want a long walk is that you can only get the full whammy of the shoreline by combining the two shorter walks. Be aware, too, that this shelf is almost completely covered at high tide and can become quite slippery in winter.

Seclusion You will not, in fact, be very far away from the unbroken line of shorefront houses. However, you won't see a lot of people here and won't feel as if you're trespassing on the neighbours, since most of the houses, atop a bank, have commendably maintained a fringe of shorefront firs and pines.

22
CRAIG DRIVE
A flat conglomerate stone shelf with a pebbly upper shore

Location, signs and parking Turn off Northwest Bay Road at Arbutus Drive, then right onto Craig Drive. Be alert as it curves to the right. The entrance to this narrow, wooded strip of public access land is right beside the house numbered 1855. You won't see any helpful signs, so will have to park and investigate yourself. Park on the shoulder of the road, since there is no recessed pull-off area.

Path Wedged between houses, the path is essentially the same length as the depth of the adjoining houses. The path drops maybe 7 m in the course of its 30 m through pretty woods, predominantly Douglas-firs. A few sections are a little steep, and the path can be muddy in winter, but a helpful local has cut some footsteps into the dirt at some points.

Beach The path ends in a patch of coarse sand and small pebbles backed by dune grass and overhung with firs. This access spot brings you near the beginning of the sandstone and conglomerate shelf that extends, with one major break, the whole length of Madrona Point. At this point the shelf has some gentle undulations and is dotted with a few large granite boulders. The lower part of the shelf drops off comparatively steeply, so at low tide the whole exposed area is some 30 m wide.

Suitability for children The pebbly area is good for nestling in, pebble searching and picnicking. The shelf is easy walking, even for unsteady little legs. A child who wants to splash is best brought to this spot at a mid to high tide, however, since the access to the water at low tide is awkward and slippery over the fucus-covered and irregular lower shore.

Suitability for groups Parking isn't great, of course, and the public area of foreshore is quite narrow, so it would be difficult to accommodate more than a few people without spreading in front of neighbour houses. Still, a couple of families could have a pleasant afternoon here without creating too much social havoc among the neighbours.

View The view from here is more open than from the other two similar access spots farther out along the peninsula, since the shoreline here is noticeably, if not dramatically, convex. On the other hand, though you get a good view into Wall Beach in one direction and up the northern Strait to the left, you will feel a little more enclosed here than at other spots if you want a good view of open water.

Winds, sun and shade This spot is a little more protected from northwest winds than the two similar spots farther along the peninsula, since the wind angles slightly away from the shore and can barely be felt up against the trees. A southeast wind can be felt more directly, but even it seems, inexplicably, somewhat muted at this point. If you want to picnic or sunbathe on the pebbly foreshore, be sure to come early in the day. Starting in the early afternoon, shade gradually spreads over the shore.

Beachcombing Opportunities abound for walking and exploring from here. To your right, you can walk through the shallows to sand and gravel bars close to Wall Beach. To your left, you can begin a walk that takes you all the way to the tip of Arbutus Point (though don't plan a round trip down the west shore of Arbutus Point, because that side is impassably cliffy).

Seclusion It is only the neighbours on either side who share this spot with you, and their houses are pulled somewhat back from the shore itself and well placed among trees.

23

WALL BEACH
A little bit of everything—
sandstone bluffs, tidal pools,
pebbly foreshores, big patches
of sand

Location, signs and parking This is by far the more obvious and popular spot to choose for visiting Wall Beach (although there is another access slightly south). Turn off Northwest Bay Road at the junction with Wall Beach Road and follow it directly to the end. A sign warns you of the danger of collecting shellfish. There is plenty of space in the area between a high fence on the left and a hedge on the right for about half a dozen cars. In the unlikely event that these spots are all taken, more cars could, with some difficulty, park on nearby shoulders.

Path A few steps take you almost horizontally through some beach grass and over a few logs. In fact, at high tide, this would be a good place to launch a kayak—but not, be warned, at low tide. The goods and chattels of beach play are easily brought to the shore.

Beach You won't find much more variety at a single beach than at this one. Wall Beach has a bit of everything. This is really a low-tide beach, however. At mid to high tide, you will find yourself facing a considerable and not wildly appealing expanse of small gravel (and, of course, barnacles). At low tide, in contrast, you will see a playground of diverse elements. Directly in front and slightly to the right, some sandy tidal pools full of little crabs and flatfish separate two large sandbars. These sandbars have been infiltrated by oyster shells straying from the gravel bars, so little swimmers might have to be careful where they put their feet down.

To the right of these sandbars is a curious Y-shaped gravel bar, looking almost artificial because it rises so steeply from the sandbars. At very low tides, the entire bay empties, making it possible to explore more sandbars extending out to both sandstone points embracing the bay. These sandstone points are themselves great potential spots for play, with their castle-like shapes and colourful tidal pools. If you're after swimming, choose a high tide, because the low-tide line is very far away and swimming conditions can be less than pleasant if the Sargassum seaweed, or Japanese seaweed (an invasive species), has decided to flourish the year you are there. Snorkelling, however, can be fascinating at low tide.

Suitability for children Oblivious children can cut their feet if they scamper heedlessly around the sandbars. In addition, there is really no place to shelter from sun. Provided they bring good sense, parents can also bring their children to this beach with the expectation of many hours of beach fun.

Suitability for groups Parking is adequate for a small group, and the diversions are plenty. Do come at low tide, though, and encourage your group to walk well out onto the beach away from the houses. The sandstone point directly across the bay, with its undulations and knobs, makes an ideal spot for a gaggle of picnickers.

View Those looking for an expansive seascape will feel themselves a little confined here. Those looking for a picturesquely framed combination of shorefront elements will be delighted. For the prettiest view (and best photographs or sketches), choose high tide, when the curve of the bay and the two sandstone peninsulas (both with gnarled firs) provide a pleasing foreground for Beachcomber peninsula and Mistaken Island in the middle distance and, across the Strait, Lasqueti and Texada.

Winds, sun and shade Wall Beach is largely protected from a northwest wind and almost fully from a southeast wind, but occasionally a north wind will fill the bay with whitecaps and breaking waves. The only shade to be had is in the afternoon at the north end of the beach—but there is no real public foreshore to perch on. Do, therefore, come to Wall Beach on a sunny day only if you really, really like sun.

Beachcombing Exploring the sandbars, pools and gravel bars of the bay at low tide is best done with water shoes. If, however, you want to put some kilometres under your belt, you can initiate a long walk from here in either direction. Turn right and keep to the upper beach to reach the sandstone shelf that will take you around the bay and deep into Northwest Bay around the corner to the south. Turn left, and you can make your way, also largely on a sandstone and conglomerate shelf, all the way to Madrona Point.

Seclusion Don't expect even a whiff of seclusion here. The deep curve of the bay and the many houses pressed up against the shoreline mean that you will always feel very much in the middle of a much-loved and much-used holiday spot.

24

SEAHAVEN ROAD
An easy, wooded approach to a secluded stretch of sculpted sandstone shore

Location, signs and parking From Wall Beach Road, simply go straight ahead the short distance to where you can see the open shore beckoning through the trees. You will have to be careful not to block the drive of house 2023, but otherwise there is plenty of space for four or five cars in the turnaround area and, if it were ever necessary, even more on the shoulder of the approaching road.

Path Short and sweet, the path is about 1 m wide and over a distance of about 10 m descends 2 or 3 m to a mini-beach of pebbles and a few logs.

Beach Where the path reaches the shore, a little nest of pebbles protected by the shoulder of grass-covered sandstone bluff to your left may invite you to spread out a lounging blanket or plunk a beach chair. Beyond this spot, you will find yourself on the wonderfully convoluted and carved sandstone shelf that extends 200 m or so to the right and, to the left, more than 100 m to the point that forms one protective lip for Wall Beach. Particularly delightful are the almost spherical, waist-high stone knobs, some of them decorated with tiny, elevated tidal pools. The crevices crossing the rock and extending to the low tide line can be filled with shells and creatures, though the rock itself does become slippery with fucus. It is possible to find fossils in this area, particularly along the little promontory to the south.

Suitability for children Children should delight in scampering and climbing over the rock formations, digging into tidal pools and playing all sorts of imaginative games involving kings of castles and the like. The lower beach at low tide, with its crevices and fucus-covered rocks, might be a bit of a challenge for the littlest of the little ones, however. Once covered with water, the shore is wonderful for snorkelling and seems to beckon with hidden chambers and swaying seaweed forests. You will give your children the greatest delight if you can arrange to be here at high tide when a warm wind blows from the northwest. Watch your wee ones shriek and leap as the waves splash around the smooth rocky bumps.

Suitability for groups You probably wouldn't want to bring a group that was planning a single mega-picnic. A group interested in wandering, exclaiming and taking photographs will find plenty of scope for a couple of hours of pure pleasure.

View The view is a little confined. You will find yourself looking straight across at the long steep shore of houses on the other side of Northwest Bay and the marina toward the base of the bay. Still, you will be able to see Mistaken and Texada islands and the Strait opening northwards to the faint shadow of Denman and Hornby islands.

Winds, sun and shade In strong winds from either direction you will find little protection, except by nestling right up against the tree-lined shore. Neither prevailing wind, however, hits the beach straight on. Both can be wonderfully cooling on hot days. The waves produced by the long "fetch" of a northwest blow hit the shore with lots of foam and spray and make for great photos. The whole beach will be in sun until about noon; thereafter only the sandstone shelf will be in sun.

Beachcombing Yes! This is one of the supreme spots for a certain kind of beach wanderer. The smooth but undulating sandstone shelf makes for easy strolling, with many intriguing variations. Extend your walk all the way round to a little secluded bay at the south end of the sandstone strip and, at high tide, take a dip in the particularly warm water to be found there. Alternately, walk all the way around to Wall Beach, either keeping to the sandstone upper beach or venturing onto the beach itself. For the latter route it's best if you bring sturdy water shoes.

Seclusion This spot is not entirely secluded, but your dominant feeling is of woods behind and untouched natural beauty all around—unless someone else wanders into your domain!

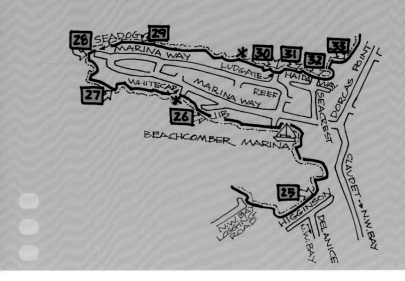

25

HIGGINSON ROAD

A pebbly beach with good views of sunsets and, in winter, sea lions

Location, signs and parking Turn off Northwest Bay Road down Delanice Way and right onto Higginson at the T-junction. Just before the road starts uphill you will see one of the small blue PUBLIC ACCESS signs that appear sporadically in this area. The shoulder of the road is the only place to park a vehicle (easiest if you drive past the path entrance, turn around, and pull over right by the shoulder here).

Cyclists' alert! This is one of the few beaches in the book best avoided by cyclists who don't want to break into a healthy sweat or who discover that there are no gears on the bike they found in their granny's garage. Most will find that swooping down to the beach is fun. Only the fit will find the return trip fun.

Path The pretty path, about 1 m wide, descends very slightly through a beautiful stand of trees—including two magnificent western red cedars, in themselves well worth the price of admission. The length of the path is the same as the length of the neighbouring lots, that is, roughly 30 m, so it would be possible to use this as a spot to launch a kayak, though the commercial launching spot of Beachcomber Marina nearby is also possible. High tide can be a bit of a trick. The high-tide water actually flows *under* the highest ridge of pebbles to fill up an otherwise empty concavity through which the path goes. At such tides, be prepared for a short scramble on the adjoining rocks.

Beach You will arrive beneath a striking cliffy area at the end of a curving pebbly shore about 100 m long. Although the beach takes its general colour from the steel-grey rock that makes up Beachcomber peninsula, don't be misled. In fact, those who perk up after a fit of sunbathing to sift through the pebbles will find an astonishing variety of colours and patterns. The trick will be not going home with pockets sagging from the weight of too many treasures—treasures which, of course, will lose much of their magic the instant they are in a house. Unlike most local beaches, which have pebbles only at the top of the beach, this one does not give way at the lower end of the beach to boulders and barnacles. Rather, the fairly steeply sloping beach is pebbly right to the low-water mark (with a sandy bottom just out of reach at low tide.) Unfortunately, because of its proximity to log booms, the beach sometimes is partly covered with bark debris.

Suitability for children The beach is safe and welcoming for children of all ages, though it doesn't provide a huge range of beach activities beyond skipping rocks, wading, treasure hunting and, at high tide, swimming. The level, comparatively short path makes getting to and from the water easy for little tottering folk.

Suitability for groups You could take two or possibly three families to this spot, but any more than that would probably seem intrusive and overwhelming, particularly since you don't have very much shore between the access point and the sequence of waterfront lawns that extend down the rest of the bay.

View In some ways the view is fairly restricted—yet, like the pebbles, varied. Because the access brings you to the southernmost end of the beach, you will find a jagged wall of rock to your right, and, beyond, the boats of Beachcomber Marina (that some will find picturesque). Farther along, your view is framed by the house-encrusted steep shore of Beachcomber peninsula. To your left, you will see a large area of log booms and beyond that, the wooded, almost uninhabited shoreline extending all the way to Wall Beach. Some will find the log booms hideous—and hideous reminders of disturbing logging practices on Vancouver Island. Others will be intrigued by the occasional thunder and crash of logs being dumped into the water, and also by the antics of the busy little boom boats pushing the logs into place. And from October to April, all will be fascinated by the incessantly barking sea lions. To see any of these views, however, binoculars are a must. A final viewing feature of this beach is the magnificent angle it can afford on sunsets.

Winds, sun and shade As the name of the bay suggests, northwest winds hit the beach straight on, while southeast winds, even when they are roaring away elsewhere, leave the water like a placid pond. Morning isn't the best time for this beach. It will be shady and even a little gloomy. Afternoons and evenings will be full of light and sun, though; if you are nursing a sunburn, you will be hard-pressed to find shade.

Beachcombing While walking along the 150 m stretch of pebble beach is entirely possible, it is not particularly comfortable. The comparatively steep slant of the beach and loose pebbles (especially at the top edge of the beach) will make anything more than a gentle stroll frustrating. The effort can be worthwhile, though; you approach the last houses, you will see that the bank at this end of the beach is the site of an ancient midden—a place where First Nations dumped the clamshells on which they feasted. If you're wondering why you see almost exclusively clamshells, you might want to remember that almost all of the oyster shells that now cover many areas of our beaches are from non-native oysters introduced early in the 20th century.

Seclusion If you stay directly in front of the access trail, you will feel reasonably uninspected by locals. Stray very far, however, and you will feel the opposite. The favourite spot for local sea lion watchers is not here but at a much closer approach off Northwest Bay Road. On weekends, when the logging operations have stopped, locals turn down the logging road off Northwest Bay Road, park in front of the locked gate and walk from there. The numbers of these California sea lions have decreased during the last few years, though whether this is a trend or a temporary dip is impossible to say. These animals, weighing up to 300 kilograms, spend their summers south in—as their name suggests—California, and move north in winter. This may strike the rest of the animal world as odd: each season the whales, hummingbirds and everything between must scratch their heads as they cross paths with the contrary sea lions.

26
THE JIB
A west-facing pebbly beach with a great view of Mount Arrowsmith

Location, signs and parking From Northwest Bay Road, turn onto Claudet Road and follow it past the turnoff to Beachcomber Marina, at which point it changes its name to Marina Way. Follow Marina Way a few hundred metres and turn left on the short dead-end road called, nautically enough, The Jib. You will see no indication that there is a public access anywhere near here. Look for the house numbered 1238 and, immediately beyond it, a swath of grass bounded on one side by a wooden fence and on the other by a high evergreen hedge. A couple of cars can park on adjoining shoulders, but there is no special parking place.

Path The length of the path is the length of the waterfront lots and gently sloping. A few steps down this narrow but clear path will bring you directly onto the beach.

Beach About 75 m long, this is a curved pebble beach that empties at low tide. Kayak groups sometimes use this as a launching spot, though launching can be a little awkward at low tide. The rocks become larger and more barnacle-covered the closer you come to the low-tide line, with a few big boulders, as there often are on such beaches. The beach is bounded on both sides by protrusions of blue-black basalt: the one on the north extends across almost the entire beach at low tide. Swimming is warmer at this beach than it is at some more exposed spots, though it is best undertaken at mid or high tide.

Suitability for children This is a good paddling, splashing and swimming beach at high tide. It is a good picnicking beach at any tide, particularly on a cool but sunny day. Skipping rocks and exploring the rocky shelf will also keep some children amused.

Suitability for groups This beach is not suitable for groups. Read the Seclusion notes and take your group elsewhere.

View The view has some of the features of the view from Beachcomber Community Park, since from here, as from there, you are looking at the mountains and shore of Vancouver Island rather than across the Strait. It is considerably more restricted, though, in part because you are entirely at sea level, in part because the headland on your right cuts off your view in that direction and virtually forces you to include the log dump in your gaze. For good or ill, the breakwater of Beachcomber Marina (actually but a short distance away) is blocked from your view by the bluffs to your left. All this being said, there are two features that make the view from this spot well worth photographing or sketching. One is the wonderfully picturesque, gnarled fir that leans out from the headland to the right. The other is the sunsets, perfectly viewed from this point.

Winds, sun and shade The upper beach is almost completely sheltered from winds from either direction. At the low-tide line, you will feel a muted version of winds from both directions. In the morning, the upper beach is in shade. By late morning, however, and through the rest of the day until sunset, it is in full sun. Indeed, it can get very hot on this beach, so plan accordingly.

Beachcombing Like any other spot on Beachcomber peninsula, this is not one from which you will want to initiate a long walk. You might, however, enjoy exploring the shore life under the rocks at low tide.

Seclusion If there were a prize for the least secluded access spot in this book, this would win. Because the houses are so close together and so close to the shoreline, and because the access is so narrow, it is impossible to escape the feeling that you are plunked in the middle of a neighbourhood—and a very cheek-by-jowl one at that.

✳ Also nearby **Whitecap Road** is a short road off Marina Way between The Jib and Beachcomber Community Park. It provides awkward access to the shore down a steep bank of jagged rock. It is, however, a great place to come to get out of the wind—all winds— while perching on one of the rocky ledges and soaking up the baking hot afternoon sun, the views of Mount Moriarty and Mount Arrowsmith, and, in the evening, views of sunsets. Two or three cars can park by the potted plants at the end of the road.

27

BEACHCOMBER COMMUNITY PARK

Winding paths through Garry oaks lead to two pebble beaches separated by an area of sandstone

Location, signs and parking From Northwest Bay Road, turn onto Claudet Road and stay on it for more than 2 km. The name will change to Marina Way after you pass the crossroads, the left fork of which goes to Beachcomber Marina. Stay on Marina Way almost to the end. Just before a significant downhill, you will see a dirt-and-gravel parking area, a wooden gate, and, a few metres below the parking area, a big new sign telling you that you have, indeed, reached Beachcomber Community Park. You will also see a litter barrel (the park's only "facility") and signs giving you guidelines on use of the park as well as forbidding fires and defecating dogs. At least 10 or 12 cars can fit in the unpaved area at the top of the hill.

Path The easiest path starts partway down the hill through the main gate. Like paths in many other community parks, it branches at various points to lead to different parts of the park. Most of the paths are wide and clear, though a few user-made tracks fade off into the undergrowth. Be prepared, too, for a fair degree of huffing and puffing on the return journey to your car, since the path drops some 10 or 15 m and, at various points, descends over rocky steps. For a first visit you might want to choose the first fork to the right, though the left fork will also bring you to a pebbly beach. Garry oaks, Douglas and grand firs, willows and arbutus are all to be found in this wooded park. Those who want a more adventurous route into the park can choose the path from the south end of the parking area and make their way down over the bumps and lumps. This second, less obvious entrance to this park is marked with a few signs pinned to a tree indicating the undesirability of fires and so on.

Beach The park is made up of two pebbly beaches separated by a headland of sandstone and conglomerate rock. If you take the right fork of the path, you will come first to a gently curving bay about 75 m wide, of smooth, golf-ball-sized rocks. The bay is flanked by steep little cliffs to the right and, to the left, by a broad but fairly flat solid rock shelf. One curious feature here is that this rocky shelf drops off vertically onto the rocky beach. While this feature is particularly noticeable at low tide, at high tide it can make for great fun for swimmers (and snorkellers).

Beyond this beach, the sandstone shelf extends some 50 m at low tide, with various bumps and crevices. It has two distinctive features. First is the "balancing rock," a huge granite boulder deposited by a glacier and looking roughly like an inverted pyramid. Every family or group of friends that visits the spot should feel compelled to pose atop this rock for a photograph—there is no choice in the matter. The second distinctive feature of this area is the clusters of fossil remains (almost entirely of broken seashells.) These are especially prolific near the high-tide level.

Snorkellers will find the southern edge of this shelf a fascinating place to investigate, particularly at mid tide, when two giant steps lead to an underwater cliff that drops straight down 7 or 8 m. A somewhat more rugged and much narrower bit of rock shelf carries on into Northwest Bay to a second beach, a little smaller than the first beach but with generally smaller pebbles near the mid- and high-tide lines. This little bay, like the first one, dries at low tide to a line of small to medium boulders.

Suitability for children Not a speck of sand is to be found here, so children who equate sand with beach are best taken elsewhere. Any other child, of virtually any age, will find lots of diversion. Both of these beaches have the best skipping stones to be found anywhere along the coast. The tidal pools, rock shelves and fossils will appeal to most children. In addition, since the two beaches face different directions, any time of day except morning (and any direction of wind) will mean a sunny or wind-free beach for watery play. Choose high tide, though, for swimming, but be prepared for a water temperature here that always seems more...bracing... than at most other nearby beaches.

Suitability for groups The relatively generous parking facilities and the many different coves and nooks mean that even a several-car-sized group could come to this park without overrunning it. There is plenty of space to spread out a picnic, set up easels, pull out binoculars or loll in the sun. Do be aware, though, that there are no picnic tables, toilets or shelters. Plan appropriately. This is a great spot for group photos, but only for those groups willing to cope with the challenging path.

View The view is approximately the same as half of the view from Cottam Point itself (Seadog Road), the next spot along. An attractive rocky promontory defines the northern extreme of the view and channels your view-line toward Mistaken Island, a short distance offshore and the Strait to the north. The distant perspectives of San Pareil extend via Madrona Point and Wall Beach all the way into Northwest Bay. Mount Moriarty, Mount Arrowsmith and, to the far north, just barely visible, Mount Washington, make a beautiful backdrop. Mountain lovers and photographers will find this a splendid viewing spot after a first snowfall, but they should come in the morning when the sun (or other more diffuse light) illuminates the mountains rather than silhouettes them. Sea lion spotters, too, might want to visit this area in winter months, since the visitors from California seem to like congregating in flotillas along this stretch of shore. Alternately barking and sleeping with flippers extended into the air, they seem to find the whole tip of Cottam Point a good gathering spot.

Winds, sun and shade The full force of a northwest blow (or even a northwest breeze) is felt on one side of the park; none is felt on the other. Wave watchers and photographers will find this a good spot to come to, since the gently shelving rock actually amplifies the effects of the waves as they curl and break. A southeast wind is little felt on either beach. (Curiously, though, the water seems to turn icy, even though the sun may be hot, when a southeast wind starts to blow.) Both sun and shade are available (on a sunny day). Seek and ye shall find.

Beachcombing You will not be able (without grappling hook and rope) to walk beyond the shore south of the park. Within the park, though, you will feel yourself invited to wander and explore, particularly if you have sharp eyes and curiosity. It is possible to walk past the houses to the tip of Cottam Point and beyond, but you will have to be well shod and nimble to do so.

Seclusion The area is popular with locals most times of day, most times of year. Some keep kayaks or rowboats pulled up into the trees. Except for the west-facing beach, however, which can be thick with sunbathers (that is, half a dozen), you can generally find a nook or outcropping to feel deliciously alone. One raised area under the Garry oaks, between the two beaches and replete with park bench, is particularly inviting.

28

SEADOG ROAD

A short scramble to the conglomerate shelves at the tip of Cottam Point and 300-degree views

Location, Parking and Signs Follow the directions for Beachcomber Community Park, but carry on 100 m past the park to the tip of Cottam Point/Beachcomber peninsula and turn left onto Seadog Road. Drive the very short distance to the rough-and-ready cul-de-sac at the end of Seadog. Being mindful of driveways, park on the shoulder of this paved turnaround area. Chances are, particularly on a weekend, you will find other cars, most belonging to scuba divers, also parked here. If your car has a high underbelly and you are confident you won't be blocking others, you can ease over the bumpy track almost to the cliff edge. In fact, during a storm or a sunset, you can drive to this spot and, without leaving your car, enjoy the view.

Path Bless their hearts, scuba divers who felt their lives and equipment threatened by struggling down the 2 m cliff onto the rock below have built irregular, steep but functional concrete steps. Although children and arthritic seniors will find these steps a bit of a challenge, the distance is short and the view is probably worth the challenge.

Beach Unlike the rest of the peninsula this area is not jagged black basalt but more or less flat (if broken) shelves of conglomerate rock intersected by cracks and adorned with various small outcroppings.

Suitability for children Having managed to get down the steps with their lives still intact, children who enjoy romping will carry on romping at this spot. The area is flat enough and irregularities interesting enough that much fun can be had exploring, climbing and investigating the few tidal pools. Needless to say, at low tide the rocks are steeper and covered with fucus and rockweed. For water play, however, the spot isn't great, though a very high tide can make wading, skipping stones and generally creating watery havoc all possibilities. Be aware, however, that a slight but noticeable current runs past this point. The water isn't nearly as warm as at more protected spots, and a child sitting atop an inflated plastic dragon might start drifting…away.

Suitability for groups Obviously, scuba-diving groups recognize the spot to be well-suited to their particular interest. Other groups could find much the same thing, particularly lovers of shore life, painters, and, in a slight pinch, even picnickers. Parking, however, is problematic for more than a few cars.

View The view is probably the main reason for coming to this spot. First off, because this is the tip of a peninsula, you have about a 300-degree view. Starting to your right, you can see Dorcas Point, Gerald and Ballenas islands all against a backdrop of the Coast Mountains, and farther north, Texada. To the north, the rounded but wild form of Mistaken Island lies a short distance offshore and beyond it, the open Strait. The distant prospect of San Pareil and Rathtrevor Beach to the left lead in turn to Arbutus Point, Wall Beach and the outer reaches of Northwest Bay. And if that weren't enough, the classic skyline of Mount Moriarty, Mount Arrowsmith and even, at its farthest reach, Mount Washington, is on full view for you to savour—and photograph.

Winds, sun and shade It is the attraction *and* the disadvantage of this spot that both a northwest wind and a southeast blow are felt here at their maximum strength. More significant for the storm lover, though, is that this is the best spot north of Neck Point to view the waves and frothing derrings-do of a strong wind. In both winds, the waves here have about as much "fetch" (distance) as they can get within the Strait of Georgia. In addition, the shelving nature of the shore allows the waves to curl deliciously (and photogenically) before throwing themselves into flurries of foam and spray. Because this shore is convex, there is some sun to be had at various points throughout the day—and some shade likewise.

Beachcombing The nearly level but deeply cleft sandstone shore allows exploring a short distance in either direction. Go very far, however, and you'll encounter rough and sometimes slippery conditions.

Seclusion Although there are houses on either side of the narrow access, the steep bank, high fences, convex nature of the land and screens of trees all combine to make this a surprisingly secluded spot. You could do much worse than choose this spot to ponder the mysteries of existence or to have that Big Conversation.

29

MARINA WAY

A little-used approach to the northeast solid-rock shore of Cottam Point

Location, signs and parking Follow the directions to Seadog Road, but keep driving as the road curves back along the northeast shore of the peninsula until you see a gap beside the house numbered 1258. You will see no other sign. Park your car on the shoulder of the road, though the proximity of driveways will make this a bit of a feat.

Path A broad strip of grass leads more or less directly to the shore. There is little change in elevation and few lumps and bumps to consider—until you actually reach the shore.

Beach The shore is rough here, but not as jagged as at some other points. It is composed mostly of rounded solid rock outcroppings interspersed with patches of large, angular boulders. The upper area of the shore is comparatively level and covered with lots of very old logs; it extends about 20 m toward the water before sloping steeply (particularly to the south). There are a few tidal pools here, but only at the mid-tide level. Snorkelling, however, is excellent at both mid or low tide. Wave watching, particularly with a southeast storm, is much better here than at points farther south along the road, because Dorcas Point provides virtually no protection from the waves.

Suitability for children This is an appealing explorers' beach, but children wouldn't want to stay here very long. The rocks don't make for easy walking, and they can be slippery and awkward near the low-tide line. Children who need water access to fulfill their beachy experience would be happiest at mid or high tide.

Suitability for groups Like the other spots on this side of the peninsula, this one isn't suitable for a group of any size. The access is narrow, the neighbours are close and the shore area is restricted. More than the others on Reef Road immediately south, though, this one does have an attractive upper area for ensconcing a few folk or setting up easels.

View The view is wonderful. From this point, you are very near the end of Cottam Point/Beachcomber peninsula. Dorcas Point and even Gerald Island are to your right, and the full range of mountains and Ballenas and Mistaken islands come into this view. The convex nature of the shore and the slight elevation of the upper shore give an impressive sense of space and depth to lovers of the Wild and Free.

Winds, sun and shade The northwest wind hits the shore more directly here than it does at points farther up Reef Road, and the southeast wind hits just as directly. If you happen to choose a windy day, you will find lots of wind here, though considerably less at the upper shore. The morning is sunny, the afternoon partly shady.

Beachcombing Beachcombing of the slow exploratory sort is the most obvious activity here, though walking—carefully—in either direction is possible for some distance.

Seclusion On either a mirror-calm day or a wind-tossed evening, it is possible to experience some sense of deep communion with the sea, but only if you keep your focus outwards. At the top of the shore, you can find a comfortable spot among the logs to snack or read while being comparatively private.

✳ **Also nearby** On **Reef Road** find the house number 1430 on a tele-phone pole and what looks for all the world like a paved private driveway. Park on Reef Road and walk to the shore. This is about as jagged and lumpy a bit of beach as you are likely to find, but it is a very interesting bit of jagged and lumpy beach and well worth the visit—if not necessarily a stay. Some will be charmed and some will be disgusted by the concrete-and-piling "ruins" of a very old dock and launching ramp, long since battered by winter storms. One of the particular curiosities is a large tidal pool created by a concrete barrier across one end of a cleft in the rocks. Small cliffs, outcroppings and jagged protrusions into the water make for a picturesque foreshore but difficult walking. The rocks drop off steeply, even at low tide, making for some great snorkelling possibilities as well as specimen hunting (there are some beautiful urchin beds just below low-tide level). During strong winds from either direction, the waves can be dramatic as they surge by the rocks.

30

LUDGATE ROAD

A slightly challenging route to a huge, gravelly tidal pool stretching to a craggy reef

Location, signs and parking Look for the anchor symbol on Northwest Bay Road and turn down Claudet Road. After about 2 km, turn right onto Reef Road. About 100 m along, when Reef Road turns left, you will have to be careful not to miss the unpaved and dead-end Ludgate Road on your right. You can pull to one side of Ludgate Road or park on the shoulder of Reef Road and walk the few metres down Ludgate Road to its end.

Path The path at the end of Ludgate is a well-beaten dirt track that can be a little tricky as it zigzags down a fairly steep bank for some 10 m. The fact that someone has installed a length of rope to help restrain runaway (or slide-away) descents will give some idea of the nature of the path.

Beach The path emerges onto a fairly flat area of large rocks with patches of huge boulders and rounded outcroppings on either side. There is a patch of overgrown seagrass on one side, but it is not very appealing as a picnic or lounging spot. The greatest curiosity here is the concrete PUBLIC ACCESS pillar sitting firmly in the middle of the boulder patch. It must have been quite an enterprise, requiring considerable strength, to get it here. There are a dozen of these old concrete blocks—but no more—in the RDN. The most noticeable feature of this beach is the "reef" after which Reef Road takes its name. More accurately, it is a tiny islet, not a reef. At low tide the intervening area dries to a broad band of barnacle-encrusted gravel with a large tidal pool in the middle. The beach is not a great spot for picnicking or sunbathing, but both could be done in a pinch.

Suitability for children This is not a good spot for swimming, and there is no sand to be had, but exploring the tidal pools and climbing over the reef in quest of adventure can amuse children of certain dispositions and with certain levels of imagination.

Suitability for groups Since picnicking isn't an obvious option here, and beachcombing is limited, it's not apparent what a group could do here, other than what children do so well—prod at hermit crabs and exclaim over starfish.

View At high tide, the islet against the backdrop of Dorcas Point and the mainland mountains provide a pretty combination of scenic elements. From this perspective, it is possible to differentiate Little Nuttall Bay from the main bay. The view, however, is fairly restricted and the foreshore at low tide is not exactly pretty.

Winds, sun and shade Any northwest wind blowing down the bay can be felt only if you walk out to the islet. A southeast wind, however, blows directly onshore here, even though if it were actually blowing from the direction after which it is named, it would not. The sun is direct, and sometimes hot, in the morning. By noon the upper shore is shady, and the shade remains throughout the rest of the day.

Beachcombing If you arrive at low tide, your automatic response will be to pick your way out to the reef. Wear fairly rugged shoes, however, and ones that you don't mind getting wet. At high tide, you will have to be fairly determined to go very far in either direction. You don't have to be Rambo, but, at a few points, you do have to be…determined.

Seclusion Rarely will you encounter more than a few locals here. On the reef itself, you will feel both far from the locals—and also, perhaps, under inspection by them from their bank-top perspective over you!

31
HAIDA WAY
A pebbly beach, reasonably well protected from most winds

Location, signs and parking Follow Claudet Road from Northwest Bay Road for almost 2 km and then turn right onto Seacrest Road. After about 100 m, take the first left onto Haida Way. A concrete public access block is usually hidden by the tall grass, so look for the gap between houses numbered 1550 and 1546. A patch of grass leads between two cedar hedges and rapidly turns into a clear, if little-used, path. Park on the gravel shoulder. The driveways here are few and far between, and the shoulder is reasonably wide.

Path The grassy path covers the distance between the two adjoining lots. You will pass a large granite boulder and enter the beach under a grove of small firs.

Beach This access point brings you to the north end of a more or less straight pebble beach about 75 m long. The upper beach immediately in front of the access spot has golf-ball-sized, though hardly golf-ball-shaped, rocks and an irregular cluster of small logs, but most of the beach is actually composed of small, smooth, many-coloured pebbles. The beach shelves off quite steeply, so the tide goes out only 20 m or so. Unlike most similar beaches, this one does not end in a barricade of boulders—even at low tide, the rocks are fairly small. To the south, the beach ends in a small jagged headland. To the north, it gradually merges into an area of increasingly large, chunky boulders. A small outcropping of solid rock at low tide and a set of tracks laid for launching a boat are the only impediments to those who might be swimming heedlessly over them at mid tide.

Suitability for children The beach is safe, well protected and comparatively free of barnacles, for a rocky beach. Probably most children would prefer to come at mid to high tide for their watery fun. The comparatively steep angle of the shore means that parents of swimmers might be more relaxed than those of non-swimmers.

Suitability for groups This is not a great group beach. At most, a family or two should come here. Even for them, the fact that they can't settle very comfortably on the foreshore at the trailhead means that they might be disturbing residents.

View The view is a good combination of foreground and background, lacking the magnificence of either extreme but nevertheless pleasing to the seascape-seeking eye. The little jagged headlands of Nuttall Bay together with the shore of Dorcas Point directly in front, give an enclosed view but not confined feeling to the south. Immediately to the north lie the "reef" that gives Reef Road its name and, beyond it, the open waters of the Strait.

Winds, sun and shade This beach is partially protected from both northwest and southeast winds, but fully protected from neither. The sun can be hot—often too hot—in the sun trap of even early morning. By mid morning, though, the shadows of a few large evergreens will spread—alternating with strips of sun—down the beach. By late afternoon, the beach is almost entirely in shade.

Beachcombing It is easy to explore the beach, but it doesn't have a huge variety of intertidal life (or much else) to look at. The curious seekers of tidal pools and under-boulder specimens will want to pick their way along the irregular shore toward the reef to the north.

Seclusion If you stay on the (uncomfortable) foreshore at the entrance to the beach, you will be reasonably secluded. Otherwise, you will not.

32

SEACREST ROAD

Primarily of interest to those wishing to launch a kayak or canoe

Location, signs and parking Follow the directions for Haida Way (above) onto Seacrest Road and follow it a few metres past its intersection with Haida Way to where it falters to an apparent halt. Beware of confusion with Seacrest *Place* in Eaglecrest. Careful scrutiny of the ground reveals another of the PUBLIC ACCESS signs in the form of a very old concrete block. You can either park on the shoulder of this rough and ready cul-de-sac or, if you've brought a kayak to launch, drive partway down the ramp-like access road that slants some 20 m to the shore.

Path At one point this "path" really was a gravel road, but the enthusiastic hedge trees from the neighbouring property have increasingly grown over it.

Beach The road will bring you directly onto one end of a short bay set at right angles to Sunset Cove beach (see next entry) and separated from it by a little jagged rocky protrusion. Unlike Sunset Cove's beach, however, this one is adorned with a bed of polished pebbles only at the end opposite the access—and directly in front of a house. The upper beach at the access point is composed of small rectilinear rocks. Immediately to your left is a kind of slanting shelf of solid rock and a cliffy point of land overhung with Garry oaks, arbutus and a highly photogenic (i.e., gnarled and moribund) fir. The lower beach is composed of jagged, geometrically odd-looking boulders covered with eager little barnacles—thus, if you are planning to launch your kayak, you will be happiest coming at mid or high tide. If your intentions are to spend a less energetic time here, you will probably want to set up your nest directly in front of the access spot. There is an undeveloped lot farther along the beach where you can equally lounge away the hours with your trashy novel. Needless to say, swimming is best at high tide.

Suitability for children Almost all children would be happier at the nearby Sunset Cove beach. If their parents do wish to come to this spot, most children will easily make their way across the little lump of solid rock that separates the two beaches. In the morning, and with a strong northwest wind blowing, the wise parent will decide that Seacrest is the better beach of the two.

Suitability for groups This is not a great spot for a group. The beach is small, and the parking is limited. A family (or even two) could be happily accommodated here, though.

View The view is oddly satisfying in spite of being very restricted. You are mostly looking into the end of Nuttall Bay rather than out to sea. However, the particularly attractive combination of the little cliffs to your left, the view of the mainland mountains and the sequence of beach and jagged outcroppings that make up the shoreline of Nuttall Bay all add up to a frame of scenic elements that cries out to be photographed or sketched. Mid and high tide best complement the view.

Winds, sun and shade This spot is perfect if you are trying to escape wind. It is well sheltered from all winds from all directions. This is a real sun trap in the morning. You might find yourself roasting to well done while the rest of the beachy world is only gradually realizing that it's getting warm enough to go to the beach. In the afternoon and evening, in contrast, the beach is almost entirely in shade.

Beachcombing Walking is very limited, though you can, like any children you bring with you, make your way along the short beach to Sunset Cove and back.

Seclusion The beach is very quiet, but you and various houses—if not their occupants—will be looking at each other.

33

SUNSET COVE
A long, pebbly beach
revealing sand and eelgrass
at very low tides

Location, signs and parking From Northwest Bay Road, turn right onto Claudet Road, and after about 2 km, take the first right onto Dorcas Point Road. After 60 or 70 m, you will see a pull-off area with a bank of mailboxes. This is your destination. One of the small blue and white PUBLIC ACCESS signs will confirm that you have hit pay dirt. The residential lots on the ocean side are so deep that all of the owners have left a welcome screen of trees along the road. There is parking here for several cars both in the pull-off and along the shoulder.

Path The wide, level dirt path, about 50 m long, leads through some scrubby alders and past a fine big cedar to the flat open area that once accommodated campers. You might be a little misled by the parallel track farther along the road, behind a barred gate currently used by locals as an access to the beach, even though it is not public access.

Beach For many years, going back at least to the late '50s, this fine pebbly bay, some 150 m long, was a campground and boat-rental facility called Clayton's. Those were the Good Old Days when it was possible to "limit out" on coho and "jacks" within a few minutes from shore, even for a two-stroke inboard. Some years later, it became "Sunset Cove." More estimable travel trailers and faster outboards moved in. Then it was subdivided and sold as waterfront lots. The shorefront's history as a resort says something about this enticing and summery beach. A fine pebble upper shore slopes quite steeply at (very) low tide to a strip of good sand, tidal pools and eelgrass. The access path leads to the most protected end of the beach.

Suitability for children While there isn't a huge amount of space backed by public land, the beach is, on the whole, well-suited for children of many ages and with many different ideas of what constitutes beachside pleasures.

Searching for pebbles with magical properties, playing inventively with wet sand at (very) low tide, and swimming or skipping stones at mid to high tide are among the more obvious possibilities. Parents whose children are still floundering more than confidently swimming, however, should be aware that the shore slopes fairly steeply.

Suitability for groups The strip of beach strictly set aside for public access is narrow, and the nearby houses are arranged in such a way that it is unlikely that either a group or the local residents would feel very comfortable in each other's company. A small group, however, could blend in and have a great experience.

View As the name "Sunset Cove" suggests, this beach faces more or less west (though, in terms of local terminology, or course, this is "north"). In fact, this is one of the best access spots in this book for viewing sunsets, though it is only in summer that the sun sets fully in view of the beach. The daytime view is considerably more restricted than the view from the average access spot, but it has its own charms. This is not the spot to come if you're after a mountain view. It is a spot to choose, however, if you are susceptible to the charms of a view composed of several overlapping treed points on either side of a gracefully curving bay, with Mistaken Island and the open water of the northern Strait far in the distance.

Winds, sun and shade Curiously, the beach receives the full fun and fury of the waves created by a strong northwest wind, but not the full force of the wind itself—particularly at the end of the beach to which the access path leads. A southeast wind, however, can be raging with whitecaps in full view a few hundred metres away, while the water directly by the beach will be as still as the proverbial millpond. The beach is in sun for most of the day, though during the morning it is less direct and its rays less baking than at the adjacent Seacrest Road beach. In the evening, depending on the time of year, the sun will dip behind a fairly solid bit of forest, but it is easy to extend the amount of time you want in the sun by moving farther along the beach away from the access point.

Beachcombing You will feel tempted to walk up and down the 150 m length of the beach, but not to go much beyond. Wear decent shoes, though, since you will be slithering a little among the loose pebbles. At either end, the outcroppings of rock make good climbing for children, but not good strolling.

Seclusion The beach is not used very much, since only a few houses share a considerable span of shoreline. At the same time, because there are no shorefront trees screening the houses and because the bay curves as it does, you will have no sensation of separation from the World of Humanity.

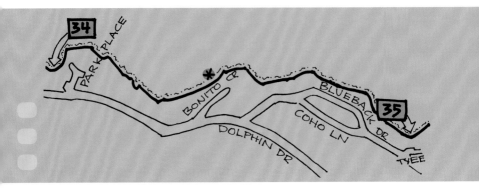

34
PARK PLACE COMMUNITY PARK
A small, wooded park with a protected and sunny, pebbly beach

Location, signs and parking From Northwest Bay Road, follow Stewart Road and turn right onto Davenham until it morphs without your noticing into Dolphin Drive. Once you find yourself running parallel to the water, keep alert at the crest of a small hill for the junction of Dolphin Drive with Park Place. Look for a discreet blue and white sign with the name of the park. If you search around a bit, you can find an ancient concrete marker inscribed with the words PUBLIC ACCESS and lying on its side. As the name of the adjoining road indicates, this spot is not just an access, but actually a park. Still, because the road is at a junction and is dominated by a group of mailboxes, the explorer can very easily miss the sign and the trailhead. A few cars can fit in the space on the wide shoulder near the mailboxes, but be careful not to take up the spots used by locals collecting their bank statements and supermarket flyers.

Path Be prepared for a considerable descent of 7 or 8 m down a wide, well-used dirt path for about 50 m through second-growth forest until it takes a sharp right and opens onto the shore.

Beach The path emerges onto an upper beach with small blue-black angular pebbles amidst dozens of logs. At low tide, the waterline is about 30 m away, revealing a gradually shelving shore with patches of variously sized rocks and boulders, though giving way to almost unbroken pebbles extending all the way to the shoreline to the left. The beach extends for 30 or 40 m to the left in front of private houses. On the right it comes to a halt with a jagged bit of steep rock. Like most community parks, this one has no facilities.

Suitability for children The smallest children will have to be toted up and down the considerable path, but once on the shore, they can be safely and cheerfully ensconced among the pretty pebbles. In fact, there is no beach in the area that has such a large proportion of small pebbles extending (in patches) so far down the beach. Larger children could enjoy some discreet romping along the shore and, feet clad in water shoes, less restrained romping in the water—particularly at high tide.

Suitability for groups The area is large enough, and the upper shore welcoming enough to picnickers, that if the conditions of shade and wind are right, a small group could spend some pleasant time here.

View The view is more confined here than at most other spots in the Dolphin Beach area, because the bay looks north almost directly into the high cliffs that extend for a few hundred metres toward Gerald Island. No spot, however, is without charms, and these cliffs themselves (notwithstanding the presence of the houses and their precipitous staircases descending the cliff faces) are well worth viewing.

Winds, sun and shade A northwest wind can waft onto this beach, though the beach is slightly sheltered by the cliffy headland directly opposite. A southeast wind skirts the beach almost entirely. Overhanging trees throw shade onto the upper beach at most times of day, though by the afternoon the sun swings around so that the shadows retreat during the course of the afternoon, providing plenty of baking heat for those in search of rays.

Beachcombing The shore is inviting to explore for a short distance in either direction. Like other spots in the Dolphin Beach area, though, this one does not make life easy for those who want to stride out for great distances.

Seclusion The beach is shared with one house (actually the "beach cabin" belonging to the house higher on the bank), and, because this is a full "park," there is considerable wooded land behind the beach. The view from the beach will not, however, create a feeling of seclusion for those wishing to Escape It All.

✷ **Also nearby Bonito Crescent**, off Dolphin Drive, ends in a small turnaround. There are no signs, but directly opposite from house number 1904, start down what seems a private driveway until you find a path onto a secluded bit of rocky shore. The path is a little steep toward the end. You will emerge onto an irregular patch of blue-black rock with various crests, ridges and bumps extending to the low-tide line some 20 m below the high-tide line. It is best to come to this spot at low tide for its most distinctive feature—its pretty array of small rocky tidal pools. At high tide, the lack of space on the upper shore will discourage you from doing much lingering, though snorkelling is interesting at high tide because of the irregular rocks over which you will be swimming.

35
BLUEBACK COMMUNITY PARK
Easy access to a small sunny bay with pebbly upper beach and barnacle-covered rocks on the lower beach

Location, signs and parking Compared to some of the other locations in the Dolphin Beach area, this access spot is easy to find. Blueback Drive is a long loop off the main road through the area, Dolphin Drive. Blueback Community Park, with a sign identifying the park, lies directly off the road at the junction with Tyee Crescent. At this point, the road descends to and runs parallel to the shore, if you are driving north. There is a paved area on the sea side of the road (actually on Tyee Crescent) for a few cars to park diagonally. Additional cars can park along the shoulder of the road.

Path A much-used 10 m path leads through blackberry bushes directly onto the shore—one of the features that makes this spot popular among scuba divers, with their heavy and cumbersome equipment. Kayakers could use the spot, too, especially at high tide. Those who want to paddle from here, however, and are willing to spend a few dollars, might want to drive the short distance to Schooner Cove Marina and its concrete launching ramp.

Beach At low tide, this is a shallow bay about 50 m long, with the water's edge some 50 m away. The beach is covered with fist-sized rocks on which barnacles grow with enthusiasm. A few outcroppings of solid rock give a little variety to the otherwise rocky beach. Of particular interest to scuba divers who arrive at low tide is the 2 m wide "path" of pebble- and golf-ball-calibre rocks cleared through the larger rocks, virtually to the low-tide line. Swimmers, too, even at high tide, might appreciate this comparatively easy way of reaching water deep enough for swimming.

Suitability for children Be sure to bring water shoes for your children if they plan on splashing or swimming. The easy access and the comparative flatness of the shore make this beach a reasonable destination for children, particularly on a very hot day. Very small children, however, will be happier at a more pebbly beach.

Suitability for groups The groups most likely to seek this area out are scuba divers. Picnickers, however, will find a pleasant pebbly area among the logs to the left of the beach. Certainly, too, there is plenty of space for most groups to park and wander.

View The view lacks some of the breadth given by other access spots in the area, though it does give good views to the north—more than most. Extending from the Yeo Islands immediately in front to Gerald Island to the north, the view also includes some particularly fine perspectives on the Jervis Inlet mountains, and especially the shark-fin peak of Mount Churchill.

Winds, sun and shade A northwest wind blows at a slight angle onto the beach, but the accompanying waves run parallel to the shore. The beach is well protected from a southeast wind, particularly at the high-tide line. The comparative lack of trees behind the beach means that it has areas of sun throughout most of the day, especially in summer, when the sun is high.

Beachcombing There is some scope for walking the shore here, though the breadth of the exposed shoreline decreases significantly beyond the end of the bay. The lack of striking features on the shore doesn't make it immediately appealing to those who wish to stroll about or explore, though the low-tide rocks shelter all kinds of interesting creatures, and the steeper bluffs at either end make for enjoyable clambering.

Seclusion Because this is not merely a strip wedged in between adjoining houses, you will feel comfortably welcome here. The proximity of the road, however, and the concave curve of the shoreline mean that you should choose another spot if you really want to feel in communion with the waves and gulls—or wish to pop a Big Question.

✱ Also nearby Gull Road ends with a pleasant view spot at the top of a small cliff. From that vantage point you will find yourself with an excellent view of Gerald and Amelia islands, with the Ballenas in the distance. If you are familiar with the landmark islands and peaks of the area, you will be interested in the unusual perspective from this spot. Storm watchers will find this to be the best vantage point in the Dolphin Beach area to experience a northwest blow, though the shore doesn't experience quite the full brunt of the waves. Finding this viewpoint involves a little navigation and faith. Turn onto Schooner Cove Road immediately north of Schooner Cove Marina (see the map that follows). Then take the first left onto Blueback Drive, the first right onto Grilse Road, and the first left onto Gull Road, and follow it to the end. The road is very narrow and a little lumpy, looking more like a paved driveway than a public road. Follow the road almost to the end, but stop a little short if you are planning to park. Walk through the grassy area maintained by the neighbouring house to your view spot.

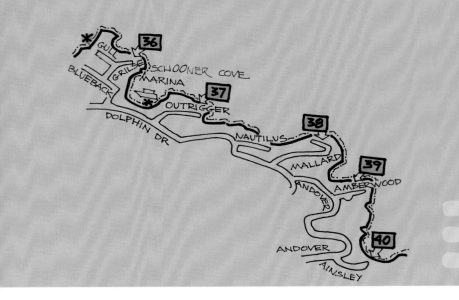

36
GRILSE ROAD
A picturesquely framed
rocky cove

Location, signs and parking In case you're wondering, a "grilse," in local usage, is a salmon that has survived the summer at sea and grown to about 30 cm. The following spring, it will graduate to being a blueback and give its name to an adjoining road. When local waters were prolific and fishing regulations correspondingly generous, local sports fishermen revelled in frying grilse for dinner or responding to the springtime call, "The blueback are running." Those days, it seems, are gone forever. As for "tyee," the name of another local road, well, ask anyone in pursuit of the Big One.

Though this spot isn't far from the "main" road—Dolphin Drive—you will have to go through a little bit of a tangle to get there. The sequence is first onto Schooner Cove Road (immediately north of the Schooner Cove marina), first left onto Blueback Drive, and first right onto Grilse Road. The road reaches a definitive dead end here with a yellow and black checkered sign. Otherwise, there are no signs indicating that you have reached the right place, so you will be forgiven for feeling a little puzzled about the configuration of driveways and parking areas. There isn't a lot of parking available, but it is possible for a few cars to pull onto the shoulders in this small turnaround area and the adjoining road.

Path Until recently, a barricade of Himalayan blackberries made getting to the shore a little adventurous. The vines have been cleared, but the irrepressible shoots are starting to reappear behind the genteel line of nursery cedars. Don't be surprised if, by the time you make it here, your way has become a little prickly. Currently the path has disappeared, but it is easy to make your way through the open dirt area—at least if you are prepared to do a little clambering over logs and large, jagged granite boulders.

Beach This is the northernmost of the publicly accessed shore spots to be composed of the pale granite that typifies the southern Dolphin Beach/ Fairwinds area. At the same time, it reverses the usual pattern of rocky beaches. Instead of having small rocks at the top of the shore and the largest rocks at the low-tide line, this shore gradually gives way to smaller rocks at the low-tide line. The tide goes out about 20 m, revealing a small rocky bay with jagged promontories and reefs projecting at either side.

Suitability for children Like most beach spots in the Dolphin Beach area, this one is best suited to the climbing and curious child, not the faint-of-heart child. Don't bring your child here for carefree water play.

Suitability for groups The beach is not well suited to groups, though a family or two could perch and picnic on the logs, and a bevy of watercolourists could find plenty of space and subject matter.

View While lacking the in-your-face extravagances of geography that some other spots in the area provide, this one nevertheless offers considerable visual delight. From this angle, the islands both to the south and to the north, from the Winchelseas to the Yeo islands directly across, seem to sprinkle themselves across the horizon rather than cluster and group. The projecting rocky points and, in particular, the smooth-shouldered outcropping immediately to the north (with a picturesquely stunted fir), cry out to be sketched or photographed.

Winds, sun and shade Surprisingly, even a fresh northwest wind largely scoots by the upper shore. Likewise, a southeast wind, though it fans the shore, does not hit it directly. The sun falls most directly onto the beach in the first part of the day. In the latter part of the day, some shade patches crawl across the beach, but do not cover it completely.

Beachcombing Even though the shore is rough, it is varied and expansive enough that it will be appealing to those who enjoy poking about the low-tide line for starfish, crabs, blennies, jingle shells and the like. Don't, however, expect to go for a casual stroll. The most off-putting part of this beach is the large OUTFALL sign implanted on the upper shore.

Seclusion The houses on either side of this spot are clearly visible, so you will not feel at the end of the earth, but the configuration of the shoreline means that you will be aware of only the ones immediately to the right and left.

✱ Also nearby You will pass **Schooner Cove Marina** as Dolphin Drive dips down to the shore of Schooner Cove. If you wish to accompany your exploration of the area with launching a kayak (for a few dollars), a cup of coffee, a seaside lunch or a glass of something cold, then the facilities of the marina will be appealing.

Grilse Road

37
OUTRIGGER ROAD
An attractive area of rocky
bluffs best suited for idling

Location, signs and parking Outrigger Road leaves Dolphin Drive immediately south of the Schooner Cove marina. It proceeds a short way parallel to the coast and comes to a halt in a dead-end bit of asphalt. (This is one time a NO TURNAROUND sign almost seems appropriate). You will have to squeeze your car onto the shoulder without blocking the drive marked HERON RIDGE.

Path Be sure to stay on the left side of the chain-link fence. A path leads through this lot-sized access chunk of land past rock outcroppings among tall grass, firs, oaks and arbutus. The path is pleasant and easy, but a little uneven for those unsteady on their feet.

Beach The shore is really a kind of rounded, rough rock shelf with tidal pools. Curious lumps and bumps give character to the shore without providing real obstacles to exploring. Picnicking or otherwise partaking in stationary pastimes can easily be done on the smooth pads of rock.

Suitability for children Children who enjoy playing in and exploring tidal pools, and are reasonably sure of foot, can easily keep themselves busy and occupied while their more indolent—or reflective—parents sunbathe, read or otherwise amble about. In fact, the bumps can be great fun to climb over for children with imagination and physical energy. Reaching the water at low tide is not easy.

Suitability for groups Parking is a significant limiting factor, and the rocky knolls and lumps of this attractive beach area seem designed to keep people separated rather than together.

View Because of the slightly convex nature of the shoreline on one side of a significant promontory, the view is wide and comprehensive. Look straight out and you feel the depth and breadth of the Strait of Georgia; look to your right and you feel comforted by the pretty overlapping shapes of the Winchelsea Islands. Nestle slightly back into the foliage, and you have your views framed by wind-worn branches of the shore trees.

Winds, sun and shade A southeast wind is directly felt at this spot, but because of the islands and curve of the land, the waves are muted a little. Otherwise, this is a good spot for viewing a southeast storm. Those trying to escape the breeze can find shelter behind a pretty little bluff at the back of the shore. A northwest wind makes itself known here, but more from the side than straight on. The sun is most direct on this shoreline in the first half of the day. Though shadows from the trees move across the shore in the afternoon, they do not completely blanket the spot at any time except evening.

Beachcombing Though the shore is uneven, it is nevertheless inviting to wander some distance in either direction, particularly to explore tidal pools or gain a slightly different perspective on the view. To your left, though, you will come to Schooner Cove. To your right, a short distance brings you to a rocky point and, tucked behind it, a small rocky beach.

Seclusion Neighbouring houses are very much in evidence, but are not obtrusive. Because there is a nearly full-sized empty lot of land that backs the shore, you can feel very much at home, rather than wedged in.

38
MALLARD PLACE
A rough track through a broad patch of oaks and firs to a steep shore of large granite blocks

Location, signs and parking If you are using a map or a GPS, be careful not to confuse Mallard Place with Mallard *Road*, north of Parksville. If you are approaching from outside the Dolphin Beach/Fairwinds area, you will have to drive the same distance to Mallard Place whether you enter the peninsula from Powder Point Road or from Dolphin Drive. Mallard winds in an S curve down a considerable hill—cyclists, beware!—before grinding to a halt in a turnaround area. And what coasts down has to puff up. A few cars can position themselves on the shoulder in the turnaround area, staying well clear of the drives.

Path This access is not a simple narrow path squeezed between two confining lots, but is actually a broad patch of land about the width of two normal lots. Rather than plummeting straight toward the shore, the path winds over crests and bluffs through oaks, firs and the occasional arbutus. It is slightly chaotic and, particularly at first, a little challenging. Infirm relatives from the Prairies are best taken elsewhere. For everyone else, it should pose no problems. After 20 m or so, the path emerges onto a granite bluff a few metres above the shore.

Beach This is not a beach for beginners or for the unromantic. From where the path emerges, a sequence of giant natural steps leads to the lower parts of the shore, easiest to descend if you turn left upon reaching the shore. Composed of granite in horizontal strata and blocks of stone, fascinating outcroppings and nooks, the upper shore drops steeply to the low-tide line.

Suitability for children Rough-and-tumble children who like the jungle gyms of life can clamber over the shore with delight, but even they will have a hard time playing incident-free at the low-tide line. Children with little sense of adventure would be happier at another beach.

Suitability for groups Depending on the function of a group, most will want to go elsewhere. Because there is a big chunk of land immediately behind the beach, a group needn't worry overmuch about disturbing neighbours. On the other hand, because of the irregularity of the beach, a group would have a hard time perching in a cluster for, say, a group picnic. A sketching, wave-viewing, or birdwatching group, however, could well enjoy a visit.

View Because of the slight elevation and the presence of the Yeo and Winchelsea islands, the view has considerable depth and breadth. There is a pleasant open feeling to the view as well, since it sweeps both to the north and south down the Strait.

Winds, sun and shade The spot is fairly exposed to both southeast winds and northwest winds, so bring a jacket if the weather is cool, and be prepared to have your easel blown about on a windy day. On the other hand, because of the configuration of the giant blocks of granite and strata, it is possible to find little nooks in which to read a novel or simply to stare and gain Deep Inner Peace. Morning is the time for sun, at least on the upper beach. By afternoon, for good or ill, some of the large trees immediately behind the shore cast considerable shade onto the shore.

Beachcombing This a shore for scramblers or perchers, not for strollers. Those who are armed with a field guide to shore life, however, will find different shorefront critters here than they will on the sand and gravel expanses to which they might be accustomed.

Seclusion The width of the treed lot behind the shore and the particular placement of the houses on either side mean that you can find a considerable sense of seclusion to feed your romantic yearnings.

39

BRICKYARD COMMUNITY PARK

A beautiful area of Garry oaks, arbutus and rocky bluffs with a well-protected pebble beach

Location, signs and parking Amberwood Lane leaves Andover Road at the south end of a golf course. At first, you will be convinced that you are on the wrong track, because a prominent set of signs informs you not only that you are about to head down a NO THRU ROAD, but also that you are about to find yourself stuck with NO TURNAROUND. The former sign is accurate. The latter is not (at least, if you stop at the park's entrance rather than drive to the very end of the lane). In fact, by the trailhead to the park there is a rather grand circular drive replete with central garden. Still, you may feel you must be in the wrong place because you will not see much indication that there is a community park to be visited here. Persevere. Largely hidden by overhanging trees, near the beginning of the dirt trail at the head of the turnaround, is a sign indicating that, yes, indeed, you have found Brickyard Community Park. Parking isn't great, but if you pull well onto the wide grass shoulder, you won't be impeding other vehicles.

Path The path winds and undulates about 100 m through maples and old, gnarled firs before splitting into a few interconnected trails. The path is wide and much used, but does have a few lumps and bumps. Be prepared to enjoy the walk not just as a means, but also as an end: the knolls, oaks, and arbutus make for a very pretty walking experience. Particularly watch out on your right for a large maple whose roots embrace some fragments of an old brick wall—a remnant of the "brickyard" from which the park takes its name. Picturesquely enough, the soil has washed away to reveal the sight of huge roots growing around the old bricks.

An additional path gives access to the park from partway up the hill on Andover Road. Parking is awkward on Andover Road, however, and this second path is comparatively rough and narrow.

Beach The path that goes straight ahead passes an attractive wood fence and private gate of a house on the left before culminating on a raised and rounded granite viewpoint. On this viewpoint, there is well-situated park bench. From here it is possible to pick your way along the rounded but lumpy shore around another small point and into a sheltered bay. Alternately, you can retrace your route slightly and take a path to this beach. At high tide, this bay is an excellent swimming spot, since the pebble and rock shore collects warm rising water and extends for dozens of metres without much change in depth. At low tide it is a little less appealing because strips of jagged boulders run through the smaller rocks. The pebbles themselves are historically interesting, because red fragments of brick are intermingled with the native rock. Since, however, the beach is so protected from wave action, the pebbles and the beach itself create a slightly dank feeling at low tide.

Suitability for children Lots of options for sun or shade, a network of trails, a variety of shorefront rocky headlands and swimming beaches make this an attractive spot for children of a wide range of ages and dispositions. Do, however, be alert to the boulders in the centre of the beach at a half tide if your child is flailing her water-winged way across the shallows.

Suitability for groups A discreet group that does not congest the road or create a major invasion will find the room and a variety of beach options to enjoy themselves through an entire range of tides. Be aware that though this is quite a large park, it has no toilets or picnic benches.

View The view from the park bench is stunningly pretty—not, perhaps, magnificent, but stunningly pretty. Even the few metres of altitude provided by the small headland give enormous charm to the clusters of overlapping reefs, islets and islands all backed by the mainland mountains. Further, because the residential wasteland of suburban Nanaimo is screened by Wallis Point, this is one of the most picturesque spots on this part of the coast.

Winds, sun and shade Southeast winds do make themselves felt on the promontory, but are slightly muffled by the time they reach the adjoining beach, particularly at the high-tide line. Northwest winds are barely felt on the bluffs and are completely absent from the beach. On a warm but windy day, it is a good idea to bring a sweater if you're going to picnic on the promontory. Otherwise, make for the beach. Because the land is relatively low, and because the various bits protrude in virtually every direction, patches of sun and shade can be found throughout the day. Be warned, though, that the upper beach area before noon can seem a little gloomy and dank.

Beachcombing This is a beach for exploring rather than combing. Prodding about under rocks, climbing over shelves of granite, peering into tidal pools, looking for interesting bits of old brick and the like are the best options for those who want to wander rather than park themselves on one spot. If you are going to wander, you will find that by going north you will round the promontory to find a reasonably wide foreshore upon which to extend your exploratory amble.

Seclusion The park is understandably popular with locals in warm weather. Dog walkers and keep-fitters ensure that the trails are busy in the first part of the day. In the afternoon, if the tide is in, swimmers and sunbathers take full advantage of the park, lolling about on the rock shelves above the swimming beach like so many seals. This is a park and not just an access spot, though, so you will feel very much as if you are part of the "community" rather than an interloper. In colder weather, because the park is comparatively large, you can expect to wander, gaze, ponder and perch without feeling part of a crowd.

40

AINSLEY PLACE

A sheltered, pebbly bay, baking hot on sunny mornings, cooler in the afternoons

Location, signs and parking If you can make your way through the Fairwinds labyrinth to Andover Road (which curves around the south end of a golf course), you should have little difficulty finding where Ainsley Place makes an enticing curve toward the sea. Like many other access points in this area, this one is not easy to spot, because it begins among meticulously groomed houses. At the right side of a large paved turnaround area, look for a path between a yellow fire hydrant and two large boulders. A tiny, virtually invisible green and white sign on the top of a small post reads PUBLIC TRAIL TO BEACH and points out that the trail is provided by the Regional District of Nanaimo. It is possible to park in the paved cul-de-sac, but take care to avoid blocking the various drives.

Path The inauspicious little track soon broadens into a well-laid gravel path running some 70 m parallel to a chain-vlink fence. The fence, as various signs remind the visitor, is the northern edge of the huge chunk of National Defence Land that encompasses the tip of Nanoose peninsula and the north shore of Nanoose Bay itself. At the end of the gently sloping section of path, 37 well-made steps lead to the beach.

Beach While the beaches immediately north in Fairwinds are composed largely of granite, this beach is made up of the blue-black basalt stone that dominates Dorcas and Beachcomber peninsulas farther north. The gently curving and banked bay is made up of sea-smoothed but angular pebbles. At lower tide levels (the tide goes out some 50 m), the stones are larger and, of course, decorated with barnacles, oysters and rockweed. The north end of the beach has a ragged outcropping and some large, equally ragged boulders. The protected nature of this bay is reflected in the fact that locals store their (not very seaworthy) canoes on the upper reaches of the beach. The beach is enclosed by a small rocky headland to the left. To the right, the heavily treed and cliffy shoreline curves around into a larger enclosing bay that ultimately leads to the tip of Nanoose peninsula (Wallis Point).

Suitability for children This spot is about as child-oriented a beach as you're going to get in this area. While you (and your children) are going to have to forget about sand play, you will find the pebbly, sunny curve of shore an excellent place for picnicking, pretty-pebble hunting, and, at high tide, splashing. Just be prepared for running the gauntlet of the 37 steps that bring you to the beach.

Suitability for groups Parking creates some constraints, though a few cars could be happily accommodated. The beach has enough room for a small group, particularly one with diversified interests. There is enough space and treed land between the south end of the beach and the local houses that you will not be intrusive as you spread out your feast among the logs and pebbles.

View The view lacks some of the drama of the views elsewhere in this section, but is otherwise charming, almost to a fault. The pretty little promontory to the left has a windswept fir exactly where a windswept fir ought to be. Little reefs in the bay, Southey Island and the other islands of the Winchelsea group overlap each other in pretty disarray. Particularly appealing is the way Wallis Point protects you from seeing the heavily built-up banks of gleaming white houses between Lantzville and Nanaimo. Altogether, you will feel protected and cozy, but not constrained or landlocked.

Winds, sun and shade One of the qualities of the spot that make it so suitable for children is that it is protected from almost all winds. Even a southeast wind, which ought to swirl into the bay, seems to be blocked enough by Wallis Point that only the strongest gusts will raise goosebumps on a bare arm or leg. On a hot day, however, the beach can feel a little too sun-baked for comfort. Morning to early afternoon is the sunniest part of the day. Particularly in summer, when the sun is high, shade never overwhelms the beach except at the extreme south end.

Beachcombing Yes, you will have lots of scope for wandering up and down, back and forth, along the 100 m beach. No, you will not have lots of scope for striding out on extended walks in either direction beyond the beach, though the sight of pebbly beaches may draw you toward Wallis Point.

Seclusion Everything thus far in the description suggests seclusion, and the visitor here will feel seclusion—but only if that visitor keeps eyes forward. After all, like almost all stretches of this highly developed coast, this beach is backed by houses—often discreetly nestled into the landscape, but houses nevertheless.

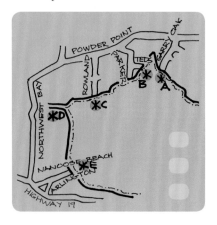

✳ Also nearby

A. At the end of **Garry Oak Drive**, off Powder Point Road, an access path leads to a rocky bluff and, at low tide, pebbles and shells. Protected from most winds, this is a good spot for warm-water swimming at high tide.

B. Drive down Powder Point Road until Parker, and, after a short distance, turn right onto **Teds Road**. A fairly steep track drops onto a gently sloping beach of gravel and a few rocky outcroppings. Although there is an oyster lease here, walking along the upper shore for a considerable distance is possible.

C. Rowland Road leaves Powder Point Road near Northwest Bay Road and leads directly to the shore. A few steps down a dirt track bring you onto a gravel shore and access to the estuary and tidal flats of Nanoose Bay.

D. Bird enthusiasts will want to note the **Wildlife Conservation Area** at the low grassy area on the shore side of Northwest Bay at the very end of Nanoose Bay. There is no easy path to the shore. Visitors most often park by the little bridge at the northern end of the strip just before Northwest Bay turns up the hill.

E. Nanoose Beach Road leaves Highway 19 just south of the traffic lights and Petrocan station at Northwest Bay Road. From a gravel parking area at the end of the road, a short level path leads through logs to the vast tidal flats of gravel and soft sand at the head of Nanoose Bay.

QUALICUM
PARKSVILLE
PART 1
LANTZVILLE
NANAIMO
LADYSMITH
PART 2
CHEMAINUS
DUNCAN
MILL BAY
PART 3 MALAHAT
GOLDSTREAM

LIKE SOME OTHER COASTLINES OF Vancouver Island, this one is remarkable for its variety. Broad tidal flats of sand and eelgrass, tiny pebbly coves and steep sandstone bluffs are among the diverse shores found here. Equally varied is the density of public access beaches from region to region. Those looking for the most beaches in the smallest area will want to go to the area between Lantzville and Nanaimo; second best is that from Ladysmith Harbour to Saltair. Three of the most remarkable parks anywhere on the island, Neck Point, Pipers Lagoon, and Biggs and Jack Point, lie within the centre of this region. Even the large city of Nanaimo has some great waterfront exploring to enjoy.

It is sad that one of the most beautiful and unusual stretches of coast on Vancouver Island—between Cedar and Yellow Point—has very few points designated for public access and even fewer that aren't tangles of wilderness. A shore of striking sandstone coves, reefs, points, bluffs, harbours and pocket beaches is almost entirely in the control of private owners. Still, there are compensations enough to make exploring this area rewarding. Some of the few spots to which the public has access are well-maintained parks. Others are charming and unusual glimpses of a striking shoreline. Anyone wanting to appreciate the area fully, though, should consider coming with a kayak or canoe and launching at Nelson Road, Blue Heron Park or even Elliott's Beach Park.

41
BENWALDUN ROAD
The better of two adjacent approaches to the large sandy tidal flats at the northern extreme of Lantzville

Location, signs and parking Benwaldun Road leads directly from Lantzville Road shortly before it joins the island highway at its northern end. Drive directly to the end of Benwaldun; you will approach between two high fences and can drive almost onto the beach itself. Signs will tell you not to park overnight and not to collect shellfish. There is sufficient room for three cars here; any additional cars will have to improvise a little on adjoining road shoulders.

Path A few steps will take you through gravel and beach grass directly onto the pebbly upper beach.

Beach The tide goes out for a few hundred metres here, as it does on the whole strip between Fleet Point and Blunden Point, a few kilometres apart. This is one of two access spots to this large beach area. The upper beach is pebbly, giving way to a band of barnacle-covered golf-ball-sized rocks, and then some hundreds of metres of sand, eelgrass and sandy tidal pools. While the beach extends both north and south, the stretch to the south boasts a higher proportion of sand. Come at low tide, though, if you want access to the sand: even at mid tide it can be underwater. Picnicking is restricted, but can be done in the pebbly-sandy area immediately below the parking spot. In fact, if you are picnicking there, don't be surprised if a workers' truck or local vehicle pulls up and unloads its occupants for a quick beachfront lunch.

Suitability for children This is a great place to bring children in warm weather. Make sure you have water shoes or flip-flops to get them across the gravel and barnacles, and then turn them loose. Choose low tide if you want lots of time for scampering through tidal pools and building castles. Choose mid tide if you want time for splashing and swimming in warm water over a sandy bottom. It is possible to swim even at low tide, but the shore drops off fairly quickly, the eelgrass is thick, and the water not as warm. One of the greatest entertainments for children at this beach is evading the water jets from horse clams that are buried in the sand and letting loose on squealing intruders. Not surprisingly, this is also a great kite-flying beach.

Suitability for groups Parking is the big issue here; otherwise, the beach itself, at least at low tide, virtually beckons even a large group of visitors to disperse themselves far out along the sand. Don't plan a boisterous picnic for a group on the upper beach, however—the neighbours are close.

View The Winchelsea and Ada islands from this angle line up like slow undulations along the near horizon. The view to the north is somewhat enclosed, but gives attractive angles of the woodsy slopes of Nanoose peninsula and the bluffs of Nanoose Hill (Notch Hill). The south view is a little more open, but because of the curve of the land, still largely enclosed.

Winds, sun and shade Northwest winds are (very) slightly muffled by Nanoose peninsula. You will feel both northwest and southeast winds but will notice that southeast winds hit the shore obliquely. The stretches of beach receive no shade, of course. Along the upper shore, however, you will find a little shade in the late morning and afternoon.

Beachcombing This is one of those beaches that makes you restless to walk: at low tide you won't be able to stop your legs from carrying you far out along the sand flats and then toward the south. At higher tides, it is possible to stroll the middle and upper shores for considerable distances as well, but it is much less appealing to do so.

Seclusion The houses at either side of the actual access point are set back, though only a little. You will feel wild and free on the open stretches of sand, but not on the upper shore.

✳ Also nearby About 100 m south along Lantzville Road, **Eby Road** takes you directly to the shore and a spot very similar to that at Benwaldun Road. It is a good alternative to Benwaldun, if parking is difficult there. Be prepared, however, for a bit of a barnacle-adorned slog to the sand if you use Eby Road.

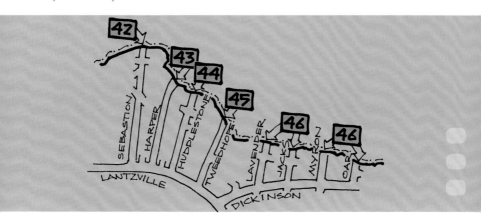

42

SEBASTION ROAD

A remarkable variety within a small area, including a striking sandstone point and a sandy beach

Location, signs and parking Sebastion Road turns directly off Lantzville Road and proceeds without twist or turn straight to the coast. Lots of signs will make clear that you have reached a public access, including a PUBLIC ACCESS sign made from concrete. In addition, you will be told that to gather shellfish is dangerous, no parking is to be undertaken overnight, and no campfires are to be lit in fire season. There is a litter barrel for your own litter and a "pet stand" for Fido's litter. Several cars can fit into the spot off the road.

Sebastion Road

Path A gradual descent brings you a short distance onto the beach. You can, with some ease, come encumbered with whatever paraphernalia will bring you beach pleasure.

Beach This spot, quite simply, is one of the most amazing on this entire section of coast. As you leave the path, you will find yourself on a broad swath of coarse sand and pebbles lining the upper shore and extending some distance below you. This pebbly area broadens out to the south to create a very large upper shore area exposed at all but the highest tides. To the north, this sand-and-pebble strip leads onto a sculpted-looking sandstone shelf that, at low tide, drops off steeply over a short cliff directly into the water below. In front, this same mini-escarpment shoots obliquely out from the shore, creating a promontory extending out almost 100 m into the sea. The south side of this angling sandstone promontory slopes gradually down to some large patches of sand, eelgrass and sandy tidal pools leading some distance to the south. You really do have to see this beach—at low tide—to appreciate how the various elements all link. The beach is great for snorkelling along the "escarpment" at mid to high tide.

View Wide and sweeping, the view includes all of Nanoose Bay to the north, to the outward curve of the wooded bank north of Nanaimo to the south. At the same time, the view doesn't feel exposed or bald because of the shorefront trees along the slightly elevated and irregular shoreline, particularly to the north.

Winds, sun and shade The biggest drawback to this spot on a windy day is its exposure to the full effects of a northwest wind (though chiefly on the sandstone projection rather than on the beach.) There is not even a whiff of shelter from a southeast wind. Sunbathers and novel readers can reduce the effects somewhat by staying high up on the shore and lying low. There is almost no shade to be had, so plan accordingly.

Beachcombing Your wandering, particularly at high tide, will be somewhat restricted if you wish to go north, though it is possible to make your way along the narrow foreshore. To the south, however, you can walk quite literally for miles. Just be aware that low tide will give you the most options for selecting the kind of walking you want to do.

Seclusion There are houses along this whole stretch of coast, of course, but at this particular spot the houses are situated in such a way and the beach itself is large enough that you won't feel cramped. At the same time, you will feel somewhat as if you are on a public beach: not surprisingly, the spot is quite popular.

43

HARPER ROAD
An alternate access to the sandy beach also accessible from Sebastion Road

Location, signs, and parking Harper leaves Lantzville Road between Sebastion and Huddlestone roads and leads directly onto the low, beachy-feeling, open shoreline. You will see a tsunami warning sign as well as signs telling you not to have fires in fire season or not to park overnight. A few cars can park in the sandy, gravelly end of this beach approach.

Path This is a good place to bring your heaviest and most elaborate picnic or your most cumbersome beach gear—even folding chairs—since you have but a few steps to bring you directly onto the pebbly shore.

Beach The upper beach of loose pebbles is unusually wide along this bit of shore, so that even on high tides you won't be crowded. Low tide, nevertheless, will be the tide to choose for many beachgoers, since that is when patches of sand and sandy tidal pools to the north are exposed. This sandy area is not one of those broad bands of 100 or 200 m that sometimes can be found along this area of coast, but, at about 70 or 80 m, is nevertheless wide enough for lots of running, Frisbee throwing, kite flying and so on. To the south, the tide goes out less far, and less appealingly, revealing only profusions of small barnacle-covered rocks.

Suitability for children Choose low tide if you and your children agree that sand is what you want on a beach. Choose a higher tide if they want to swim or paddle. Choose any time at all if they want to sift through the pebbles looking for the world's prettiest, whitest, or weirdest pebble.

Suitability for groups The sufficient parking for several cars, the easy access and the scope and variety of the beach make this beach a practical choice for most groups. It may not be the first choice of sketchers or photographers.

View The curve of the shore blocks much of the view of the northern Strait. A smaller (and attractively treed) curve of shore to the south likewise gives this beach a comparatively enclosed view. Still, this is hardly a cove; the wide sweep across the Strait and south toward Howe Sound will not make you feel the least bit cramped.

Winds, sun and shade Of all the beaches in the Lantzville area, this one is probably most protected from a northwest wind, and to a lesser extent from a southeast wind. On a hot day, in fact, this beach can become almost uncomfortably hot—though the water provides an instant and obvious remedy! One obliging tree in the parking area provides a little afternoon shade on the upper beach, but otherwise you and the sun will be very well acquainted with each other by the end of a long day.

Beachcombing Good walking is to be had in either direction, though a little less easily to the north. After a few hundred metres in either direction, you will have to make your way over headlands of solid rock before finding more pebbly shore to carry on. Low tide will give you most options for the kind of walking you probably want to do.

Seclusion The waterfront residential lots are unusually large adjoining Harper Road, and the houses are set well back. You can feel comfortable that you are not intruding or being intruded upon—but you won't feel you've found a little piece of wilderness.

44
HUDDLESTONE ROAD
A little-used access with a narrow pebbly shore and a low rocky headland

Location, signs and parking Huddlestone Road is another in the sequence of roads that turn directly off Lantzville Road and plow in a businesslike and forthright manner directly to the shoreline, though you will find the opening to the shore is considerably less extensive than that of many similar access spots farther south. There is room for only a single car directly in the access road, but room for several more along the adjoining shoulders. You will see a concrete barricade and a litter barrel, as well as a "pet stand" for cleaning up after your Irish wolfhound or chihuahua.

Path The bushes here (sometimes whacked back) tend to block the beach access, but enterprising souls have chopped a 30 m path through the growth, laid down gravel and inserted small log steps. Be prepared, though, for a 1 m drop directly onto the gravel upper beach from the end of the path. Those wanting to drive their mega-cooler and beach chairs directly to the shore can do so at most of the nearby access spots, most attractively perhaps at Harper Road and Sebastion Road.

Beach The beach here is unusual in several key ways, though you will fully appreciate its characteristics only if you come at low tide. Even the upper beach has its odd yet pleasing qualities, comprised as it is of loose golf-ball gravel and large, sculpted sandstone chunks. Somehow the word "boulder" doesn't seem appropriate for these strangely shaped slabs. To the south these chunks are interspersed with the gravel. To the north you will find a crest of these slabs running toward the water, and beyond that, more open gravelly shore. At low tide this gravelly shore trails undramatically down to the tide line. To the south, however, the shore does something much more interesting. Below the sandstone chunks, you will find yourself walking onto a long, irregular sandstone shelf that drops off a couple of metres onto the lower gravel-and-boulder shore. This area makes stunning snorkelling at mid to high tide and interesting exploring and climbing at low tide.

Suitability for children This is a good cool-weather beach for children, if you are willing to supervise them as they climb and jump over the nobbly and cliffy bits. In addition, at the corner of Lantzville and Huddlestone roads is a park with the usual paraphernalia of slides and swings and an open grassy area. This is not a great hot-weather beach, though, if you are looking for a swimming spot.

Suitability for groups Parking limitations are the most significant issue here. At low tide the beach itself will accommodate two or three families or a clutch of like-minded shore-goers without crowding out each other or the waterfront residents.

View The angle of the shoreline is such that the headland immediately to the north steers your view south across the Strait and toward Nanaimo. The shore, not the view, is the main reason to come to this beach.

Winds, sun and shade The headland that partly blocks your view does have the advantage of slightly reducing a cool northwest wind if the day happens to be blowy. You will find some shelter from a southeast wind as well, particularly if you find a nook below the low-tide cliff. Because the bank is a little higher here than at spots to the south, and because there are some shorefront firs, significant patches of late morning shade fall onto the beach and make their way along it as the day progresses. Finding shade in the late afternoon—just when you might want it most—is considerably more difficult.

Beachcombing The varied terrain makes this a good beach to explore for those who are interested in what lies under their feet and not merely what horizons lie in front. Long-distance striding-out in both directions is possible, especially to the south, but wandering and poking about are the more obvious forms of beachcombing suited to this beach.

Seclusion The bushes that crowd onto the upper shore, together with the slight bank and the particular arrangement of adjoining houses, make this a surprisingly secluded beach, particularly on the upper shore.

45
TWEEDHOPE ROAD
One of a series of short, gravelly shores in the most settled area of Lantzville

Location, signs and parking Turn down charmingly named Tweedhope Road directly off Lantzville Road and follow it to its sandy end directly at the edge of a small bank. You will be warned about harvesting shellfish and about not having fires or parking overnight—but not about the danger of tsunamis, despite such warnings popping up at very similar spots in the immediate area. Parking is limited, though a few cars could fit in the space between the adjoining houses and, for a couple of cars, directly overlooking the shore.

Path Two or three steps through the large boulders (evidently in place to prevent erosion) take you directly onto the beach.

Beach The upper beach is a wide strip of coarse sand and pebbles dropping gradually over several metres to a lower beach with mixed patches of barnacly rocks, some large boulders and some fine patches of sand and sandy tidal pools. The tide does not go out a long way here, so even at low tide it is easy to reach both the sand and the water.

Suitability for children This is a good beach for children of a wide variety of ages and interests. Make sure that delicate feet have protection against the patches of barnacles and that sensitive skin has protection against sun and wind. Then sit back and watch your child play to her heart's content.

Although the patches of sand are not nearly as extensive as at nearby Sebastion and Harper roads, the waterline is much closer. At a half tide, a child frolicking in waist-deep water on a sandy patch could flail into one of the patches of boulders hidden, at this tide, from sight. Other than that, the beach could hardly be safer.

Suitability for groups The beach itself is good for a small group set on eating sandwiches while sifting through pebbles. The limited parking and somewhat intrusive access, however, means that discretion in parking is important.

View The shoreline here angles south in such a way that you will find yourself looking primarily toward the southern Strait and the mountains above Howe Sound. Since your view of the northern islands is restricted and no shoreline trees frame your view, you will find that the view here, though pleasant, lacks some of the picturesque charm afforded by similar spots in the Lantzville area.

Winds, sun and shade Northwest winds reach the beach on a blowy day, but will generally come ashore at an oblique angle. Southeast winds, however, face little impediment as they sweep up the Strait. Nothing provides shade at any time of day, so bring whatever beach umbrellas and sunscreen you need to protect yourself.

Oar Road

Beachcombing Bring your beach shoes if you fancy a long walk in either direction, though you will probably want to choose a low tide for maximally interesting and varied walking, particularly because the upper shore has lots of loose pebbles and sand.

Seclusion It is hard to imagine a less secluded spot. Low fences on the close adjoining houses, a virtually non-existent bank, lack of vegetation, continuous houses along the flat, open shore—all add up to very, very little seclusion.

46 LAVENDER ROAD, JACK ROAD, MYRON ROAD AND OAR ROAD

Four nearly identical access spots close by each other in the middle of residential Lantzville

Location, signs and parking All four roads lead directly off Dickinson Road and end directly on the shore. Signs vary a little, but whether you are told not to gather shellfish, not to park overnight or to keep your antennae alert to the first sign of a tsunami, you will need no such signs to tell you that these are obviously beach accesses with strikingly similarly characteristics. Parking, too, is similar: all four spots are road-width, allowing space for three or four cars. About two of these spaces with ringside seats.

Path Although the particular details vary slightly, the end of all four roads are separated by but a few steps from the coarse sand, beach logs and pebbles of the upper beaches.

Beach At none of these is the low-tide line a great distance from the upper shore. Oar Road opens onto the broadest expanse of low-tide shore, followed by Myron, Lavender and, smallest of all, Jack. Kayakers will find Jack Road a particularly easy spot to put in their kayaks, even at low tide—though they will have to be a little careful of the barnacle-encrusted small rocks that cover the shore. The surfaces of all four shores are covered, more or less, with small rocks and barnacles, except above the high-tide line, where coarse sand and pebbles can make for pleasant picnicking and sunbathing spots. A drainage pipe running down the beach at Lavender Road a few dozen metres north somewhat spoils the otherwise pristine feeling of this beach. All four spots are good for foul-weather car picnics: you will feel little separation between you and the shore. Such winter car-picnickers will generally find that Jack and Oar roads provide the most exposure to spanking southeast storms.

Suitability for children Children can easily get to the water at low tide to splash and explore, yet can do so without stumbling too much over slippery or uneven ground. At high tide they can readily splash and swim over the smooth and pebbly upper shore. The proximity of the car can, with children of certain ages and dispositions, be a huge advantage of this spot. Needless to say, however, most children will prefer one of the sandy alternatives farther north or south.

Suitability for groups All four spots can handle small groups reasonably well, depending on what the group has in mind. Picnicking, birdwatching, even (at high tide) swimming can all be pleasant and comfortable here.

View Although the view is, of course, much the same as that at spots both farther north and south, it seems especially pleasing here. The pilings visible at low tide from Lavender Road seem picturesque (except to some). The slightly varying arrangements of Winchelsea and Ada islands off Nanoose peninsula are probably the chief scenic feature and the one most likely to make it into sketches and watercolours. Nevertheless, this is a sea-level view, so it lacks some of the feeling of space and depth of the high-bank views in the area.

Winds, sun and shade Both northwest wind and southeast winds are felt here, though the northwest wind seems to be particularly bent on blowing directly onshore. Only a little midday shade is cast on the upper shores at Myron and Oar roads. On a hot day, come prepared. The pre-noon sun will seem stronger, because it will be mostly from the front.

Beachcombing Walking through the loose pebbles is a little slow and walking over the gravel farther down the beach can lead to a few stumbles, but, on the whole, strolling in either direction is both possible and inviting. Obviously, choosing the right footwear is crucial to enjoying walking here.

Seclusion You will find no seclusion here, though neither the beach nor the neighbourhood is busy or crowded.

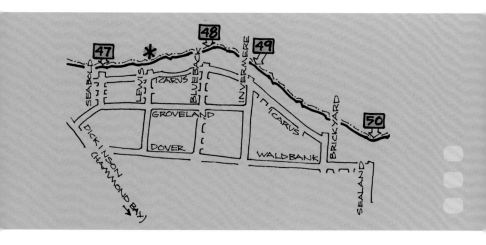

47
SEABOLD ROAD PARKETTE
A giant wooden staircase high in the trees of a wooded bank down to a large expanse of low-tide sand

Location, signs and parking There are several approaches you can take through the tangle of roads in this congested suburb, but it is perhaps easiest to drive down Groveland Drive from Dickinson Road and thence Seabold. When you get onto Seabold Road, simply follow it to the end. A sign identifies the spot as Seabold Rotary Park and provides information about the volunteers who developed the park. Some maps identify it, oddly, as a "parkette," while Lewis Road "park," close by, is much smaller and less developed. Parking is a real problem. The road is not particularly wide and has a curb, and so no shoulder. In addition, many driveways crowd the area. Visitors will simply have to park as considerately as they can along the road.

Path The "path" is really something of a minor engineering masterpiece. Before you come to the spot where you can descend to the beach, however, you will pass (or, possibly, hesitate at) a pretty and manicured area with four picnic tables and a playground, embellished with a pleasant little stand of arbutus and fir. At the end of the area, you will come to a magnificent flight of suspended wooden stairs descending in a sequence of rest stops, 179 steps to the beach. In fact, the descent to the beach is part of the pleasure of this spot, since you will almost have the feeling that you are high among the big trees.

Beach Where the path reaches the shore, the beach is not at its best: a little stream enters the beach at this point, and a large gravel area fans out about 30 m in all directions. Beyond this circle of gravel, most will feel that this is a beach to rival the best sandy beaches of this whole section of coast—if, that is, you prize vast, long flats of sand stretching hundreds of metres out to a low-tide line. Patches of eelgrass and large tidal pools give variety and colour to the wide beach. Occasional big boulders protrude up from the sand.

Suitability for children Sand-loving children will have a wonderful time here, at least at low or intermediate tides. There is vast space to galumph, warm tidal pools to splash in and so on. You might want to bring flip-flops or beach shoes for traversing the gravel patch, however. You may also find your child is the sort who finds the eelgrass beds creepy rather than fun. There are a few other flies in the ointment. The beach has little to offer the sand-loving child at high tide—and particularly because the upper beach is in deep shadow for the entire day except the early morning. In addition, of course, 179 steps is a large number, especially when you are going up those steps rather than down. Even with the rest areas and platforms, the staircase can lessen the pleasure of bringing children of certain dispositions to this beach.

Suitability for groups The beach itself has heaps of room for lots of people to frolic and wander about. The biggest impediment to bringing more than just your immediate family, however, is parking.

View Both the view from the top and the view from the beach itself are splendid, in large part because of the same mountains and islands that appear in slightly different arrangements along this whole section of coast. Because the beach line is somewhat concave at this point, you may find your eyes drawn most to the north, where the bank drops closer to the shore and the Winchelsea Islands pattern the horizon.

Winds, sun and shade The beach can be breezy, especially with a northwest wind, but also with a southeast wind. This, of course, can be an advantage for kite-fliers. In spite of its pleasures, this beach is not a sunbather's beach, nor much of a picnicker's beach, either. The gravelly and shady upper shore does not invite anyone to linger. It is possible, though, to wander a few hundred metres to the north, where the bay curves gradually south and the bank is lower. Here the shade line disappears altogether until mid afternoon, and the upper beach provides pretty, sandy spots among the logs for picnickers and loungers.

Beachcombing If you choose your tides—and to enjoy this beach, you really need to come at a low tide—you can stroll, stride or even run to your lungs' content. You will probably be happiest, however, if you wear beach shoes or flip-flops, since it is impossible to walk very far without crossing a large, though shallow, tidal pool.

Seclusion This is probably the busiest of the various similar beaches along this section, in large part, no doubt, because of the beautifully built and maintained stairs and upper park area. Still, you can expect to walk alone—or hand in hand—along the empty stretches of low-tide sand, free of crowds and free of curious shorefront residents.

✱ **Also nearby** Where Dover Road leaves Dickinson Road, turn toward the shore at the Lewis Road T-junction. Follow the road to the end, and you will find yourself at **Lewis Road Park**. If you are planning a sequence of beach explorations, you can drive among the Lewis Road, Blueback Road and Invermere Road accesses via the interconnecting Icarus Drive. Since a short stump of Lewis Road extends past Icarus Drive, parking is a little easier here than at some of the other access spots in this congested suburban area. In fact, this is really just a viewpoint, though it is designated as a beach access. The bank is as high here as at other spots along this stretch of coast. Two picnic tables, a bench, a litter

Seabold Road Parkette

barrel and a sloping grassy field have been provided for proper enjoyment. At the end of the grassy area, you can see where a few suicidal folk have slithered down the dangerously steep bank, but only the desperate will feel tempted to follow suit.

The view is probably best when the tide is low—a pleasant vista of sand flats and pools below, in addition to the views through the treetops. You will have less of a view out across the Strait than north toward the islands off Lantzville. In fact, even though you might feel frustrated at not being able to descend to the beach here, you will, in an appreciative frame of mind, enjoy the wonderfully "treetop" feeling of looking out through the trees and, in particular, past one large cedar leaning out from the bank.

48

BLUEBACK ROAD

A long descent down a wooded bank to a wide expanse of low-tide sand

Location, signs and parking If you can make your way onto Icarus Drive by any one of many different routes, you will discover that this spot is not only easy to find, but clearly designed to welcome, organize and contain visitors. (Do, however, be alert to the fact that there is a Blueback *Drive* near Schooner Cove in the Nanoose Bay area.) On Blueback Road, look for one of the red and white PUBLIC ACCESS signs common to the city of Nanaimo. You will also see a rectangular parking area surrounded by a sequence of concrete barricades and a chain that can be closed to prevent unsavoury overnighters. A list of city regulations on one side will tell you what you can and cannot do (dog owners take note). Ten cars could fit in this carefully organized area, so there is no need to park on the street and irritate local residents.

Path Be psychologically and physically prepared: this path has 296 steps! The top section of this high bank is set back a little, providing visitors with both a bench and a litter barrel. The top part of the path is a sequence of wide steps constructed of chunks of timber and gravel. Evidently some visitors find the angle and width of the steps awkward, since the path is worn into the grass and earth beside these steps. As the path descends into a stand of alders, it remains a wide swath until it comes to a skookum, strongly constructed lower staircase. Passing the remains of a giant fir, the path descends through a stand of large cedars and emerges onto a fine sandy beach.

Beach While the upper strip of the beach is composed of boulders and ostrich-egg rocks, the lower beach, some 100 m out at low tide, reveals big tidal pools and broad stretches of sand. The beach is wider to the left than to the right. While some sandy beaches are dense with eelgrass, these sandbars are mostly bare. Those who want to test their balance will find this a good spot to practise their skim-boarding techniques. The biggest limitation of this beach, other than its difficulty of access, is its lack of a good picnic spot. The upper beach can be used, but is in deep shade well before noon and is largely overhung with shorefront trees.

Suitability for children The path, naturally, can be more than a bit of a trial for unmotivated children, but the beach is well worth the price of patience and cajoling (or piggybacking). Children (and their happy parents) will find lots of scope for sand and water play here, though they will want to check tide tables to gauge how much exposed sand and how much water-covered sand they want and when.

Suitability for groups Because of the well-planned parking, this is a good spot for a group. The beach clearly allows lots of room for spreading out or gathering, depending on the nature and interests of the group. Unfortunately, the remains of a beach fire scar the upper beach. Any group should remember not only the restrictions on beach fires, but also the etiquette of ensuring any remains are not visible.

View Except for the islands clustered in the distance off Nanoose, the view is open and wide, extending as far south on the mainland side as Bowen Island.

Winds, sun and shade Like the rest of this shoreline, this section is exposed to northwest winds and southeast winds. While the morning floods the entire beach with sun, the late morning and afternoon spread increasing shade, though not out as far as the sandbars.

Beachcombing Wander to your heart's content, though do mull a little about what footwear to choose, considering the tide and season. Flip-flops will allow you to shift easily from barefooted strolling on the sand to protected strolling on the small rocks. Beach/water shoes will provide a little more protection on the rocky sections. The longest stretch for sandy walking, if that is what you're primarily after, is to the north.

Seclusion How likely are flocks of visitors to take on 296 steps? Most visitors you will see—and you will see some—will be approaching along the beach from either side. The high, heavily wooded bank will shield you from the stares, too, of waterfront householders.

49

INVERMERE ROAD
A steeply sloping path down a high wooded bank to gravel shore with expanses of low-tide sand

Location, signs and parking Follow Invermere Road to the end of a suburban cul-de-sac, paved and curbed. PUBLIC ACCESS and NO OVERNIGHT PARKING signs will confirm that you are in the right place. This is, of course, road parking, but in the cul-de-sac you can be reasonably out of the way, though no more than a few vehicles can fit here.

Path Invermere, another of three descents from the top of the very high wooded shore (Waldbank/Sealand Park and Blueback are the others), is perhaps the easiest, not because the path from here is any shorter, but because the bank is least steep here, allowing a somewhat more gradual descent and ascent. At the same time, the path isn't quite as kempt as the paths at the other spots. A litter barrel marks the beginning of the path. The path begins as a wide, curving dirt track among maples and alders, the S-curve clearly planned to reduce the angle of descent. In addition, loose earth is interspersed with patches of concrete slab steps where the track becomes a little steeper. As it descends closer to the beach, it leaves the small trees and enters a band of larger trees, though they are hardly old-growth giants.

Beach At very low tides the pilings from an old brickyard are visible emerging from the sand. Whether you see these as picturesque opportunities for artistic photos or blights on the pristine beach is a matter of taste. The tide does go out a significant distance, exposing a wide band of barnacle-crusted rocks before the sand begins, so consult tide tables if it's sand that you want. At low tides, the largest swaths of sand can be found if you go a little distance north, though there are some to the south as well. The great advantage of this beach over the two similar ones to the north is that it is much better for picnicking or sunning. Because the shore faces (north)east rather than north, until noon, at least, it offers a pleasant chunk of sunny upper beach among the few beach logs.

Suitability for children As with other beaches in this area, children have to be game to ascend where they have descended, or parents of smaller children have to be game to engage in a little hefting of reluctant children. You will probably want to choose either a low tide for children to scamper barefooted over the sand or an incoming tide for them to splash over the sandy bottom.

Suitability for groups If groups can park without congesting the street, they will find that the beach itself is well-suited to even a large group. You will find plenty of room to spread out and few locals with whom you will be exchanging sights or sounds.

View Because the shore is slightly convex at this point, it has an expansive feeling. The open Strait, mainland mountains and high, wooded bank sweeping back in both directions make for a sense of space and depth.

Winds, sun and shade All winds will have some impact on this beach, though the impact is reduced the closer you are to the high-tide line. You will be slightly sheltered from a cooling northwest breeze if you turn right as you arrive at the shore. While there is plenty of sun in the first part of the day, shade seekers will find the second part of the day provides a broad swath of shadow from the high bank behind.

Beachcombing There is plenty of scope for wandering along the fine gravel and long upper band or down through the boulders and interspersed sandbars at low tide. The large tidal pools among the sand patches can make barefoot wandering pleasant, too, so easily removed sandals or water shoes might be the best footwear for this section of beach (at least during the warmer months).

Seclusion As with the other access spots along this stretch of shore, this one brings you to a place where the high, wooded bank virtually guarantees you lots of opportunity to be your own sweet self. Technically, the whole strip of foreshore and bank is designated park area. Given the geography, however, the beach is equally secluded in either direction.

50

SEALAND PARK

A dramatically wooded ravine
ending in a gravelly beach
with a few sand patches

Location, signs, and parking Actually, there are two road approaches to this large park and the extensive strip of forest that leads to the shore. Recommended is the entrance from the paved cul-de-sac at the end of Waldbank Road, near a bank of mailboxes. A red and white PUBLIC ACCESS sign reassures you that you have found the right place. You will also see a sign reminding you of city-park regulations. It is also possible to enter the area where a dirt track descends off Sunset Road, near the house numbered 5954. At this point there is no sign, and since the first part of the ravine walk is not actually in the park, you will have to go by faith and a sense of direction. Although a sidewalk lines the cul-de-sac at the end of Waldbank Road, parking for a few cars is fairly easy, largely because the turnaround isn't lined with houses.

Path The first few minutes will provide you with as colourful and dramatic approach to a beach access as you are likely to get. A series of airy wooden staircases and platforms descends, at some points very steeply, through a steep bank of cedars, maples and swordferns. Disappointingly, once you have descended to the bottom of this striking ravine with its rainforest feeling, your way is marred by an ugly dirt road leading toward the coast. It seems that this dirt road was necessitated by a drainage system buried beneath it, for both the gurgle of water and a faint sewage smell can be discerned as you carry on perhaps 100 m toward the water. As vegetation regenerates here, visitors can reimmerse themselves into the wonderful, hidden world of the emerald-forest ravine. A huge chain-link fence and concrete drainage structure are firmly in place at the end of the dirt road, but a dirt path to the right allows you to scuttle and slither down onto the beach.

Beach The upper margin of beach is made up of small gravel that gives way to increasingly large and barnacle-covered boulders. Beyond these boulders at low and mid tides, however, patches of sand become available for barefoot scampering. Until noon at least, picnicking or lolling can be done in full sun, particularly if you turn right as you come down to the beach.

Suitability for children Some children will delight in the jungle gym part of the staircase descent, as long as they will tolerate the more rigorous ascent at the end of the visit to the beach. Otherwise, the beach will afford the usual pleasures and the usual pains of this kind of shorefront.

Suitability for groups As long as parking doesn't become an issue, this area is secluded enough and big enough that quite a healthy clutch of folk could move unimpeded, and unimpeding, through the forest and to the large, expansive beach.

View Since this is a sea-level view and the banks are high behind, it does not have the expansive feeling of the view from the high points south of here. Still, you will have fine views across the Strait toward Bowen Island and the Howe Sound mountains, as well as down the concave curve of the steep wooded shore.

Winds, sun and shade The high curving shore will slightly reduce the effect of winds from both directions, but the closer you get to the waterline, the more you will feel the wind. As the morning wears on, so does the amount of shade increase; by afternoon there is a significant swath of shade across the upper shore.

Beachcombing Beachcombing in both directions is easy, but it's easiest at or near the high-tide level, where the gravel is finest. Low-tide walking, requiring sturdy water shoes, is best done if you turn north.

Seclusion Because there are few close access points and because the walk to the beach is considerable, not many people will be found on this section of shore. The high, wooded bank gives a wonderfully natural feeling to the shore as well, even though the fastidiously kept gardens of suburbia lie not very far away.

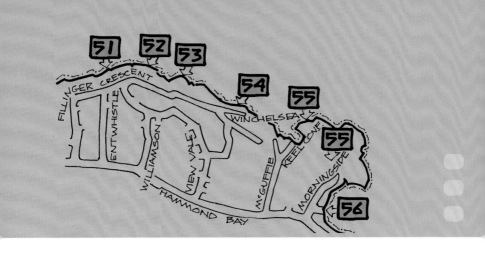

51
ENTWHISTLE DRIVE
A peculiar approach to a steep sandstone shore with tidal pools

Location, signs and parking Compared to some in this area, this access spot is ridiculously easy to find. On Hammond Bay Road, you will see both a red and white PUBLIC ACCESS sign and the road sign for Entwhistle Drive. Follow the road a couple of hundred metres to its end. Parking is a little awkward but possible along the curbed road. Your heart may sink when you see the sign saying VIEWPOINT, since such a sign elsewhere means you have access only to the view and not the shore. The sign is misleading. You will see a strip of manicured lawn and a gated asphalt drive leading straight toward the coast. At the end of this asphalt road, an odd, semicircular wall, evidently part of a municipal utility, apparently bars you from the shore. Persevere.

Path At the end of the 30 m gated asphalt road, you will see two benches at the top of the concrete structure and a set of steps curving down in front. The concrete steps lead not to just a "viewpoint," as the sign says, but directly to the beach about 5 m below.

Beach The beach directly ahead and to the right of your point of arrival is an interesting sandstone shelf approximately 15 m wide, pocked with tiny tidal pools. At the end of the shelf, the shore drops away steeply into a tangle of large sandstone rocks. To the left the shore is mostly boulders decorated with rockweed and barnacles. Not many people would choose this spot for a picnic, but, a small patch of beach logs and gravel at the upper part of the beach makes an unusual—and pleasant—picnic site.

Suitability for children If you can convince yourself that the faint whiff of sewage you detected descending the stairs does not suggest a threat from pollution, you should enjoy bringing the adventurous and tidal pool-loving sort of child to this beach. If the child is only interested in getting into the water as quickly and splashily as possible, however, the beach is not a good choice: beyond the sandstone shelf the shore is steep, the rocks large and slippery with seaweed.

Suitability for groups Heaven knows where a group would park, though they could legally disperse themselves along the curbed street. In any case, the spot's appeal is its isolation from groups. It's not clear why a group would want to come here.

View As the sign indicates, this spot really does provide views, and very good ones, both from the top of the concrete structure and from the beach below. From this far south, the islands off Nanoose peninsula look romantically tiny and clustered. The mountains across the Strait extending from Jervis Inlet to Howe Sound are particularly appealing. On a clear day you might see Mount Baker as well—though, as few people realize, this ghostly white triangle is just the top of a very large mountain, most of which is below the horizon. Most striking about this spot is that it is probably the best place along the whole central coast (with the possible exception of Neck Point) to view a northwest storm. Without the protection of any intervening land, the wind and waves charge down a great distance (a "fetch," as nautically tongued folk say) and hit the shore directly. A southeast storm is likewise a good bet for wave watchers.

Winds, sun and shade The spot is exposed to just about all wind. Some shade starts falling on the upper shore in late morning, though the trees and bank aren't high at this point along the coast.

Beachcombing The sandstone shelf makes great walking in either direction, though of course walking will also involve occasional bits of scrambling, and the shelf can get slippery in winter.

Seclusion The banks are just high and bushy enough that, even in the heart of suburbia, you will feel happy that you have found your way to this largely unvisited section of shore.

52
FILLINGER CRESCENT A
A broad, paved path to a gravelly pocket beach and jagged, steep shore

Location, signs and parking Like the other spots close by, this one can easily be reached by turning off Hammond Bay Road, either onto Fillinger Crescent or onto Entwhistle Road. In both cases, turn right to follow the shore along Fillinger Crescent. The spot you are looking for is opposite a house numbered 5040. A red and white PUBLIC ACCESS sign should confirm that you are in the right place. A large gravel parking area can accommodate 10 or so cars off the road—but, strangely, two driveways lead from one side of this parking area.

Path At the end of the parking area are concrete barriers and two vertical stanchions locked in place. The path is a narrow paved road that curves down, dropping 7 or 8 m over the next 40 m. This little road goes through a pretty wooded area (there is a fine little stand of arbutus near its beginning) and is bounded by a wooden fence on the right. Although kayakers and canoeists will have a bit of hike here, the path is a good, clear, smooth one on which to carry their pleasure craft—and because of the nature of the beach, they will find (at high or half tide, in calm waters) launching easy.

Beach The path emerges onto an area of angular but slightly smoothed fist-sized rocks, an area that, at high tide, extends toward the water on the left. Directly in front, the short and fairly steep shore is made up of a series of solid rock and somewhat jagged ridges. The water drops off quite quickly right by the shore, so both scuba divers and snorkellers will reach deep water quickly. Picnickers should make a special note of this spot, since it is one of the few along this section that scoops up afternoon sun—but also offers some patches of shade.

Suitability for children The access is easy for children, and supervised little ones could be happy hurling rocks into the water or finding their way up and down the shore looking for critters. The fact is, however, this is not going to be any child's favourite beachfront haunt.

Suitability for groups Certainly there is easy parking for a bridge-club-sized group. Whether they find the beach suits their tastes is another question. There are, of course, no facilities.

View On a clear day, the view is wonderful. The shore is angled in such a way that the view seeker will be tempted to look more north than south. Nanoose peninsula and the adjoining islands are clearly visible in this direction, while to the south the shore-side view comes to a halt half a kilometre away with a high point. The Coast Mountains, and particularly the Lions, seem especially fetching from this spot.

Winds, sun and shade A northwest wind is (almost) fully felt here. A southeast wind comes ashore obliquely, but is not much muffled unless you are sitting on the little beach and facing the late afternoon sun, in which case a southeast wind will be at your back and therefore little felt. Patches of shade crawl across the upper shore all afternoon, interspersed with some broad sunny patches, particularly toward the later half of the afternoon.

Beachcombing At low tide, the intrepid investigator of tidal pools can go a short distance in either direction. At high tide, small cliffs make venturing very far more of an adventure than a pleasure.

Seclusion The distance between houses and the drop to the shore are big enough that you will feel you have your own piece of shore and some sense of belonging—but you will be very visually aware of houses along the coast.

53
FILLINGER CRESCENT B
A wooden staircase through a large, wooded lot to a jagged, steep rock shore

Location, signs and parking Turn off Fillinger Crescent from Hammond Bay Road and follow it as it begins to parallel the shore until you see a huge black boulder on your left and, on your right, a house numbered 4999. Because the public land is some 70 m wide at this point, the shoulder in front of it is unpunctuated with driveways. It is not easy, however, to get completely off the road, because there is a paved curb.

Path There are two paths. The first you will see is actually a paved road that leads down from the high bank beside the giant boulder. The other, more suitable for most visitors, leads down from the opposite end of the park area. Here some fine, solid handrailed wooden steps take you down 10 steps, and, after you wind down a well-defined track for some distance, another flight of equally fine, solid handrailed wooden steps takes you right down onto the shore. The path leads through a treed bank dominated by cedars, alders and firs and cut through with a small stream, wet even in the driest summer.

Beach The beach is fairly steep and jagged, but full of small tidal pools. The shore drops off quickly into deep water. While the water doesn't get particularly warm here, the steep shoreline and jagged rocks can make for some fascinating snorkelling. A pair of reefs slightly offshore to the right prettifies the beach. Picnicking is possible, but probably not comfortable.

Suitability for children The limited range in which a child can roam and the limited range of activities in which a child can engage will put this spot low on most people's list of child-friendly spots. Still, the sure-footed child who loves molesting hermit crabs and sculpins can be happily occupied for some time here. Don't forget, too, that the child who cheerfully goes down won't necessarily cheerfully come up.

Suitability for groups The significant size of the parkland, the length of exposed curb, and the well-planned path make this a good destination for a group picnic or sketching venture, though, of course, there are no facilities.

View The view has a slightly more "bay-like" feel than the view to be had at the two other shorefront spots nearby: rocky headlands on either side frame your perspective down the coast. That being said, you still have something close to 180 degrees of wide-open vista with all the glories of the Coast Mountains before you.

Winds, sun and shade This spot seems a little more protected from both northwest winds and southeast winds than spots close by, though certainly both can be felt. For many, the big drawback of this spot on all but the warmest days is that even by late morning the shore is in heavy shade—and, because the shoreline is so narrow, you can't walk into the sun even if you want to.

Beachcombing With this kind of shore, the beachcombing is restricted in scope but—because of the tidal pools and interesting rock textures—enriched by foreground interest.

Seclusion The strip of woodland behind creates a pleasant parklike aura. You feel close to the burbs, but not actually in them. Don't be surprised if you are alone at this spot for as much time as it takes you to find Deep Inner Peace.

54
WINCHELSEA PLACE
A small park with a spectacular bank-top view and steep descent to a rocky coast

Location, signs and parking This is the southernmost of four spots off Fillinger Crescent, though it is the last you get to as you approach from Hammond Bay Road. Just before Fillinger Crescent turns away from the water and begins a climb, Winchelsea Place, a short cul-de-sac, branches off. The only sign you will see is an alarming warning sign. From this sign you will learn that you are at Rocky Point Parkland, and not only should you be aware of dangerous conditions—particularly of potentially slippery rocks—but you should also wear a life jacket! No doubt the spot can be dangerous, and has been for some, but on a sunny day it seems not just harmless, but idyllic. Two driveways take up part of the turnaround, but otherwise there is room for a few cars to pull over.

Path Not everyone will decide to take the path down to the waterfront, since the viewing spot—with bench and litter barrel (not to mention the guardrail between the bench and an unhealthily steep cliff)—is so well suited to pausing. The well-used but admittedly steep and rocky path drops some 20 m vertically over not much horizontal distance. This is not the kind of path on which to take those infirm of limb or those encumbered with paraphernalia.

Beach The path actually arrives near the water on a roughly level little shelf with some grass. Otherwise, gaining the water's edge is a foray through jagged points of upthrusting basalt ridges. In spite of the challenges, it is well worth coming down the path to the actual shore, not only for the view, but also for whatever exploring you feel up to doing. Because the shore drops off so deeply, for example, sea lions can (and do) swim by within a few metres. In fact, it is possible to fish from the rocks if you have a good casting rod. Picnickers can find a pretty spot here but can hardly expect to spread out a feast with teetering dishes of four-bean salad.

Suitability for children Older children should have little difficulty making it up and down the path and scrambling over the rocks. The lifesaver on a post, however, suggests that some have found the spot to be dangerous, so you will probably want to stand reasonably close guard.

Suitability for groups A family group will enjoy a visit, but don't bring a much larger group, even though the actual patch of parkland extends some 30 m along the road front.

View The view from the top of the path is probably the best high-point view of any in this area. This is not to say that it is broadly expansive and uncluttered. Part of the charm of the view is that it is seen through a latticework of medium-sized fir and arbutus. From below, in contrast, the view is one of the most expansive of any you're going to get. The shore is roughly oriented southward, framed by cliffs, and beyond, jutting slightly out, one of the promontories of Neck Point. To the north the shore extends as far as Fairwinds and the offshore islands. On a clear day, it goes without saying, the mountains are stunning.

Winds, sun and shade Both northwest and southeast winds hit at oblique angles here. As with many other spots along this coast, shade starts to creep across the shore by late morning. The angle of the bank behind and the lack of lower limbs on the trees, however, make it a primarily dappled shade.

Beachcombing This is not a beach for beachcombing, unless by that you mean making your way with curiosity and a sense of adventure in the confined area of dramatically jagged foreshore.

Seclusion Except for a few large houses on the clifftop to your right, you will neither see nor be seen from your brooding spot on this shore.

55 NECK POINT COMMUNITY PARK

A large, full-facility day-use park with a network of trails, rocky headlands and several pebbly beaches

Location, signs and parking Signs on Hammond Bay Road point down Morningside Drive to both Neck Point Park and Morningside Beach Area. It is also possible to approach the park through the little-used and slightly convoluted Keel Cove Road off McGuffie Road, though almost all visitors will prefer the Morningside approach. The main parking area accommodates several dozen cars, but there is a gated access to a small handicapped parking spot closer to the main park. If you decide to come via the "back door" at Keel Cove, you will find parking for only a few cars at the end of a narrow, uneven road.

Path This is a large park with an equally large and complex network of paths—far too large to be described here. Simply come assured of finding a huge variety of trails and trail surfaces. Some inland trails, like the one that goes from the main parking area to Sunset Beach, are almost like small, level roads through fine stands of maples and cedars. Others are actually boardwalks with raised viewing areas, particularly on bluffs, but also between Keel Cove and the main part of the park.

Beach This is a magnificently scenic area with great variety. As the name of the park suggests, it is a headland, roughly anvil-shaped (though also, if one is very free with analogies, with what looks a little like a "neck"). The result is that the various pebble-and-gravel beaches—Finn Beach, Indian Beach, Last Beach and Sunset Beach—all have different exposures, however much they are roughly similar in size and type. No matter what the direction of the wind and the direction of the sun, you can find a beach on which to picnic, loll about, swim or read a biography of your favourite rock star. Picnic benches, for those who eat best from a solid perch, are situated at each of these four beaches. Many will not want to spend their time at these four spots, but will seek out unique ones among the various outcroppings, bluffs and headlands. Lots of interpretive signs will, besides identifying various species, ask you to stay on the paths, particularly in areas where such springtime species as camas and nodding onions can be easily trampled.

Suitability for children If your children need sand to feel they are at proper beach, make the short drive from here to Pipers Lagoon, where they will find the sand they need. Otherwise, bring them to Neck Point Park, confident that they will have a great time exploring the various beaches and trails.

Suitability for groups This is a good spot for just about any size of group. All group activities aren't easily done here, though. If you want your group to do a physically boisterous activity together, take them for their egg-and-spoon races to Pipers Lagoon, where there is a large grassy area. For picnicking and wandering, however, for swimming and snorkelling, for birdwatching and photographing, this park offers lots of options. Washrooms at the parking area give a practical spin on selecting this spot for your Annual Picnic of the Society for World Domination.

View The views are too numerous and varied to describe here. Each bay, cove, headland and beach offers a wonderfully picturesque foreground (often spiced up with a gnarled and windswept tree or two). Having seen everything at one time of day, you owe it to yourself to come back at a different time of day, when different tides make everything look completely different. Even then, what you see in spring will look completely different from what you see in autumn or winter.

Winds, sun and shade If there is wind, there will be a windy spot—but also a sheltered spot. You need only wander and find what you want. Again, if there is sun in the sky, there will be a sunny area—but also a shady one. If you are intent on finding shade, though, be aware that most of the beaches are not backed by thick groves of trees (Sunset Beach is the exception), so you will find a lot more sun than shade.

Beachcombing At some points the shore is steep and jagged enough that you will have a hard time circumnavigating the whole point from the shore. In any case, you will want to do at least some of your walking on the paths to appreciate the full view.

Seclusion You wouldn't expect to find seclusion in a developed park so close to the city. A surprising number of people don't know the park exists, however, and an equally surprising number will choose a sandy beach like that at Departure Bay or Pipers Lagoon. Even when the parking lot is nearly full, though, the park is large enough and the nooks and coves plentiful enough that you can find a spot where you can wander hand in hand with a Significant Other, or let your mind go completely and utterly blank.

56

MORNINGSIDE BEACH AREA

A protected pebbly beach with picnic tables and an excellent view of the "shack islands"

Location, signs and parking This park is well-signposted, though its location can be a little confusing because both this one-acre park and the much larger Neck Point Park lie down Morningside Drive. The smaller park is immediately on the right down Morningside Drive. Parking is plentiful (for eight to ten cars) in the recessed parking area off Morningside Road.

Path You have plenty of room on the gently sloping grass of this spot to manoeuvre, and won't be stumbling over impediments, but the distance to the beach is much longer than it first appears. This is not a great spot for launching a kayak or canoe, though. You might be better off driving the short distance to the Charlaine boat ramp (see next entry) if you want to save energy for leaning into your paddle. Otherwise, the stroll to the beach through the open grassy area is easy and pleasant. At the end of this area is a short asphalt ramp, 1 m wide, leading directly onto the beach. You may even wish to stop at one of the two seats or at the picnic table en route.

Beach Pebbles with small sandy patches make up the upper shore of the beach. About halfway to low tide, larger rocks dominate. The park actually lies in the centre of a pebbly bay about 150 m across and enclosed by a headland. Plenty of beach logs act as backrests or uneven tables for teetering bowls of potato salad, though some will prefer to lay out their feast on the picnic tables. For swimming, high tide is best, though even then water shoes are not a bad idea to get you past the rockiest area.

Suitability for children The combination of grassy open area and gently sloping beach make this an excellent spot for even small children, unless their idea of a beach is restricted to building sandcastles.

Suitability for groups Any group that doesn't bring hordes will find plenty of space here. If, however, you are after multiple picnic tables to set up a mammoth picnic, you would be better off heading to a larger public park, even Neck Point Park, a short distance down Morningside Drive.

View The view is more restricted than that from the access spots farther south in Hammond Bay. You won't have the same view of either the mainland mountains or the summer cabins on the small islands at the south end of the bay (called the "shack islands" by locals). You will, however, have a very pretty view of the overlapping shapes of small islands and Lagoon Head in the foreground and, in the distance, Gabriola Island and the open Strait.

Winds, sun and shade If you love this part of the coast but a cool northwest wind is a-howling, you will find that this beach is probably the most protected of any of the beaches in this area. What wind there is will, in addition, be coming over your shoulder as you sit on the beach, so will have minimal cooling effect—something to keep in mind as well on a sweltering summer day when you want reprieve from the heat. In contrast, a southeast wind will hit the beach more or less full force. While the sun is most direct in the first part of the day, you will be in sun throughout the day. A couple of trees in the grassy area, however, can afford welcome shade.

Beachcombing The beach has enough of a pleasant sweep and curve to allow strolling in either direction, but don't expect to walk great distances. A rocky outcropping lies beyond the end of the beach for clamberers. If you want to combine exercising with your beaching, be aware that a twin brother of this park, replete with tennis courts, lies kitty-corner across the road.

Seclusion Because the beach curves in on itself at the enclosed end of Hammond Bay, it doesn't provide much sense of seclusion. You will be looking in part at a line of houses, and may feel that they are looking right back at you—a fact that, for those who have been working on their Summertime Abs, might be a positive feature. For those who want to mull over their failed romance or investment scheme and do so without benefit of an audience, this beach is not ideal.

✻ Also nearby Piper Crescent is a short loop off Hammond Bay Road between Lagoon Road and Morningside Drive. Halfway along this road, photographers with a particular interest in the "shack islands" will find a meticulously kept concrete-and-gravel walk between two houses leading to a short set of stairs—and a not very inspiring bit of shore. Outcroppings of rock to your left, chunky boulders and the feeling you are more or less in local householders' front yards don't provide much incentive to linger.

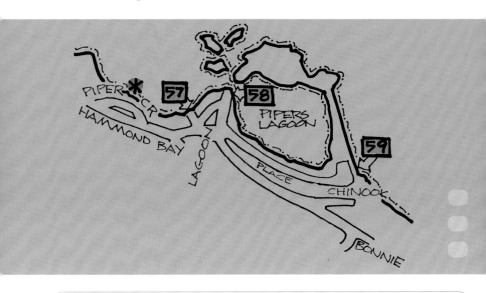

57
CHARLAINE BOAT RAMP
A free concrete launching ramp, great for kayaks and canoes, but also for shore seekers and those interested in unusual views

Location, signs and parking The ramp is clearly signposted at the corner of Polaris Drive and Hammond Bay Road. A shellfish warning will tell you that you're not going to be spending your time at this beach collecting your supper. Two small parking areas, an upper and a lower one, provide lots of parking, even in good weather. In case of crowding, however, it would only be fair to leave the parking for those who are putting their boats into the water while you push on to another of the many access spots nearby. Before you make a beeline for the shore, note (and admire) the huge triple-trunked black cottonwood tree in the wooded bank that separates the two lots. Another special feature of a somewhat different sort is the portable chemical toilet perched at the end of the lower parking lot.

Path You can simply walk down the concrete launching ramp and hop off to the side.

Beach The light gravel beach curves prettily around in both directions at high tide and, at low tide, drops only enough to create a little more walking space.

Suitability for children The beach is safe and pleasant for children, but without any particular features to entice them or keep them entertained for long—other than the nearby water itself, of course.

Suitability for groups A small group could enjoy the views or picnicking or strolling the shore. If you are part of a photography or sketching group, you owe it to yourself—and them—to bring them to this spot.

View The real point of coming to this spot is for a different view of the cabins on the little islands opposite (see the description for Wheatcroft Park in the next entry). In fact, this is probably the best viewing angle open to the public. You won't find a similar spot anywhere else on the east coast of Vancouver Island, so enjoy the uniqueness of the sight. The view is further enhanced by the spiky peaks of Jervis Inlet across the Strait and, farther north, the whale-like lump of Texada Island.

Winds, sun and shade The spot is largely exposed to a northwest wind, but fairly protected from a southeast wind. The shade of a few trees creeps across parts of the beach in the afternoon.

Beachcombing It is possible to meander in both directions along the pebble beach, but the beach doesn't encourage much more than peering and prodding. Most appealing is the walk to the south and Wheatcroft Park at the entrance to Pipers Lagoon.

Seclusion You won't find much seclusion here, particularly if you turn right. The locals' gardens come virtually down to the shore, and all of them are long on groomed lawn and short on trees. Toward the left, however, because the house is high up on a bank, you can spread out your picnic blanket, dig out your diary or prop up your easel without feeling you're intruding.

58
WHEATCROFT PARK
A tiny but striking bit of geography, allowing access to Hammond Bay and the flow channel for Pipers Lagoon

Location, signs and parking For this spot on Lagoon Road, don't turn right onto Place Road, which leads you to the main beaches and parking lot, but instead drive straight ahead the short distance to the circular turnaround. You will see a spanking new sign with the park name and the swirly logo used by Nanaimo. There is room for a few cars in this circular turnaround, but no more than that.

Path You have no path to speak of to get to the water's edge, simply a rounded bank from the edge of the parking spot nearly at sea level.

Beach Although at first glance you might feel you have gained a "back door" access to Pipers Lagoon and the surrounding parkland, it won't take you long to realize you haven't. Virtually at your feet is the watery entrance and exit to the lagoon itself, the narrow channel through which all of the water flows into and exits from the lagoon. Unless you're willing to get wet (even at low tide), you won't be able to cross this channel to get to the shore opposite. Once there, however, you can cross Lagoon Head (the rocky headland on the seaside of the lagoon) and make the complete loop. This spot can be quite fun as the water rushes past in either direction, and it does provide an interesting perspective on the rest of the lagoon— and the shack islands. It would be quite easy to put in a kayak or canoe here, but probably easier to go the short distance instead to Charlaine Boat Ramp.

Suitability for children This spot can be fun for children as they splash in the current, but parents will have to keep a close eye on small children so that they don't get themselves into difficulty. Obviously, small children atop inflated sea creatures would be safer bobbing their way through the channel on an incoming tide. On the other hand, the water is much warmer as it rushes out of the lagoon rather than into it.

Suitability for groups The area is too small and the entertainments too limited for most groups to spend any time here. Sketchers, however, will want to put this high on their list of "must comes."

View Most striking about the view from here, aside from the interesting perspective on the rest of the lagoon, is the angle it affords on the cabins dotting the little cluster of rocky islands at the southern end of Hammond Bay. Some will see these cabins as an eyesore, no doubt. Most, however, will be either charmed or intrigued by their irregularity, by their picturesque clustering among the islands and by the contrast they make with the serene suburban elegance of the upmarket houses that line the waterfront of the whole area.

Winds, sun and shade Northwest winds can be felt here, and, to a lesser extent, southeast winds. Trees provide some shade if it's shade you want; if not, you will get most sun on the shore until about noon and in the latter part of the afternoon.

Beachcombing As already noted, the only strolling going on will be by those who make their watery way across the channel that separates the spot from Lagoon Head. It is possible, if you really want a walk, to head along the gravelly shore through Hammond Bay itself. Walking around the edge of the lagoon offers few pleasures: the yards of the local houses force you onto squelchy flats where each step can be a chore.

Seclusion You will find little seclusion here, since there are houses all around, but at least you won't feel you're in someone's front yard. The space is big enough and separate enough to give you some sense of being genuinely at an intriguing bit of shorefront.

59 PIPERS LAGOON PARK

A full-facility park in a striking setting, incorporating a sandy beach, rocky headlands, three secluded pebbly beaches and the flow channel for Pipers Lagoon

Location, signs and parking Except for the beaches in the large provincial parks, the beach at Pipers Lagoon is probably the best known and most visited in this area. Still, it is a strange fact that very few people from outside of the immediate area visit this stunningly beautiful spot. Indeed, many are the fine folk living, for example, in Parksville or Qualicum (not to mention Calgary or Halifax!) who, tragically, do not know it exists. So, for such folk, here is the scoop. Look for the large and enthusiastic sign on Hammond Bay Road. It will guide you to turn onto Lagoon Road and then almost immediately right onto Place Road. Place Road will lead you along the edge of the lagoon itself to a large paved parking lot with plenty of space for dozens of cars.

Path There is no path to speak of if your goal is to get straight to a beach—*a* beach, that is, rather than *the* beach for, in fact, there are several. You can walk through the grassy field and over the logs to the popular main beach on your right, or turn left to find easy access to the lagoon beach. A well-maintained gravel path runs the 200 m along the grassy isthmus between the two beaches and out to the rocky headland.

Beach The outer beach is like so many of the best local beaches. Its upper strip is composed of pebbles leading down to fine sand flats, thus making for excellent swimming at high tide and romping at low tide. Those who like sunbathing in icing-sugar sand will want to tote their towels and sunscreen to the end of the beach closest to the rocky headland. Here the sand extends well above the tide line into the rows of beach logs. The lagoon beach feels slightly swampy, but it, too, is very pleasant. Those who find the water temperature of the outer beach just a little too bracing may enjoy lolling in the shallow water of the lagoon, once it has filled up with a high tide. Those who want to escape the sand altogether can make their way along the neck of land to the rocky, treed promontory that forms the ocean-side of the lagoon. Lagoon Head, as this promontory is called, is interwoven with many picturesque paths. As a bonus, too, you will find more small beaches on the outer shore of the head.

Suitability for children This is a perfect spot for children of all ages and types, since the various beaches and rocky spots provide a great diversity of entertainments. The large grassy field near the parking lot is perfect for kite flying and (discreet) Frisbee games, among other things. This is one of the few beaches in this book with washrooms.

Suitability for groups Although it would be unfair to everyone to bring an entire convention to this beach (or any other in this book), a group of, say, 20 would have plenty of space to gather—and, as the mood hits, disperse. On a sunny summer weekend, expect the parking lot to be full, so plan around prime times.

View The view is best from Lagoon Head. You will be surprised how even a slight gain in elevation will reveal the picturesque sweep of land around the lagoon. From the promontory, too, you will be able to look out on the islands that dot the entrance to Nanaimo Harbour and across to the mainland mountains above Horseshoe Bay and Howe Sound.

Winds, sun and shade While the spit itself is exposed to both northwest and southeast winds, those who wish to bask and lie low will be generally out of the wind. In addition, it is wind blowing toward you that always seems most chilling, so you can also significantly reduce the amount of wind simply by changing beaches. Those wishing to settle down with an easel or trashy novel might prefer to find a spot completely out of the wind on the treed promontory of Lagoon Head. Sun lovers will find sun here as long as there is sun to be found in the sky. If you wish to escape the sun, you will have to go to a spot among the trees on the Head; there is not a speck of shade to be had on the beach.

Seclusion Surprisingly, you will find some seclusion among the trees and rocks of Lagoon Head, since almost everyone spends the bulk of their time on the main beach. At the same time, the phalanx of houses lining one side of the lagoon will remind you that you have found a little gem of nature at its best on the edge of a congested suburb.

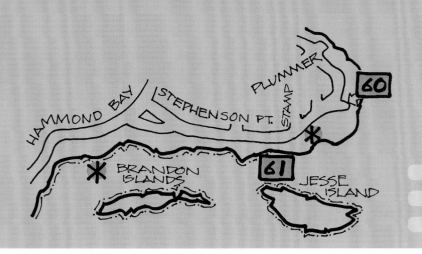

60
STEPHENSON POINT ROAD A
A wooded bank-top picnic area
and path to a small beach
of mixed pebbles and rocky
outcroppings

Location, signs and parking The signs here are a little confusing.
Approaching the northern end of Stephenson Point Road, as you pass Stamp
Way on your left, look for signs with the puzzling information that if you
go ahead you will continue on Stephenson Point Road but if you turn right
you will also be on Stephenson Point Road. These signs actually do make
sense because the road to the right—which you will turn down—is really
just a kind of public driveway to three addresses technically on Stephenson
Point Road. A helpful red and white PUBLIC ACCESS sign will reassure you
that you are on the right track. As you turn right, you will find it easiest to
pull off onto the shoulder immediately and walk the short distance down
the asphalt road. You will see signs telling you that if you park at the end
of the turnaround or farther down the access road you will be towed away
(because, apparently, you will be blocking emergency routes). If you have
elaborate equipment or passengers with walking difficulties, however, you
can continue to drive down this short road, drop off your imponderabilia,
and return to a discreet parking spot.

Path From your (legal) parking spot, you will walk down an asphalt road through a pretty parklike area where the access road circles and divides. In an open grassy area overshadowed with maples and firs, you will find a picnic table, a park bench and a waste bin. Although you might want to eat a picnic in this small park, sooner or later you will want to descend to the beach. The beach is actually on the Stephenson Point after which the road is named. To get there—and back—you will need a little energy to negotiate the 40 very skookum wooden steps.

Beach The pretty beach is composed of patches of pebbles among stone ridges running roughly parallel to the water. A giant sun-bleached stump is perched decoratively at the top of the beach. A low tide will expose enough beach area to allow some picnicking, exploring and lounging, but even at low tide the area is comparatively confined.

Suitability for children The beach is suitable for those children who like clambering, poking in tidal pools and wading, but not those who want to scamper unheeded or those who are unsteady on their little feet.

Suitability for groups A small group, as long as it is careful with parking, could comfortably picnic either at the upper spot or on the beach.

View Immediately in front is an interesting reef, covered at high tide. Behind it loom the Hudson Rocks and Snake Island, with the large bulk of Gabriola Island creating an attractively diverse seascape. Clearly visible in the distance are the mainland mountains above Horseshoe Bay.

Winds, sun and shade The beach is only slightly exposed to northwest winds, but fully exposed to southeast winds. If you want lots of sun, you will find the most from morning to early afternoon.

Beachcombing At low tide particularly, it is possible to wander in either direction for some distance, picking your way among the slabs of rocks and investigating cracks. Don't, however, expect to be able to stride quickly if you bring your MP3 player and launch into a "power walk" for exercise. If you do want an extended walk, you can finish off your venture to the beach by crossing the road from where you parked and entering the so-called wilderness parkland of Planta Park. Although the park is not huge, it will provide you a good half hour of walking among the arbutus, oak and firs of this beautifully and laudably preserved bit of woodland.

Seclusion Because of the height of the banks, the houses above the shore are largely out of view. Thus you will be able to enjoy the sense of being on a beach rather than in someone's front yard.

✳ **Also nearby** Partway along **Stephenson Point Road,** opposite a house numbered 3351, you will see a beautifully constructed series of wooden steps descending the open but wooded bank. A sequence of flights and landings comes to a grinding halt at a viewing platform a few metres above the shore. Apparently, original plans were to extend the steps all the way to the tiny pebbly cove, but protests from a local resident resulted in the change of plans. Still, from the viewing area, it is possible to have only partially screened views of Jesse Island and behind it, the north shore of Newcastle Island. The land that extends to the shore is public property, and some local residents have managed to bypass the wooden staircase by making their own trail down.

61
STEPHENSON POINT ROAD B
A long flight of stairs to
a narrow shore with
unique views

Location, signs and parking Although a local map shows that this public access leads down Marine Road, the map is misleading. In fact, it is easiest to find this access simply by driving down Stephenson Point Road a short distance past the Pacific Coast Biological Station. Look for house number 3328, one of the City of Nanaimo perky red and white PUBLIC ACCESS signs, turn right after a few metres and drive a short distance before pulling over. There is room for several cars on the side of the road.

Path Be prepared for a little bit of a hike. This might not be the beach to which you take your aged great aunt. Eighty-six steps will take you down, down to the beach. The construction of the steps is a little odd. They are more like a gravel walkway with a wooden tie every so often. The first 30 or 40 steps are too wide to take a step at a time and too narrow to take two steps at a time. Still, the step builders made an otherwise slippery descent very civilized and manageable.

Beach The shore itself is narrow, even at low tide, and not particularly well suited to lolling about, but, in its own way, is both attractive and interesting. Bands of solid sandstone and conglomerate rock are interspersed with patches of pebbles, giving way at lower levels to large boulders.

Suitability for children Children would have to be fairly chipper to enjoy the long descent to the beach and fairly patient to endure the oohing and aahing adults. A few squidgy things can be found on the beach, but the average child will not be charmed.

Suitability for groups This one is not suitable for groups, though a few friends headed for Planta Park, for example, could troop down for a short stay.

Hammond Bay Road

View The view is well worth the visit, primarily because this is the only public spot from which you can view the bizarre sandstone cliffs and formations of Jesse Island directly in front. Some people will find the ruins of a wharf picturesque as well and enjoy the unusual views of Nanaimo Harbour, the ferry traffic and the shoreline of Newcastle Island. The only really unpleasant part of the experience is auditory: the dogs on Jesse Island seem to spend much of their lives barking... at kayakers, at sailors, at anything that moves.

Winds, sun and shade The beach is well protected from northwest winds, but exposed to southeast winds.

Beachcombing Abandon all hopes of strolling happily along, because there is no place to stroll on this narrow and rocky shore.

Seclusion Houses high on the bank behind are largely out of sight. Be surprised if you are not alone on the beach.

✱ Also nearby Near 3100 **Hammond Bay Road** you will spot one of the distinctive red and white PUBLIC ACCESS signs unique to the Nanaimo area. The road shoulder is too narrow to allow you to park safely, so continue past this point an additional 100 m. A well-kept, pleasant asphalt path between discreetly spaced houses descends about 5 m to a set of 25 aged but apparently safe stairs that will bring you to a rough rock-and-boulder shore. Not many people would want to stay here for very long, but the spot is well worth visiting for those who would like an interesting and unusual view of Nanaimo, Departure Bay and Brandon Islands immediately in front. The odd floating structures 100 m down the shore to your left are used by the Pacific Coast Biological Station for research projects. The spot will most likely appeal to photographers or artists looking for some unusual subject matter (see illustration).

Nanaimo Those interested in exploring the shorelines of this part of the island may not know of some of the pleasures that Nanaimo itself offers. Three very different parts of Nanaimo are of particular interest.

At Departure Bay, you will find **a large, sandy beach**, a smaller version of the kind of child-friendly beach you otherwise see at Parksville. Departure Bay Road is well marked from the highway at the junction that also leads to the Departure Bay BC Ferries terminal. At this beach, well protected from most winds, you will find not just the stretches of low-tide sand and sandy tidal pools typical of this kind of beach, but also picnic tables and washrooms.

If you want to paddle around Nanaimo Harbour, seek out the **public boat ramp** near the Departure Bay BC Ferries terminal. Go straight through the traffic lights at the bottom of the hill but, instead of turning left for the terminal, head into a large parking area. You will have to pay for parking, but otherwise will have free access to the ramp and the wonderful opportunities for paddling along the coast of Newcastle Island and Nanaimo Harbour itself.

A beautifully maintained, **4 km long urban path** for cyclists and walkers starts from a spot just south of the Departure Bay BC Ferries terminal, extends past Matteo-Sutton park, and ends near the Port Shopping Centre. The views of Newcastle and Protection islands, the busy boat and seaplane traffic, and the commercial fishing harbour make for a varied and eye-pleasing walk. En route you will find washrooms (at Matteo-Sutton park) and refreshments (near the south end of the route).

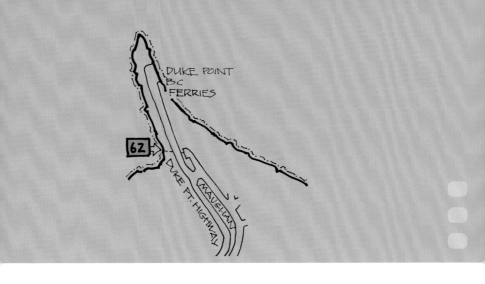

62

BIGGS AND JACK POINT PARK

A long narrow sandstone peninsula near the Duke Point Ferry terminal with several water-access spots and many kilometres of shoreside path

Location, signs and parking You may be a little confused in looking for this spot, since there are two signposted routes from the same superhighway to the Duke Point ferry. It helps to make sense of the double approach if you realize that the park lies on the Nanaimo side of the narrow point along which the giant access road to the ferry sweeps. Once on the ferry highway from Highway 19, keep your eyes peeled long before you get to the ferry for a large green and white sign with the name of the park. An additional signposted T-junction will take you onto a road that runs parallel to the ferry access and to the pulp mill. After a couple of kilometres you will see a paved parking area and a large sign with the City of Nanaimo logo and the name BIGGS PARK JACK POINT.

Alternately, you can stay on the main ferry approach road until you approach Duke Point. Another large, fresh sign will direct you to turn right and into the parking area. At least a dozen cars can park in the rectangular paved parking area. You (and presumably those who are looking for free parking) will be told that overnight parking is illegal. Forgive yourself for feeling a little confusion if you've read the Nanaimo information web page, which tells you that Biggs Point is the name of the park on one side of Duke Point, and that Jack Point is the name of the park at the point of Duke Point. All your senses tell you that there is but one park and one point. Putting such confusion aside, head through the concrete underpass, past two additional signs that tell you the area is closed to shellfish and that you should clean up after your dog.

Path Unusually, this is not a path to the shore, but a path beside the shore. For 2.5 km, including a 1 km loop at the tip of the narrow peninsula, you can walk with virtually uninterrupted views. Those in wheelchairs or with walking difficulties can easily use the first few hundred metres of the path, since it is horizontal and more or less paved. Along this section, a high hedge provides a visual barrier, but not a sound barrier, from the traffic rushing to and from the terminal. At the end of this section, though, you leave behind both the ferry traffic and ease of access as a complicated series of 40 wooden steps and landings takes you into a wider and more treed section of the trail. One of the curiosities of the (increasingly rough) path is that on your outward journey all three of the stairways go *up* (40, 40 and 64 steps respectively)—and yet you end up at sea level. The geography and fauna of the trail are striking. As you go, you will be treated to the kind of oak-and-arbutus ecosystem and wildly sculpted sandstone formations you find almost exclusively on south-facing shores of the Gulf Islands. If you're after some of the amenities you would expect in a city park, you will find a litter barrel, a few benches, and, partway along the trail, a portable toilet.

Beach If your primary interest is in reaching the water, not just walking, you have a few options where the trail dips to low bluffs and tiny bays. Don't choose the dusty scramble onto the shore at the beginning of the trail, but carry on to much more attractive options, including the very tip of the peninsula and its gently curving sweep. At low tide, muddy tidal flats (with dozens of great blue herons) extend from the sandstone shelf for the first part of the trail. Toward the point, though, the sandstone shelves and lumps drop off into increasingly deep water. Because of the length and variety of formations along the trail, there are plenty of options for curling up in a sandstone basin, perching atop a sandstone couch or peering into tidal pools.

Suitability for children Children who don't like to walk, and parents who don't like carrying children who don't like to walk, will be happier elsewhere. Other children, though, will find lots of play and splash areas after about a kilometre, and, at one low, grassy bluff area in particular, a small spot of pebbly beach to complement the sandstone lumps and bumps. If your child wants to include a good deal of splashing in the outing, though, it is best to choose a mid to high tide, since the low-tide rocks can be something of a hurdle.

Suitability for groups Although not as well suited to a large group as some other parks, this one can accommodate certain kinds of group well. Those interested in birding, walking or photographing will be happier than those wanting to picnic as close to the car as they can.

View Naturalists of various hues will want to come at low tide. Everyone else will be best pleased at mid to high tide, when the less conventionally attractive lower shore (and mud flats) are well out of sight. At high tide, indeed, lovers of varied views could do no better than come to this park. Starting with views of the island mountains, Nanaimo Harbour and Protection Island, visitors will find, as they round the point itself, vistas of the mainland mountains, the stunning Gabriola cliffs, and, of course, the ferries churning busily in and out of the BC Ferries terminal.

Winds, sun and shade The tip of the park could hardly be more exposed to northwest winds. Indeed, many a northwest wind seems to become particularly enthusiastic as it approaches. A southeast wind can, likewise, be more than a little fresh on the Gabriola-facing side. The Nanaimo-facing side, however, is well protected from these cooling winds.

The shore is so varied, and the patches of trees equally varied, that you can expect to find plenty of both sun and shade at any time of day. At the same time, though, be aware that the Gabriola-facing side will be sunniest in the morning. The side facing Nanaimo will become sunniest mid to late afternoon.

Beachcombing At many points the shore itself becomes too steep or even cliffy to walk along. The long-distance shore walker will be happiest, therefore, in using the trail as a means of gaining access to the sandstone shore at several points. The tip of the point facing Gabriola provides the longest stretch of smoothly shelving rock and tidal pools for those who would like to stroll next to the water.

Seclusion The park is not heavily used. Regulars, however, and particularly those with small dogs in need of exercise, make this a favourite destination. Because of the considerable length of the trail and the often convoluted shoreline, those in need of solitude should have little difficulty in finding a sculpted nook in which to be alone—or not quite alone.

Beachcomber Community Park

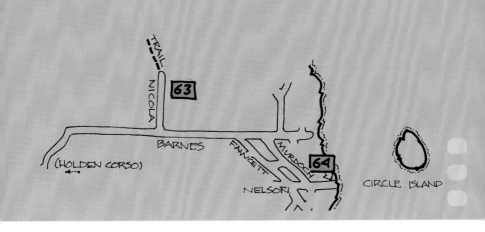

63

CABLE BAY TRAIL

A long, forested trail passing a small narrow bay and, in a rough form, leading along the rocky shore to Dodd Narrows

Location, signs and parking While you need to go through a bit of a labyrinth to get to this trail and shorefront, once you've made your way here you'll be close to a couple of other interesting watery spots. Take the Cedar Road exit from Highway 19, south of Nanaimo. Cedar Road will morph into Harmac Road. Turn first onto MacMillan and then Holden Corso Road. Follow it until it turns into Barnes Road. After some distance, Nicola Road and a signed parking lot will be on your left. Since this is a park, and one that doesn't provide instant beach-gratification, parking is never a problem.

Path For some, the path to the water will be the major attraction. For others, it will be the main detraction. In either case, the path, involving a 5 km tromp, can hardly go unnoticed. It varies considerably during its length and has some side branches or cross tracks. In general, though, the main route is clearly just that. Be prepared for considerable descent on the way out and, unsurprisingly, a bit of a slog on the way back. Your first point of seashore is the small, narrow, steep-sided bay that lives up to its name—rusty chunks of cable abound. From here, you can carry on over a fine footbridge and cross a bit of a headland to the shore facing Gabriola. Approximately a kilometre's rough tromp along the shelving sandstone upper shore of Stuart Channel will bring you to Dodd Narrows. Most will choose to return via the same route, but it is possible to continue, on a sketchy trail turning directly inland back toward the main trail. Check out www.trailpeak.com to get the extra security of GPS settings.

Beach Cable Bay is not a place to picnic, dabble your toes, or, indeed, linger very long unless you are observing the local duck population up to their tricks. Squelchy with mud at low tide, the beach offers only a steep-sided rock shore at high tide. In contrast, the gently shelving sandstone shore farther along the trail offers lots of opportunities for lingering and picnicking. Don't even think about entering the water, though. The currents that sweep through Dodd Narrows (up to 18 km per hour!) churn up icy water from the lower depths. In addition, the same currents, with their whirlpools, eddies and wellings, become extremely dangerous.

Suitability for children Only children who are small enough to fit into a backpack or old enough for a considerable hike will enjoy coming here. Similarly, only children who go past Cable Bay to Stuart Channel will get any watery compensation for their walk. Even then, they will be restricted to skipping stones or climbing over the sandstone shelves.

Suitability for groups This is a great location for a sizable group who want to get some kilometres under their feet in a natural setting and, possibly, stop for a (highly portable) picnic. It is not a great location for a group who want easy access to a picnic site or shore view.

View Most of the way, of course, you will be in second-growth forest. The view from Cable Bay itself is highly restricted, offering only glimpses toward Duke Point. Once you have reached the shore facing Gabriola, you will find that the farther you walk toward Dodd Narrows, the closer the foreground becomes. The great attraction for many coming to the trail will be the view of Dodd Narrows itself and its whirlpools, standing waves and back eddies. Choose maximum current conditions for the most drama. Several websites and publications offer tide and current information. Search "Dodd Narrows current tables" and choose the site that suits you best.

Winds, sun and shade Winds are not a major factor here, though a northwest wind can seem a little fresh along Stuart Channel. Only the sandstone shelf gets very much sun, and then mostly during the first part of the day. During the afternoon, if you enjoy your strolling in the sun, choose low tide, when you can walk below the shadows of the trees.

Beachcombing Walking is what this spot is all about, although much of it will be through second-growth, but reasonably mature, forest. You can walk for a considerable distance along Stuart Channel and find some interesting tidal pools to explore, particularly at low tide.

Seclusion You will find seclusion in abundance here. You are likely to cross paths with only a few other strollers. At the shore, too, you can enjoy the view or a snack in a completely natural setting far from housing developments or thronging crowds—for now. A major development is slated to obliterate much of the natural setting of the area.

64
NELSON ROAD
A public launching ramp beside a sandy beach, rocky outcroppings and tidal pools

Location, signs and parking Getting to the end of Barnes Road is a little tortuous from the main highway—but kayakers and canoeists will be more than willing to engage in the map reading required to get to this convenient launching spot (and all the more because it is the only such spot for many kilometres of coast). While there are various routes here, most visitors will want to leave the highway at the more northern of the two Cedar Road junctions. From Cedar turn onto Macmillan Road, and then right onto Holden Corso. Stay alert for an odd configuration of roads, requiring careful sign reading. After taking a sweep to the left, Holden Corso suddenly turns sharply right. At this point you will want to shift your car's allegiance to Barnes Road, which, in any case, looks for all the world to be an extension of Holden Corso. From here it is probably easiest to stay on Barnes Road until Murdoch on your right and then go the single long "block" to Nelson and its launching ramp.

Because this is intended largely as a launching ramp, the various signs are directed toward boaters. Thus you will be told to park at an angle, to limit your stay to six hours, and, for most of the large turnaround area, not to park at all. There is space for a good dozen cars, though the spot is rarely crowded, perhaps thanks to the depletion of fish stocks. On a holiday weekend, expect to find the shoulders of the adjoining roads lined with vehicles whose owners plan stays longer than six hours.

One of the truly scary shellfish warning signs, skull and crossbones prominent on it, warns you to check with Fisheries and Oceans Canada before collecting chowder ingredients. The sign indicating that beach fires are not permitted is not odd; what is odd is that a parallel sign prohibits camping in a place where it is difficult to imagine anyone wanting to camp. An important feature for anyone planning several hours on a beach is the chemical toilet usually ensconced in the parking lot here.

Path The "path" is actually a road-width asphalt launching ramp that, at low tide, merges into the underlying sandstone rock shelf. From either side of the ramp, and particularly toward its end, past the low concrete barrier, you can reach one of the adjoining beaches. In fact, another, narrower concrete ramp angles back to the right, allowing easy access onto the sandy beach. Those in wheelchairs could be brought to this spot for a pleasant shorefront visit—but be aware that the first part of the ramp is quite steep. Likewise, in winter or stormy weather, when you are not likely to be in the way of someone trying to bustle a boat into the water, you could come here for a perfect waterfront car picnic.

Beach You can choose from two beaches. That to the left offers on its upper shore a short stretch of pebbles and small rocks, ideally suited to those who prefer to picnic on the shore without benefit of sand in their sandwiches. Most will head for the short bay of fine white sand to the right, though—and all the more because of the layers of sun-bleached logs that make for a great Vancouver Island beach. Those expecting to launch a boat would be happiest coming here at a mid to high tide since there is a bit of a trek to the water's edge at low tide.

Suitability for children Although this isn't intended as a family beach park, in fact, it is one of the most child-friendly beaches in the entire area. The combination of fine white sand (on the southern beach) and gently sloping beach, easy car access, and, of course, toilet, make this a great spot for any child, from toddler to teen. You won't find the neighbouring children disagreeing with you as they frolic around their swimming raft.

Suitability for groups Although this spot is lovely, it isn't suited to more than a small group—perhaps a few kayakers back from a morning's paddle or a pair of families. Larger groups would be better off going to Blue Heron Park (see entry 69), unless they are really determined to have a sandy beach.

View The view from here is much more varied and extensive than that from spots farther south along the Cedar/Yellow Point peninsula. Immediately to the north, Gabriola angles toward Dodd Narrows, while Circle Island sits almost immediately offshore. From the tip of Gabriola the chain of Mudge, Link, De Courcy, Ruxton, and Pylades islands extends south. In fact, to the south, because of the curve of the shore, you will see the charming overlay of many distant Gulf Islands (from north to south): Valdes, Galiano, Kuper, Thetis, even distant Salt Spring.

Winds, sun and shade You're better off coming here if a cool northwest wind is blowing rather than a cool southeast wind; though both can be felt here, the southeast hits more directly, particularly on the sandy beach. Even so, on the beach it is possible to tuck into the shelter of the ramp if you are a little chilled. Bring your whole arsenal of protective sun gear, as there is almost no shade here until late afternoon.

Beachcombing You can pick your way some distance along the shore past the two beaches. The shore narrows as you head south, until walking becomes more of an adventure than you probably want.

Seclusion The strip of public land is not huge, and is bounded by houses on both sides. You won't be able to wander as lonely as a cloud, but you will not be in the middle of a madding crowd. The ramp itself can be busy on a sunny summer weekend.

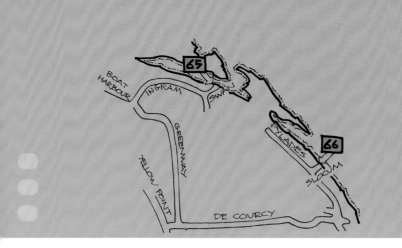

65
SWAN ROAD
An isolated small bluff at the entrance to a tidal channel cutting deep into the woods

Location, signs and parking You will have to follow the map carefully to get to this unusual spot. Like other parts of the Cedar/Yellow Point peninsula, this area bristles with peculiar shifts in road name and surprising twists in road direction. Thus, taking Tiesu from Yellow Point Road, you will watch with bemusement as it changes to Boat Harbour Road, and, long before it reaches the boat harbour, changes into Ingram Road. Don't bother, however, following any road map to the end of this road sequence as it turns into Kendall and arrives at a set of docks. Many exclamatory signs will rid you of any delusions you might have that you can visit here. No: the marina is very, *very* private. Instead of looking for the harbour, therefore, keep your eye open for a small gravel road leading from your left off Ingram, and follow it through its twists a short distance to the end. The only sign that indicates that this is a public access is a shellfish-warning poster. There is no real parking area. If you have a four-wheel drive and plan to stay only a few minutes, it is possible to make your bumpy way down a dirt track virtually to the shore. More sensibly, however, you will squeeze onto the side of the gravel road, being careful not to block the single private drive here.

Path From the end of the dirt track, a short, slightly slippery path leads over what appears to be a First Nations midden (ancient shell heap) onto a rounded sandstone shelf. Launching a kayak here is reasonably easy and, indeed, the only spot in the area where you can easily do so. You will have to confine your entry and exit times around high tide, however.

Beach What might bring you here, in spite of the difficulty of route and the unmaintained path, is the fascinating geography. As you come down the path, you will find yourself near the mouth of a narrow inlet cutting more than 100 m into the forested land. At low tide, the shore is more interesting than attractive. The sandstone formations on which you find yourself drop steeply toward the water on the right, but to the left, slope easily to the lower shore. At a low tide, a considerable stretch of gravel and barnacles leads into the inlet. The adventurous could probably make their way across the weedy and variably deep stretch of water to the opposite shore of meadows and woods. If you're looking for a picnic spot, this one offers a suitable sandstone shore for you to linger over your celery sticks.

Suitability for children Children might enjoy playing on the sandstone and throwing rocks, but most will feel constrained by the small area available to them. Apprehensive parents, likewise, will find lots of opportunity to issue dire warnings about falling on the steep sections.

Suitability for groups Limited parking, limited usable shore and limited potential for activities make this spot suitable for no more than one or two cars' worth of explorers.

View There is probably no more restricted view anywhere on the Island. At the same time, it is probably the view that will bring beach lovers and visual artists to this shore. Choose mid to high tide, however, for the most picturesque views up the inlet, or across the water the short distance to the prettily treed headland opposite. Because of the angle of the shore, you won't be able to see the little harbour well. There is no other viewpoint accessible to the public in the whole area.

Winds, sun and shade Choose morning if you want to perch in the sun. Choose afternoon if you want to see the prettily wooded shore opposite fully lit. Any wind from any direction is hard-pressed to make its way into this protected inlet.

Beachcombing Don't choose this spot with an eye (or foot) to shore walking. If you are truly adventurous, though, at low tide you can make your way over the slippery shore to your right, the soft, gravel inlet to your left, or, possibly, even across the stretch of water to the shore opposite.

Seclusion If seclusion is what you want, seclusion is almost certainly what you will get. Expect neither to see others nor to be seen by others. Indeed, this may well win the prize as the most secluded access spot covered by this book!

66
SLOCUM ROAD
A pretty, secluded bluff and small area of varied, steep shoreline

Location, signs and parking Do a Google Maps search for Slocum Road and you won't find it! Otherwise, the route here is straightforward if you leave Yellow Point Road at De Courcy, turn left onto Pylades Drive, and watch on your right for the SLOCUM ROAD sign onto what appears to be a private gravel track. The road sign—and an accompanying NO EXIT sign—are the only permanent signs you will see at this spot. In dry summers, though, expect to see a temporary plasticized notice warning against fires. Parking is not easy, though you can squeeze into a spot at the end of the gravel road or, at a pinch, along one side (the other side has a ditch).

Path You might not see the path at first, since some St. John's wort is busily engaged in covering it. Persevere, however, and you will soon find a short dirt path winding past a large arbutus to a lovely lookout with a memorial bench. To get onto the shore, don't scramble down the short, steep incline straight ahead but, instead, turn left for a much easier descent. An enterprising soul has built a short set of stairs through the tangle of boulders, using local stone and mortar. It would be possible to get a kayak onto the shore here, but difficult to get it to the water, unless you come at high tide.

Beach The shore is primarily solid sandstone, but more jagged and broken, less rounded and scooped, than it is at similar spots in the area. At the same time, it packs lots of variety into a small area, with nearly horizontal sections leading to small cliffs and, at low tide, to some pebble and broken shell flats and tidal pools. If you are thinking of a dip, choose high tide and bring a mask and snorkel—the variety of formations makes for a magical snorkelling experience! Picnicking, however, is awkward here, unless a romantic couple uses the bench. The rocks above the high-tide line are mostly steep or jagged.

Suitability for children Do consider bringing an older child, or at least one who is well shod and sure-footed. There are many bits to explore at low tide, though some patches of rock are slippery and awkward. Don't bring a toddler unless you want to spend your time on rescue missions.

Suitability for groups The parking is much too limited, and the size of usable shore much too small, for more than a few people at a time.

View The view is surprisingly varied and complex. A picturesque reef and wooded peninsula to your left are the most distinctive elements. Otherwise, expect the same chain of islands you will see from other points in the area—Mudge, Link, De Courcy, Ruxton, and Pylades. Valdes and a piece of Thetis are visible farther south. You can even see the high points of Galiano and Salt Spring, if you know what to look for. On a clear day, the peaks of the mainland mountains above Howe Sound loom behind Valdes.

Winds, sun and shade Winds run largely parallel to the shore, but there is little shelter from any wind. This spot receives a lot of sun throughout the day. In the afternoon, the arbutus provides shade over the lookout spot and upper shore.

Beachcombing Don't plan to get your exercise by walking a long distance along the shore here. The rocks are too steep, jagged and slippery to allow easy walking. Do, however, come—at low tide—if you love poking and prodding along an interesting bit of shore.

Seclusion The houses on both sides are in clear sight of the shore, but the spot is understandably quiet and little used, except by a few locals.

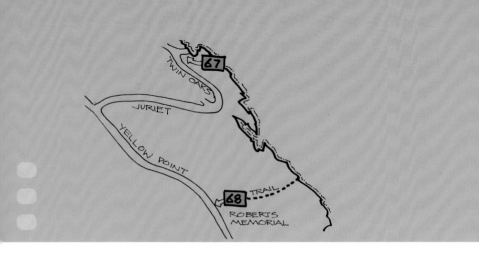

67
TWIN OAKS DRIVE
A quiet, wooded access
to a rocky shore and
expansive view

Location, signs and parking Although getting to this access point
involves few twists and turns, it is easy to miss the turn onto Juriet Road from
Yellow Point Road. Likewise, keep alert to the facts—first, that Twin Oaks
Drive will seem like an extension of Juriet Road and second, that you will
have to take a very sharp turn to reach the end of the road and the beginning
of the access trail. This spot is a little more welcoming than most other public
accesses in the Cedar district. The gravelly end of the road broadens into a
parking space for two or three cars. In addition, once you have spotted the
leaf-screened trail—to the right side of the parking area—you will see one
of the cube-shaped concrete signs that occasionally appear between Nanoose
and here. In summer, expect to see a plasticized sign prohibiting "open fires,"
roughly translatable, one supposes, to beach fires.

Path A smooth dirt path winds almost horizontally about 15 m through
light, open woods. Bringing a kayak down this path would be fairly easy, but
be prepared for a little bit of fancy footwork negotiating the flat sandstone
boulders that act as a transition onto the shore. It is possible to launch a kayak

even at low tide since, to the left at least, once you are past a few large rocks, you will have little difficulty getting down the smoothly sloping solid rock shore. Just be aware that the rockweed (fucus) can be slippery.

Beach This is another in the series of sandstone shores that typify the whole area. It is a little less dramatic than some other spots, though. Except for a small vertical drop a short distance from the mouth of the path, the shore offers a restrained mixture of patches of boulder and rounded, sloping rock. Even at low tide, the water is not far away. Swimming is best at high tide. Picnicking is pleasant in the area of rounded sandstone directly in front of the access path, but do be aware that you will be sitting on solid rock rather more forgiving pebbles or sand.

Suitability for children Children would be happier here than at some of the other small access points nearby. Here, at least, they can clamber over the rocks with only a little struggle and get to the all-important water's edge with only a little care. Still, choose Blue Heron Park or Nelson Road if you want a largely carefree afternoon with your scampering, wet children.

Suitability for groups Two families could come here for a picnic or a swim, but no more.

View Although the broad expanse of Stuart Channel and the chain of small islands across the channel dominate the view, it is prettily framed by overlapping wooded points to the north and a single, closer point to the south.

Winds, sun and shade If there is a cool breeze blowing and you want a warm spot to sit with a sizzling novel or just your thoughts, you will find that the upper shore is moderately sheltered by the points on either side. Morning is by far the sunniest part of the day, but the low, lightly wooded bank doesn't cast deep or extensive shadows in the afternoon.

Beachcombing You can stroll easily on the upper sandstone shelf for several hundred metres to the north. It is generally easier to keep to the upper shore to prevent slipping on the weedy lower rocks.

Seclusion Although the narrow public strip lies between houses, both houses are set well back into the bushy shore. Particularly if you stay on the upper shore, you should be able to have undisturbed conversation.

68

ROBERTS MEMORIAL
PROVINCIAL PARK

A kilometre-long trail through a
beautifully forested provincial park
to a sculpted sandstone shore

Location, signs and parking Cedar Road is a loop off the main highway and Yellow Point Road is, in turn, a loop road off Cedar Road—so whether you are driving from the north or the south, the directions are more or less the same. Once you are on Yellow Point Road, simply keep an eye open for the **Roberts Memorial Park** sign. The parking lot is just a few metres from the main road. Among the interesting signs in the parking lot, including a map and various warnings about fires, pets and the like, is one telling you to watch out for *aliens*. In this case, though, the aliens are not little green men, but little grey squirrels—an invasive species that has wrought much havoc among the gentler, less aggressive local squirrel population. Don't be surprised if, as sometimes happens, you see a sign warning you about another unwelcome animal, one a little larger than a squirrel—the black bear!

More than a dozen cars can park in the gravel parking area. You are not likely to find the lot full, but you can expect a few cars there during sunny and summery weather.

Path For those who want to get to their beach with minimum effort, there is good news and bad news. The good news is that this park path, unlike many similar ones on this part of Vancouver Island, is gently rolling. The not-quite-so-good news is that the pretty, wooded path is almost a kilometre long. If you are planning to launch a kayak or set up an elaborate picnic, you should be prepared either to work for your pleasure—or select another shorefront. Once you have made your way through the Douglas-fir forest, with its many fine samples of the species, expect the path to divide into several equally usable branches as you get close to the shore. Keep an eye open for an interesting pair of juniper trees, usually found on only south-facing banks of the Gulf Islands.

Beach Far from being a beach in any conventional sense, this bit of shore is nevertheless wonderful in the way that only a few spots on Vancouver Island—and many spots on the Gulf Islands—can be. The sculpted shelves of sandstone that are so characteristic of the Gulf Islands are found aplenty here. At the south end of the shore, these formations become increasingly cliffy and dramatic. Keep your eyes open for a wonderful little petroglyph—a recent embellishment of a First Nations design postdating that of ancient petroglyphs. During winter months, I'm told, both California sea lions and their larger cousins from the north, Steller's sea lions, haul their considerable bulks onto the rocks here. Because of the configuration of the rocks, snorkelling can be excellent, particularly at a mid tide.

Suitability for children Some children need the instant gratification that comes with a beach abutting a parking lot; some children require sand for their beachy pleasure. If your children are superior to such mere mortals, they will find much to give them pleasure at this beach. Most such pleasures will come with romping over the rocks and prodding at low-tide creatures (not including sea lions!). At low tide, though, be warned that the lower shore is quite steep and slippery in sections. Choose high tide for splashing around the rounded lumps and miniature bays. Be aware, too, that the cliffy area to the south is dangerously high for little wobbly creatures. The (pit) toilet near the shore is one advantage here for children.

Suitability for groups The stroll through the forest and the search for seabirds, sea lions, eagles and great blue herons make this an ideal location for a nature-loving group. Picnic tables near the shore and toilets at both ends of the 1 km long trail are other group-friendly features.

View From your perch on the sandstone shelf, you will find the view considerably more open than that at most spots between Nanaimo and Goldstream. Stuart Channel is a few kilometres across to the chain of low islands—Mudge, Link, De Courcy, Ruxton, Pylades. Beyond them, Gabriola to the north and Valdes farther south rise higher, but not so high that you can't glimpse the mainland mountains rising above them.

Winds, sun and shade Neither northwest nor southeast winds hit the shore full on—but both can be felt. Indeed, there is little to impede either wind as both scud up and down Stuart Channel. The upper beach is in sun only during the first few hours of the day. Though no high shore blocks the sun, plenty of high trees provide some shade. Still, particularly in mid-summer when the sun is high and the tide is out, the lower shore is in sun during much of the day. Even in evening some channels of sunshine cut through the trees.

Beachcombing Consider yourself to have done your walking on your way to the shore. Once on the shore, you can make your way a considerable distance in either direction, but you will be very much "making your way" rather than striding out. This is a shore for walking slowly and peering, not for stretching legs.

Seclusion Sunday morning is dedicated to the walking of large dogs: the park is justifiably popular with locals. On the other hand, most don't seem to linger on the shore. In addition, the curve of the shore and the width of the treed park make for a wonderful feeling of serenity.

✱ **Also nearby** **Raise Road** is a tiny road, not appearing on most maps, that leads off Yellow Point Road immediately opposite Paulson Road (see next map). Impressive care has gone into building a winding mulch path through recently planted shrubs. A few steps will bring you to the ridged sandstone shore. It is only the unusual and interesting geography that justifies your coming to this small, obscure spot, crowded in between adjacent houses. At low tide, you will find yourself looking at a deeply inset bay, its bottom covered with soft, almost muddy sand and eelgrass. If you want to satisfy your curiosity and get a pretty view, come at a mid tide, when you can also make your way to the left along a gently sloping gravel beach backed by a farm field. You probably won't, however, want to linger here, because of the cramped parking and the sense that you are ensconced in a close neighbourhood.

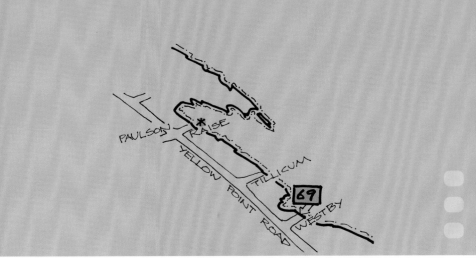

69
BLUE HERON PARK
A small park with washrooms, picnic tables and smooth sandstone shore, good for launching kayaks or swimming

Location, signs and parking From the north or south, turn onto Cedar Road (a loop off the highway). Since Yellow Point Road is, in turn, a loop off Cedar Road, the directions work from both north and south. Keep an eye out for Westby Road and a discreet but clear sign as you drive along the southern portion of Yellow Point Road: the park is, in fact, but a few metres down Westby Road. Probably the most lovingly produced park sign in the area—executed on a tree slab, and complete with bas-relief carving of the eponymous blue heron—perches prominently at the end of the parking area. Other signs will tell you—indirectly—not to plan starlit beach parties with marshmallow roasts and, during the day, to come equipped with plastic bags if Fifi or Brutus is accompanying you. There is plenty of parking for about a dozen cars, though be careful not to block the private drive that—oddly— cuts through the park's grassy area near the end of the parking area.

Path Two paths are relevant, one for your comfort, one for your pleasure. From the road end of the parking lot, be mindful of the path into the stand of cedars and firs—and, after a few metres, to an outhouse. From the other end of the parking area, 10 broad gravel-and-tie steps take you gradually to the shore. This is a reasonably comfortable spot for someone who has walking difficulties, though there is no handrail on the steps. Kayakers will find this an easy spot to put in their boats (even at low tide)—indeed, for many years this was the starting point for the kayaking leg of the Yellow Point Pant and Paddle adventure relay race. Picnickers, likewise, will be pleased with the three picnic tables in the grassy area immediately above the shore.

Beach Like most of the shore along Yellow Point, the shore here is mostly sandstone shelves with occasional tidal pools and patches of broken shell, gravel and the odd boulder. Unlike most of the shore on the Cedar/Yellow Point peninsula, this part is nearly level, without the convolutions and steep drops common elsewhere. The water recedes about 30 m at low tide, revealing sandstone covered with rockweed, tiny periwinkles, barnacles, ochre stars and all the other required shore-life species.

Suitability for children The beach offers little in the way of sand, but this is nevertheless a highly child-friendly park. Pools and sea creatures are there for low-tide entertainment; (sometimes) warm, safe paddling and swimming water offers itself for mid and high tide fun. Add the convenience of the tables and toilets, the grassy area for less watery play, the mix of sun and shade—and you have a comfortable and pleasant spot even for toddlers.

Suitability for groups The same features that make this a good spot for children also make it good for even a medium-sized group of 15. The wedding group that wants that shorefront setting for its photos, the eco-club that wants its annual picnic and meeting in an unusual place, the kayaking group that wants to follow up an afternoon's paddle with a picnic—all of these would find this a great spot.

View There is little remarkable about the view from here, in large part because many kilometres separate you from the generally low, even contours of the islands opposite (Reed, De Courcy, and, behind them, Valdes). Still, on a clear day, the forested shores all around and the coastal mountains looming in the distant are everything your soul needs for a refreshing quaff.

Winds, sun and shade Both northwest and southeast winds (particularly the latter) can get rambunctious here, though neither strikes the shore directly. At the same time, if the wind is a little too cooling for extended lounging or reading, the screen of low bushes and trees between the grass and the shore will allow you considerable protection.

Except for the late afternoon and evening, this park has plenty of both sun and shade. If you want most sun on the shore itself, however, you will want to come during the first part of the day.

Beachcombing You can walk some distance to the south along the primarily sandstone shelf, though after a couple of hundred metres you will find yourself on the low rounded sandstone bluffs in front of Yellow Point Lodge. To the north, you are more limited; in fact, another lodge and a narrowing shoreline make life difficult for the would-be shore walker.

Seclusion This is a quiet but nevertheless popular park. Only in ugly weather or unlikely times of day can you expect to have it to yourself. Except for one neighbouring house, though, and the lodge a short distance to the north, you will feel uncrowded and free from (much) scrutiny.

Hunting for sculpins

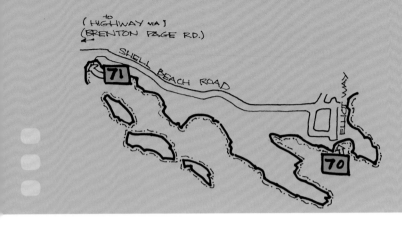

(to HIGHWAY VIA)
(BRENTON PAGE RD.)

SHELL BEACH ROAD

71

ELLIOT WAY

70

70
ELLIOTT'S BEACH PARK
A small, pebbly bay with picnic table and views toward Vancouver Island

Location, signs and parking Leave the highway a few kilometres north of Ladysmith and take Brenton Page Road until, with a little gyrating, it turns into Shell Beach Road. At the T-junction turn onto Elliot (spelled, oddly, with one "t") Way and carry on the short distance to the end, where a sign welcomes you to Elliott's (two t's) Beach Park. This beach also seems to be known, ominously, as Coffin Beach, though no signs here indicate that. More signs will tell you that this is a Cowichan Valley Regional Park—though very far from the centre of the Cowichan Valley! Other signs will remind you of the prohibitions against midnight carousing (this is a "dawn to dusk" park, after all) and midnight snoring (this is not a park for camping.) A gravel parking areas provides spots for several cars—though the arrangement is peculiar, since these spots are arranged around the edges of a rough T-junction.

Path The path could almost not be easier. In fact, it is really a short gravel service road with a locked gate that keeps cars out. The regular surface, short distance and lack of vertical drop make this a perfect spot to bring a complicated picnic. At high tide, at least, it also makes this a perfect place to bring a kayak.

Beach Shell Beach Road brings you most of the way to Elliott's Beach Park (Shell Beach itself is within a First Nations reserve and not open to the general public). The upper part of this prettily curving little bay is almost entirely crushed white shell. The shore is bounded on the left by a steeply jutting (and—as yet—beautifully treed) point of land, and on the right by some shelving sandstone formations. At low tide the beach is mostly pebbles and shells, but an interesting sandstone lump protrudes from the middle of the beach, surrounded by a few boulders. Because no currents sweep past these shores, this is bound to be one of the warmest swimming beaches along this stretch of coast. Tender feet will probably have to be protected from the odd sharp bit of rock or barnacle, however, so water shoes should be part of the swimbag inventory.

Suitability for children This is one of the best children's beaches in the area—particularly for the wee 'uns who want a beach that is warm, protected, gradually sloping and well provided with amenities. Even the picnic tables and the (small) grassy area will be welcome for this class of beachgoer. Finding little crab treasures at low tide, paddling at high tide, trotting to the nearby car or toilet when needs arise—a day at the beach could hardly be easier. And, who knows? Those first splashy strokes just might turn into the beginnings of a great dog-paddling future.

Suitability for groups Everything is here for a *small* group, just as it is for a small child. Much will depend, however, on what the small group has in mind. The park calls out for a family picnic, a group of watercolourists, perhaps some birdwatchers. It does not call out for those who wish to celebrate under the stars or play a round of touch football.

View "Charming" is the first word that comes to mind. Indeed, one of the qualities of this spot that would make it appealing for photographers or painters is the unusually pretty combination of close, treed points (with the ominously monikered "Coffin Point" to the left), and distant, overlapping hills and islands. It is also one of the only spots on the southern island where you can look back at Vancouver Island. Even better, Ladysmith is tucked out of sight, so you have only the southern part of the community of Saltair and the high hills above to soothe your eyes.

Elliott's Beach Park

Winds, sun and shade Somewhat exposed to southeast winds, though slightly sheltered by the point to the left, this little gem of a beach is completely protected from northwest winds. In fact, you have to be careful on a hot day, because you may find you will need a refreshing dip just to cool off. This is a beach for sun lovers, particularly in the middle part of the day. Throughout most of the evening, you will still be in full sun, but because it will be coming from slightly behind you as you lie on your favourite beach towel, you will feel its effects a little less directly. A huge, magnificent maple tree spreads over part of the grassy area, but, on the whole, this is a beach for sunscreen, beach umbrellas and your trendiest shades.

Beachcombing Extensive beachcombing is one thing that this beach doesn't offer. To the left you can go only a short distance, unless you're good at inching your way along a small sandstone cliff. Because of the low shelving rock to the right, it is easier to browse your way through the pools and rocks to the right. Don't, however, expect to jog or even stride.

Seclusion You will see only other beachgoers at this relatively popular little park. There is a private house on one side of the beach, but it is set well back and is partially hidden behind some trees. Enjoy the relative solitude!

71

RAVEN PARK

A picnic table in a small grassy area with, at low tide, a short path onto muddy tidal flats, and at high tide, a pretty kayaking area

Location, signs and parking Follow the same directions as in the previous entry to get to Shell Beach Road. Keep an eye open on your right for what appears to be a descending asphalt drive. Look for a large, shingle-roofed sign with the name of the park. In spite of its size, the sign is easy to miss. With its unusual font and equally unusual combination of yellow and green, it is easy to mistake as a commercial sign for a trailer park. This sign will, on closer inspection, remind you that you cannot park your camper here overnight or light fires. It will also provide you with a map, but be prepared to be confused if you are using it as a guide to local beaching. Elliott's Beach Park, for many the ultimate destination for a beach-exploration trip along this road, is given its old name "Coffin Beach" on this sign. A paved circular area, just a few metres off Shell Beach Road, provides space for half a dozen cars.

Path Beside the parking area are two picnic tables in a pretty grassy area separated from the shore by a light lattice of small firs and cedars. A smooth gravel-and-moss path leads down a gentle slope some 20 m or so to the water. So far so good. It is when the path reaches the shore that it disintegrates into an eroded dirt clamber. At this point you will see two signs, one warning you that you have reached the park boundary, the other saying, a little mystifyingly, CAUTION: TIDAL MUD FLATS: CREEK BED NOT VISIBLE AT HIGH TIDE. Presumably, this means that you won't realize that there is a slight drop-off into the—very small—creek bed that runs through the flats. It is not clear why this information is a matter of caution, unless you are engaged in a highly unlikely bit of wading near high tide.

Beach This is not a beach. It is mud. Even the government charts are unambiguous on the subject. "Mud" is printed over the whole area. Not only that, but at low tide, the mud flats extend far, far into the distance, making it virtually impossible to get to the water's edge. Why bother with this spot at all, then? The answer is: high tide. At high tide, this makes a lovely picnic spot, and, even more strikingly, the starting point for a unique paddling experience. If you can cope with the slightly dodgy business of getting your kayak or canoe the last 2 or 3 m onto the shore, you will find the nooks and crannies among the clusters of islands provide one of the most charming paddling experiences in the whole area. It is important, though, that you plan carefully so that you can get back to your starting point while the tide is still in. The alternative is not pretty to contemplate.

Suitability for children Children might enjoy a picnic or a bit of Frisbee throwing on the grass, perhaps. Otherwise, go directly to Elliott's Beach Park a few kilometres along the road. Children who catch one glimpse of the mud flats will be forgiven for unleashing a tirade of "icks" and "yucks."

Suitability for groups For a pleasant picnic, or an even more pleasant bit of photography or painting, this is a good place for up to a dozen people. Most groups will not want to stay for more than an hour or so, though, not least of all because there is no toilet.

View It is really the view of the overlapping clusters of islands and wooded coves that make this spot worth visiting. There is nothing quite like it anywhere along this coast. Do, however, time your visit with high tide if you want to find the view charming rather than the opposite.

Winds, sun and shade It is hard to imagine a more sheltered spot from wind or waves. Indeed, even on a blowy day, you can paddle here with impunity (again, though, only at high tide). For most of the day, you will find patches of sun and shade as the shadows from the small trees in the area make their way across the open spaces.

Beachcombing No other public access spot on the island has so little to offer the beachcomber—unless you really, really, like sinking deep into mud.

Seclusion Be surprised if you find yourself with company when you come here. This is not complete wilderness, though. A small housing development extends along the curving shoreline and is clearly visible (but not obtrusive) from the view spot on the shore.

LADYSMITH Three waterfront spots might interest those who drive through Ladysmith without ever stopping because they are not sure what they will find there. The spots are so close to the highway, however, that they need no detailed description or maps. If you wish to explore more, here is what you might expect.

Well signposted from the highway, **Transfer Beach**, a popular family beach, has many facilities. It is possible to rent kayaks here or launch your own.

Look for a post along Transfer Beach Boulevard that marks the beginning of the **Marine Walk**. The route, which runs for about two kilometres beside Ladysmith Harbour, passes through woods and along old railway tracks. Signs en route provide interesting historical background.

Though not designated for public use, **Slack Point**, immediately north of Transfer Beach, is popular with weekend strollers. It takes its name from the loose black "coal slack" remaining from the days when Ladysmith was a harbour for shipping coal.

Sunrise over Nuttall Bay

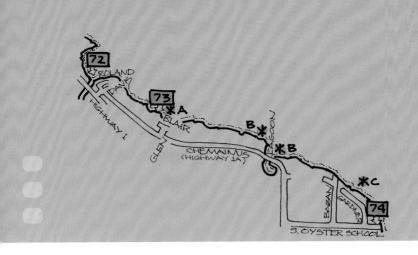

72

HOLLAND CREEK PARK

A wooded path south of Ladysmith leading down a bank to the mouth of Holland Creek and the rocky shore toward Ladysmith

Location, signs and parking At the traffic lights opposite Coronation Square shopping centre at the south entrance to Ladysmith, turn toward the sea onto Davis. After crossing the railway tracks, turn immediately left onto Chemainus Road for a short distance until you see the Roland Road sign on your right—and the trailhead immediately in front of you. Here you will see one of the monumental rock cairns reminding you that the Town of Ladysmith makes public beach access signs like no one else does! The sign will not only provide you with a reproduction of a fascinating historical photograph but will also tell you that here you will find a BEACH WALK TO HOLLAND CREEK ESTUARY, only 0.7 km distance, adding that there is NO ACCESS AT HIGH TIDE and that you should USE CAUTION. All of these points are worth noting, but all are just a smidge misleading (see Path section). A few cars, but only a few, can pull off onto the narrow shoulder of the road, and then everyone will have to pile out of one side of the car, because the only way to get properly off the road is to sidle up to a virtual wall of leafy green.

Path When you proceed down this interestingly varied trail, you may start to agree that the signs have created some false impressions. This is not really a "beach walk" so much as a walk *to the shore*, approximately .7 km distance. No one will want to walk out onto the "beach" very much—though some will enjoy the walk along the upper shore to Transfer Beach. After a highly groomed beginning behind an equally groomed hedge, the trail becomes a little more basic as it traverses a wooded band while descending some 10 or 15 m toward sea level. A combination of concrete stairs, tie-and-gravel stairs and switchbacks will bring you past a concrete bench down almost to sea level. From here, one trail branches out onto a lightly wooded spit, while another parallels the shore before dropping onto it.

Beach The word "estuary" says it all. Dispense with any expectations of strolls out to the water's edge. Holland Creek winds through a long stretch of gravel, intertidal salt-marsh vegetation and pools. Like most estuaries, this is a great place for viewing our feathered cousins, for sketching, or finding some solitude, though most will find it far prettier at high tide than low tide. This could well be one of those places, though, that you want to save until autumn. The brilliantly coloured maples, and, more excitingly, spawning chum salmon in the "enhanced" stream can make for a particularly memorable visit.

Suitability for children Estuaries aren't for most children, though a picnic on the grassy spit could be enjoyable, particularly at high tide, when driftwood-boat floating or pebble throwing can divert a child long enough for a parent to soak up a little atmosphere and view.

Suitability for groups The parking limits the size of the group; the unusual features of the access limit the form of the group. Those interested in birdwatching, photography, sketching, possibly a little lightweight picnicking, will want to make this spot a must on their list of desirable spots. Those wanting an interestingly varied sequence of low-tide walks will be less enthusiastic, perhaps, but nevertheless generally pleased with what they find here.

View Especially when framed by overhanging maples or cedars, the view is often lovely. Because the paths twist and wind along the shore, too, the view is interestingly varied. From the distant contours of Salt Spring Island in the south to Coffin Point across from Ladysmith, the view is full of the unspectacular but varied geographical lumps and bumps that enclose the large body of protected water along this stretch of shore.

Winds, sun and shade The path and upper shore within the estuary itself are almost completely protected from a northwest wind and can, in fact, become quite hot on a summer's day. A southeast wind, however, blows more freshly onto this area. The early and middle parts of the day are the sunniest, but overhanging trees provide patches of shadow throughout the day.

Beachcombing Considering the fact that the walk is officially endorsed, it would be churlish not to recommend the (low-tide) walk along the shore to Transfer Beach a kilometre or so distant. The fact is, though, the walk isn't great. Expect to do some boulder hopping along the first section and slip-sliding through loose gravel along the second section. The shifting views can be pleasant; less pleasant is running the gauntlet of massively engineered concrete walls of a waterfront housing development, heavily larded with vehement NO TRESPASSING signs.

Seclusion That the enticements of this spot are subtle means that you are unlikely to have much company here. While picnicking or painting on the grassy spit, you will feel a little under the inspection of a battery of houses along one side, but they are far enough away that you can relax and let down whatever hair there is to let down.

73
GOURLAY-JANES PARK
A walk through woods to the site of a former homestead on a gentle, gravel shore

Location, signs and parking There are few beach access spots that are as easy to get to yet as difficult to actually find! Gourlay-Janes Park is but a kilometre or so down Chemainus Road from its intersection with the highway on the southern outskirts of Ladysmith. A spanking new sign has been planted directly in front of the park. If you are interested in driving to this pretty little park, read the description for Blair Place, since getting into the park via Blair Place, though requiring more navigating, is actually easier.

The difficulty in getting to the park arises from the fact that, commendably, a new sidewalk has been built along this section of Chemainus Road, with "lanes" indicated for bicycles and pedestrians. Less commendably, the curb for this sidewalk has been made passable for vehicles at only one spot, where it is possible to pull off the road onto a raised gravel area big enough for a single car. Apparently, improvements to car accessibility are being actively encouraged. One strategy is to park along the edge of Woodley Road, in the Ladysmith direction from the park, and walk the short distance back along Chemainus Road.

Path More than one path leads down through the wooded area of 100 m or so to the shore. Locals seem to use a gated dirt track at the park's right-hand limit as the easiest way to get at least partway to the shore. At that point a pleasant trail branches off into the woods. Another trail starts near the road but, at present, requires a bit of bushwhacking to reach. The pretty, winding trail leads through woods dominated by small maple and alder, though apparently there are plans to plant other native species as well. The path drops about 15 m vertically until it opens on a lot-sized grassy area—the former homesite of the owners who donated the land. On the sea side of the grassy area, past a couple of fruit trees, is a park bench and the open vista onto the shore. A few concrete steps lead through a gap in the concrete retaining wall directly onto the pebbly upper shore.

Beach The beach itself is not going to win any prizes for beauty or popularity, although on a sunny day it is a pleasant enough place to sit or, at low tide, to poke around, looking among the small barnacle-covered rocks for shore crabs and other critters. Like the waterfront along most of this stretch of coast, this is a gradually sloping decline of golf-ball-sized rocks leading, at the lowest tides, to some patches of soft sand.

Suitability for children While the beach is perfectly safe and, at high tide in warm weather, the water warm, it is not the kind of place where most children will be happy for very long. If they join their friends or parents nudging aside rocks, however, or strolling in either direction, then they may well enjoy themselves—particularly if they are allowed to get wet.

Suitability for groups Because of the wretched parking situation and the lack of facilities, a (small) group would be coming here only for a specific purpose, like a wander along the shore or a picnic (best accomplished on the lawn).

View Pleasantly enough, the curve of the shoreline allows a view onto the shore of Ladysmith and the peninsula opposite ending in Coffin Point. The broad basin formed by Thetis and Kuper islands gives some sense of openness, but the view is essentially confined.

Winds, sun and shade Both northwest and southeast winds blow roughly parallel to the shore. Because the land behind the shore slopes gradually and a grassy area lies immediately above the shore, this spot is sunnier for more of the day than any of the other spots between Ladysmith and Chemainus. For those who need to get out of the sun, though, there are plenty of patches of shade under the trees surrounding the grassy area.

Beachcombing It is possible to walk for several kilometres on the gravelly shore. At low tide, about 30 m of shore is exposed, but most will find walking on the middle to upper shore the easiest. Do, however, come with tough shoes or ones you don't mind getting wet, if you want to be most flexible about where you walk.

Seclusion One house's lawn is virtually contiguous with the park's lawn, but on the left, the trees provide the impression of a wooded area rather than a subdivision.

✳ **Also nearby**
A. Immediately south of Gourlay-Janes Park, Glen Avenue turns off Chemainus Road. Follow it to a T-junction and turn left onto **Blair Place**. Another monumental stone-cairn beach access sign indicates a public access route to the beach, even though you will have the impression you have to walk through someone's side garden to get there. Since, in fact, this route is so close to Gourlay-Janes Park and arrives at the shore just a few metres south of it, most will choose to go to Gourlay-Janes Park itself. If, however, parking is not improved for the park, some will want to choose this spot for the sole reason that at least there is room off a busy road to park along a curb.

B. Chemainus Road drops to the shore and crosses a bridge over the tidal stream that fills and empties a small lagoon. **Lagoon Road** theoretically leads from near this bridge to the shore, but the configuration of public access and private drives means that the access does not function as shore access. If you really want to get to the gravelly shore here, it is easiest to do what many locals do and park on either side of Chemainus Road immediately south of the bridge. From here, it is only a few steps down to the water's edge, though the soft, gravelly beach is not particularly enticing at this point.

C. Bazan Road, off South Oyster School Road, ends in a small turn-around and, to the right, a flight of wooden stairs. The beach is generally pebbly and gently sloped, but most will find that nearby Boulder Point (entry 74) has quicker access to a more extensive and welcoming shore.

74
BOULDER POINT
A well-maintained path with 50 steps dropping down a wooded bank to a pebbly upper shore and low-tide sand

Location, signs and parking The very old highway between Ladysmith and Chemainus changes its name as it meanders through this historic area. As you pass through the area known as South Oyster (charmingly or hilariously, depending on your viewpoint), turn toward the sea on South Oyster School Road and follow it to its end—even though it seems to fizzle out into a largely unmaintained asphalt-and-gravel strip. A venerable, hand-carved wooden sign will tell you that you have come to a "Beach Trail," the responsibility of the "Saltair Recreational Commission." A much more eye-catching sign will tell you not only that Fang must be leashed, but, even more insistently, "Scoop The Poop." Come prepared.

Parking is limited, though the area is quite large and the access well set up. There are two perfect spots at the very end of the road under some fine maples and a cedar, but otherwise you will have to park as inoffensively as you can along the side of the approach road.

Path Before you start down the asphalt path sloping down from the left side of the parking lot, take the time to walk to the edge of the grassy area beyond the parking spots—the view from the top of the bank is worth the few minutes' detour. The smoothly sloping path has a civilized air, with its tidy strip of grass on one side and concrete retaining wall on the other. Don't be misled, however, if you are with others who have difficulty walking. After a few metres, and after going by a portable chemical toilet, the path gives way to a full 50 steps to the shore. This chemical toilet is itinerant—don't always expect it to be in the same place (or the same colour!). The stairs, over four flights, are in excellent condition, however, and handrails make life comparatively easy. Along the path, you will be warned of the danger of collecting shellfish.

Beach Come at low tide to experience the beach at its best. Although the upper beach, with its one giant boulder and several small ones, does offer some sand, it is really the lower beach, with its broad stretches of sand, sandy tidal pools, and eelgrass, that is the best feature. To the north the beach is comparatively narrow and rocky, so most will automatically turn toward the south. Because you will have to cross a strip of golf-ball-sized rocks and barnacles to get to the sand, do come prepared with flip-flops or water shoes.

Suitability for children This is a great spot for children, especially at low tide, and especially if you come fortified to meet head-on the usual difficulties a child can encounter—wet shoes, stubbed toes, sunburnt nose, wet clothes. Because there are only the slightest of currents here, too, expect the water to be warm, especially on an incoming tide over the sand flats. The chemical toilet is an obvious feature appropriate to little ones with little bladders.

Suitability for groups Parking is the most limiting factor for groups, though, with care, it is possible to come with several cars' worth of beachgoers. Once on the beach, such a group has plenty of space to spread out and wander with little worry about feeling as if it is crowding into a private neighbourhood. Picnicking, though, will have to be done on the patches of high-tide sand and rocks—don't expect to lay out fried chicken and apple pie on a picnic table, because there isn't one.

Boulder Point

View Although this is more a slight bulge in the shoreline rather than the "point" its name suggests, it does provide sweeping views. To the north, you can look across Ladysmith Harbour, distant islands and a few tips of mainland mountains. To the south, Thetis and Kuper islands, with their low, undulating skylines, dominate the scene. In all, the view is uncluttered and protected, lacking in striking features but nevertheless pretty.

Winds, sun and shade The southeast wind runs almost parallel to the shore here, but can be felt quite strongly on the lower part of the beach. Much the same is true of the northwest wind but, because of the curved shore, it is possible to snuggle up among the boulders to feel sun-baked (during the morning). The first part of the day is the sunniest, although there is plenty of sun on the beach itself well into mid-afternoon.

Beachcombing At low tide, expect to see a few locals strolling along the low-tide line, especially in the sandy areas—and expect to feel drawn to join them. Wear water shoes for such walking, though, since if you go very far, you will be crossing not just tidal pools but also areas of gravel and barnacle.

Seclusion This quiet area is not much used, but do expect a few locals who may look—perhaps curiously—at you. Houses are set well back among the trees, especially on the south side.

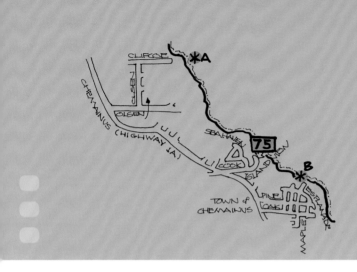

75
COOK PARK
A tiny park within a new development, combining a small treed bluff and a pretty pebbly beach

Location, signs and parking Cook Road leaves Chemainus Road just north of Chemainus itself. Island View Close on the right takes a turn through a newish housing development before coming to an end in an odd, paved cul-de-sac beneath a concrete retaining wall that puts the Great Pyramid of Egypt to shame. On the sea side of this cul-de-sac, you will see a dapper little blue and white Comox Valley Regional District sign telling you that, indeed, this is Cook Park. There is easily space for half a dozen cars in the large asphalt turnaround; in the unlikely event of a pinch, more could park along the edge of the road.

Path A gracefully curving, smoothly surfaced crushed gravel path leads about 30 m down a gentle incline. Managing a pair of kayaks or a canoe down this wide, well-maintained path would present few difficulties, though you would be happiest coming at mid to high tide to get your vessel into the water. En route you will pass a pretty grove of firs and arbutus, two picnic tables and a litter barrel.

Beach The beach is at its prettiest—and it is a very pretty beach—at mid to high tide. The overhanging arbutus, the curve of the small, enclosed pebble bay, and the low rocky outcroppings at either end make this not only visually varied, but also ideal for all sorts of shore activities—or sun-soaking inactivity. This is the kind of beach that, on a warm day, you will find perfect for leaning against the sun-bleached logs among the pretty pebbles while basking, reading or just dreaming.

Suitability for children Forget the sandcastles if you come here—but do remember the other playthings for a water-loving child, particularly in warm weather. If you choose the right tide and a warm day, most children will find this shelving shoreline perfect for splashing or swimming.

Suitability for groups Don't bring more than a small group here. The park, however beautiful, is not large, and the shoreline doesn't allow much spreading out. If you keep in mind that there are two picnic tables, you will have a good idea of the restraints you should put on your invitations for a day at the beach.

View Both the view from the descending path and from the shore itself are, like most along this stretch of coast, pretty rather than awe-inspiring. To the north, you will see the low wooded slopes of South Oyster and, many kilometres in the distance, Yellow Point. Directly across are Thetis and Kuper Islands, with the little Thetis Island ferry plying its way to nearby Chemainus. You will see only glimpses of mainland mountains.

Winds, sun and shade Winds tend to be light here, and none strikes the shore directly. Because of the open stretches of water, though, when the winds decide they are going to be strong, you will feel them a lot here, no matter what the direction. While the first part of the day is the sunniest, sun and shade are both available throughout the day. You will have to move your spot as the shadows move, of course, but you can come to this beach sure to find patches of both.

Beachcombing The chief imperfection in this otherwise nearly perfect little park will be felt by those who want a good soul-stirring tromp. At low tide, it is possible to make your way—properly shod—in either direction, but at any other tide, you'll find yourself struggling over a narrow bit of steep rock with overhanging trees if you try to venture too far.

Seclusion Because this is a park—albeit a small one—you have some green buffer between you and the houses in the small development that surrounds it. For the very same reason, though, you will find yourself falling into conversation with local residents and their dogs as they stroll onto the beach.

✱ Also nearby

A. Turn onto Olsen Road from Chemainus Road until you hit Clifcoe. From the end of **Clifcoe Road**, a broad path leads through a newly developed area to a dramatic flight of stairs. Enjoy the view of the Gulf Islands from the top of the stairs, or descend for access to a gently sloping gravel shore.

B. Kin Park, in the very centre of Chemainus, is worth a visit on a hot day if you have been buying ice cream and antiques in the well-known part of town but a few blocks from the beach. Kayakers and canoeists will be particularly interested in the Rotary Club-sponsored launching ramp here. From Oak Street, in the centre of commercial Chemainus, take either Maple or Willow to the north. At the shore you will find a grassy treed area with picnic tables, washrooms, a launching ramp and a small but pleasantly sandy beach. The tide does not go out a long way, but the gently sloping shore is great for children. The beach is fairly exposed to northwest winds but well sheltered from southeast winds. Although there are patches of shade on occasion, during most of the day you will find sun on the beach.

Chemainus Kin Park

QUALICUM
PARKSVILLE
PART 1
LANTZVILLE
NANAIMO
LADYSMITH
PART 2
CHEMAINUS
DUNCAN
MILL BAY
PART MALAHAT
3. GOLDSTREAM

PART 3 Chemainus to the Malahat

ALTHOUGH THE AREA FROM CHEMAINUS to the Malahat is geographically the largest of this book, it provides the smallest number of places for public access. This fact may arise partly from the unenlightened values of those responsible for zoning. More significant in this area, though, is that huge chunks of the shore are too rugged for development (Maple Mountain, the north shore of Cowichan Bay and Saanich Inlet beneath the Malahat). Others are inaccessible because of intervening forest lands (Stoney Hill). Some areas, primarily estuaries like that at the head of Cowichan Bay, are the kind of place few would want to visit even if there were access. Other chunks are allocated to industry, to First Nations reserves and to private housing estates (Arbutus Ridge). Then, of course, many spots have been allocated for public access, but are tangles of wilderness, impossible to find without surveying equipment and difficult to traverse.

The spots along the shore to which there is access are largely clustered (as, for example, around Crofton, Maple Bay, Cherry Point and Mill Bay). The advantage for beach explorers is that—with maps very firmly in hand—they can navigate through the labyrinth of roads while enjoying picturesque farms, hills and forests. They will arrive at several charming shorefronts close to each other. In addition, though sandy beaches are few in this section, the sheer variety of shorelines and dramatically shifting views of nearby peninsulas, coves and the Gulf Islands make for some great shorefront exploring.

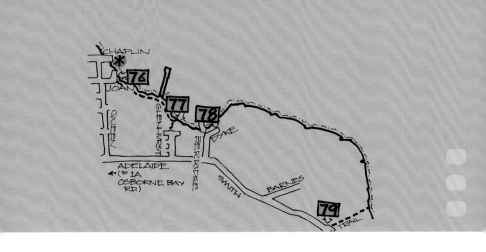

76
CROFTON COMMUNITY SEAWALK—TOWN CENTRE
A well-developed harbourfront walk leading south from the centre of Crofton

Location, signs and parking As one might expect, this walkway has two ends—and therefore two approaches. But only from one end can you, the water-seeking walker, gain easy and direct access to the shore itself. From this end, you will have to postpone stepping easily onto the shore until after you've treated yourself to about a kilometre's worth of waterside promenade. Driving through Crofton on Highway 1A as it changes its name to York Avenue, you will come across the Crofton Old School Museum. Joan Street leads three blocks to the waterfront and a substantial little parking lot. A rather grand little roofed entrance to the walkway bears one curious sign saying CATALYST PAPER WAY as well as CROFTON COMMUNITY SEAWALK. A plaque proclaims the source of funding for the impressive wooden esplanade to be the Western Economic Diversification Canada's Community Economic Adjustment Initiative. The walkway was built to commemorate the first century of the village now 2,500 souls strong. More pragmatic signs will tell you of the dangers of collecting shellfish and direct you toward a "pet stand" and the necessaries for coping with your dog's... movements. Feel free to bring your whole Saturday morning walker's group here: you'll find plenty of parking not only in the little parking lot provided, but also on the adjoining streets. A litter barrel and planters add to the welcoming atmosphere.

Path Those in wheelchairs or with walking difficulties should find this a great place to amble beside the ocean. Smooth and largely horizontal surfaces from vehicle to the elevated boardwalk ensure an easy time of it.

Beach From this end of the walkway, at least, you will initially encounter no beach as such. Farther along the asphalt path, it is possible to scramble down to a strip of gravel and barnacles. Even better, you can make the goal of your amble the community beach, about a kilometre distant.

Suitability for children For children who like to scamper ahead of strolling parents, this a good, safe walking spot. For those who want to play on a beach, they are best off waiting for the end of the walkway, where they can poke about on the gravelly shore or at the sandy community beach.

Suitability for groups A whole group can easily park and stroll here, but if they are intent on picnicking, they will have to carry their egg sandwiches to the end of the path before they can feast. A picnicking group, or one wishing to make the village pub their mid-walk destination, would be better off starting at the opposite end of the walkway.

View Crofton Harbour may not seem the most scenic spot for a stroll. However, on a sunny day, turning eyes away from the pulp mill to the north of the town, you will find it both interesting and pleasant to watch the ferry and tugboats. Across the open stretch of water rises Salt Spring Island and, to the south, the wooded hills crowd above the curving bay at the end of the harbour.

Winds, sun and shade This is a harbour for a good reason! It is well protected from any southeast squalls—though a northwesterly can whisk through. Because the path curves around the shore, it cuts through different patches of sun and shade. Bring your sun hat and sunscreen, though, for a summer stroll. For most of the walk, at most times of day, you will be in full sun.

Beachcombing You won't walk very much off the walkway itself, though it is possible to do a little, slightly squelchy strolling along the shore itself. More important, once you reach the southerly end of the walkway, you can extend your walk along the gravelly shore for 100 m or so.

Seclusion The walkway is not even marginally secluded: it is a walk along the edge of a village, and at one point, a trailer park. At the same time, even on a warm summer day, it is extremely quiet.

✱ Also nearby Those looking to launch a kayak or canoe will be interested in the **public launching ramp** at the end of Chaplin Street in "downtown Crofton." This launch is all the more valuable to note, since at no other spot nearby can you launch a small boat so easily.

77 CROFTON COMMUNITY SEAWALK—SOUTH

A small pebbly beach at the suburban beginning of the seaside walk that leads to the village of Crofton

Location, signs and parking This is the southern terminus of the lovely little seawalk described in the previous entry, which also includes the information relevant to planning your Sunday morning outing. Those seeking only a short stroll or quick access to the shore (or both) will want a little more.

Access to this end of the walk is through a small subdivision off Adelaide Street past Glenhurst Street, south of downtown Crofton. Look for a wide, smoothly paved asphalt path. A yellow and black diagonally striped sign planted in the middle of this strip presumably blocks vehicles of some sort from using the path or, possibly, mistaking it for a very, very small road. Don't be discouraged that the path seems to go through the side yard of a house. Even from the start of the path, you'll be able to recognize—by a refuse bin and a small sign on a post—that you've arrived at the Crofton Community Seawalk. There is less parking available here than at the opposite end of the seawalk, but enough for several cars. Even on a summer day, you will have no trouble finding a spot, if you are alone.

Path Those with wheelchairs or walking difficulties could use this access to the walkway, but less easily than at the opposite end. The initially skookum asphalt path gives way to a gravel (but fairly smooth) S-curve path—past a pair of benches for resting and, possibly, contemplating whatever needs contemplation. Handrails both on this part of the path and across a sturdy little bridge are helpful.

Beach No one is going to seek out this spot for the beauties of the beach at the end of the approach path. At a high tide on a sunny day, though, it can be pleasant enough to spread out snack supplies. The facts that a little stream exits onto the shore here and the fine rock is coal-black make it a little odd. The broken remains of an asphalt ramp leading toward the water's edge are likewise more curious than attractive.

Suitability for children Safe and solid, this end of the path, like the other, is fine for cooperatively scampering children—but not particularly obvious as a play spot. At the same time, this is a perfect shore stroll for children who like watching ferries and barges—or, even more likely, who can be best coaxed on a shore walk when there is ice cream to be had at the end, in this case in Crofton village at the far end of the walk.

Suitability for groups Because of parking limitations, a group would be better off starting at the opposite end of the path. On the other hand, those groups who would like a little refreshment mid-stroll will find this one of the only places on this part of Vancouver Island where they can make their shore-walking destination a village cafe, pizza parlour, a quaint museum—or even a fine little pub.

View The little harbour, with its occasional boat traffic, is quaintly interesting from the start of the path and is framed by views of distant Thetis Island, mainland mountains, and the sweep of the bay to the south. A photographer or watercolourist will find plenty of material here for discreet, rather than obvious, charm.

Winds, sun and shade This end of the walk is almost completely protected from a southeast wind, but fairly exposed to a northwest breeze. The whole strip of shore and walkway is pretty much in full sun, except partway along the path in the afternoon. Think: sun hat/sunscreen.

Beachcombing Again, the shore is best enjoyed from the walkway, not the shore itself, though it is possible to pick your way along the gravelly upper shore both to the north and to the south.

Seclusion The village access to the walkway affects seclusion; see the description in the Crofton Community Seawalk—Town Centre access point, above.

78
CROFTON BEACH PARK
A small park with grass and trees, picnic benches, washrooms, and a small but pretty, sandy beach

Location, signs and parking Turn off Highway 1A south of central Crofton first onto Adelaide Road, then left onto Berridge Street. You can either stop here or carry on a short distance along Dyke Road. The first access to the park is indicated by only a small sign at the curve of the road along with a dog owner's sign. Watch for a gap in the concrete barrier and a black and yellow checkered road sign, other clues to the fairly obscure access to this end of the park. The other access to the beach to the right, down Dyke Road, is more clearly marked by a larger sign and important warnings about closing hours and shellfish gathering. The first access spot provides parking for half a dozen cars in a gravel area along the right side of the road. The second access spot provides another dozen or so spots. Even on a summer weekend, though, parking is generally easy.

Path Those with walking difficulties or with cumbersome amusement equipment in the form of painting easels or portable barbecues will want to choose the second parking lot. Such beachgoers can step directly from their car into the grassy park and, from there, make a gentle descent to the beach. Others preferring a more direct route to the beach can park in the first spot and descend the dozen or so broad, gradual gravel-and-tie steps, first to the grassy area and then to the soft sand.

Beach This is a perfect spot for (afternoon) sunbathers. Unlike most beaches on the east coast of Vancouver Island, it has a broad area of sugary dry sand fully exposed to afternoon sun. Those eager to paddle, build sandcastles or swim will find a good area of (slightly soft) sand at the water's edge.

Suitability for children For a day at the beach with children, you could do much worse than bring your children here. The treed, grassy area between the parking area and the beach call out to have Frisbees thrown or games of tag played. The ease of access and proximity to cars (with the snacks and equipment they can provide) are additional bonuses. Most of all, though, children with the least capacity to enjoy themselves by the sea will find exactly the requisite proportions of dry and wet sand—though don't come at high tide if your children have sandcastles on their minds.

Suitability for groups This is close to a perfect spot for a large family picnic or a group of friends to spend a few hours on a warm summer day.

View Don't expect much in the way of wide-open nature vistas from here. From this side of the Crofton bay, your view-seeking eyes are primarily directed across the bay to the village, the barges, the docks and the Catalyst paper mill. At the same time, because of the small scale of all of these signs of civilization and "progress," you might find yourself oddly charmed by this hidden little corner of Vancouver Island.

Winds, sun and shade Come here on the blowiest southeast day, and you won't find much more than a slight ripple on the calm water. Come here on a day when a northwest wind is kicking up its heels, though, and expect the reverse. One of the features that makes this a good spot for children and all-purpose beachgoers is the mixture of sun and shade in the leafy, treed grassy area above the beach. If, however, you come with only the morning free to sunbathe, you will find much of the beach in shade in the early part of the day.

Beachcombing This is a small beach, and largely restricted to the north. Turn left as you approach the beach to make your way—if the tide is not too high—a couple of hundred metres along the shore to the beginning of the raised shore walkway that will lead you to the village of Crofton and the creature comforts it can afford the hungry or thirsty walker.

Seclusion This is a public park, but a small and quiet one. If you want an intimate chat or if you feel a little contemplative, you can come to this park with the expectation that you will find plenty of space and few prying eyes or ears.

79
OSBORNE BAY REGIONAL PARK
A long trail through woods leading down a high bank to a pebbly shore

Location, signs and parking Making your way to this park is a bit of a (scenic) trek, though an excursion here could well be combined with exploring the offerings in the immediate vicinity of Crofton. Leave Highway 1A at Adelaide Street (the highway is called York Avenue in the northerly direction and Osborne Bay Road in the southerly direction). Adelaide will, in turn, transform itself into Smith Road. Watch out for Barnes Road on your left, but stay on Smith almost to the end of the road. Be warned, though: the approach to the park itself is peculiar. As you drive cheerfully along Smith Road, look for a gravelly branch angling slightly uphill to the left and coming to a stop 50 m later in a gravel area outside a wooden-fence-enclosed grassy field. You may feel you are in the middle of nowhere, but a few small signs will reassure you that you are, indeed, at Osborne Bay Regional Park. The gravel area has space for seven or eight cars, but, in the kind of pinch that is unlikely to occur in this area, more could park along the edge of the road.

Unlike most signs at shore access spots, the ones at Osborne Bay Park are worth pausing over. You will want to notice, for example, not only that you will be fined a whopping $100 if you are caught in the park after dusk and before dawn, but also that your dog is being addressed: "Grrrrr, ruff, woof woof. Good dog." In case you are not up on your dogspeak, you are provided with an English translation: "Supervise and pick up after your dog." An additional sign is full of all sorts of prohibitions and warnings; if you have your small children with you, though, you will particularly want to watch

Osborne Bay

out for the warning that the "edge drops off sharply from pathway" and that the path is bristling with "trip hazards due to root and rock outcroppings." A raccoon-frustrating chain-suspended litter barrel is good to note as a place to dump your picnic leftovers on your return from the shore.

Path In spite of the warnings of the conscientious sign makers, the path is generally very good. It is also very long. Fortunately, the grass is generally cut in the field between you and the beginning of the wide, crushed gravel path that enters the second-growth forest of firs. Keep an eye out for the purple and chartreuse birdhouses decorating the route. After a couple of hundred metres, the path turns parallel to the shore—visible some 30 m below through the firs and some of the largest arbutus you will see anywhere. A user-made dirt trail soon branches down the shore, but, being sensible, you will carry on down the main gravel path. Those who want to get to the shore quickly can opt for a series of 30 tie-and-gravel steps; others will carry on down the gradually sloping main trail.

Beach The upper beach is a pleasantly sit-on-able stretch of fine gravel, crushed shells and many, many logs. Even at low tide, the water is not very far away.

Suitability for children Most children won't be thrilled by the long walk from the family car (or even less by the trudge back up the hill). Most, however, should find the long, level shore affords lots of opportunity for romping, log jumping, stone throwing and the like. An improvised rope swing suggests that other children have been eager to find diversion here.

Suitability for groups If a medium-sized beach-questing group is not expecting picnic tables or any other of the accoutrements of a group outing, they certainly will have enough room in this park to get up to whatever they wish to get up to. Space is not an issue, and the likelihood of overcrowding very small.

View Few spots on the east coast of Vancouver Island provide such a virtually untouched sense of forest and ocean. In part, this is because the steep wooded bank that sweeps to the south is undeveloped—and will not be easily developed. In part, too, this sense of wilderness is created by the fact that the even steeper shore of Salt Spring Island, only a few kilometres away, is also largely undeveloped. The only surprising intrusion into this mostly empty seascape is a mysterious structure (related to mariculture?) a couple of hundred metres down the shore and extending well into the water.

Winds, sun and shade Even on a windy day, beachgoers will not be buffeted here. Particularly sheltered from a southeast wind, this bit of shore is only slightly exposed to a northwest wind. Catching full sun in the morning, the upper shore is completely sunk in shadow for the later part of the day. A beach explorer who is also a sun lover could do worse than start the day at Osborne Bay Park and afterward backtrack a few kilometres to Crofton Community Beach, just as it starts to be flooded with afternoon sun.

Beachcombing Because the shore is flat and without awkward boulders or slippery shelves, the beachcomber can walk a considerable distance in either direction. If you are such a beachcomber-to-be, however, try to avoid high tide where the upper shore, though passable, is overhung with trees.

Seclusion Except for a few fellow beachgoers, you are not likely to run into many people here—nor will you be exposed to binocular-wielding house owners. In short, you will be more than able to Be Yourself.

Maple Mountain Forest Reserve

MAPLE MOUNTAIN FOREST RESERVE is a huge chunk of rugged forest land between Crofton and Maple Bay. Steep bluffs lead down to Sansum Narrows, which separates Vancouver Island from Salt Spring Island. A network of trails—roughly in the form of three parallel trails—runs between the north and south approaches to this area (Chilco Road on the north, Arbutus Avenue on the south). One of these trails runs next to the steep rocky shore for several kilometres and thus can be—roughly—considered a shore trail. Don't, however, expect to find any isolated little pocket beaches along this coast—there aren't any! Those interested in exploring these trails can find a trail map by searching the Municipality of North Cowichan website at http://www.northcowichan.bc.ca/.

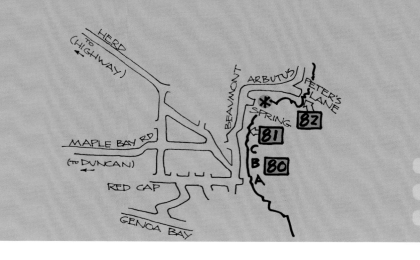

80
MAPLE BAY A, B AND C
Several different access spots to this pebbly beach in the middle of a charming village

Next to the huge chunk of wild, steep shoreline south of Crofton lies the tiny village of Maple Bay. Nestled into a friendly bit of geography, the village has four points of access within a short distance of each other. A short drive north out of Maple Bay brings an additional two.

Getting to Maple Bay from the main highway is both difficult and easy. It is difficult because the village is a long way from the highway; it is easy because there are so many routes you can choose. Additionally, because Maple Bay itself is a village, it is well signposted along the various routes. Herd Road and Maple Bay Road (obviously) are the two main roads in the near vicinity to Maple Bay.

Few will probably want to seek out Redcap Steps (A), located at the end of the quirkily named street from which the well-developed access takes its name. This, the southernmost access, provides parking for a few cars and, as the name suggests, a route to the shore down a flight of 58 well-maintained steps. Anyone wanting to spend time on an attractive beach, though, is better off going to Maple Bay Beach access (see next entry), the northernmost of the four close access spots.

Less than 100 m north is the small parking area for the public docks (B), possibly of interest to those toting a canoe or kayak on their roofs and finding it easiest to launch from docks rather than a ramp. Most kayakers or canoers, however, will want to go to Maple Bay Boat Ramp (C) a few houses farther north.

Maple Bay Boat Ramp (C) is the main access point for Maple Bay.

Location, signs and parking Moving from south to north brings you to this, the third in the sequence of public access spots off Beaumont Road (the road that runs parallel to the shore of the tiny village of Maple Bay). The ramp itself is clearly visible from Beaumont Road, particularly since a small parking lot allows a clear view toward the water. At the head of the concrete ramp itself is a sign indicating the conditions of use and, in the process, evincing a good deal of common sense. The paved parking area has room for a dozen cars, but, if the lot happens to be full, more parking is possible along the street.

Path There is no path as such, since you can step out of your car and walk directly down the ramp a few steps away. At the same time, though, be aware that many use this spot rather than the Beach Park slightly to the north as an access to the beach, presumably because, ironically, it is so easy to park close to the beach.

Beach The beach is much used by locals, even into the warm days of September, and well past the warmest part of the day. Although the strip of gravel and sand of the upper beach is backed for most of its length by a high concrete wall, the beach retains a surprisingly cheerful and attractive feeling—particularly at high tide, when swimming (or snorkelling) are the most obvious alternatives to kayaking. Kayakers will be pleased to discover, in fact, that the waters of Maple Bay are well protected from foaming wind-waves in all but the very most vehement weather. They will likewise be pleased that the beach's sand-and-pebble shore makes a welcome spot on which to pull up their kayaks after a hard paddle.

Suitability for children Parents planning to stay here a long time may prefer to take their children to the public beach access a little farther north, if only because of the picnic tables and toilets provided there. Otherwise, they will find that this is a great spot for their children to wander along the shore and, even in moderately warm weather, that this is one of the most delicious swimming beaches in the area.

Suitability for groups Limited parking and the comparatively narrow beach, especially at high tide, make this spot suitable only for a small group. A minivan-sized family, accompanied by Granny and Gramps, for example, will be welcome here. The entire McRumpus Clan will not.

View This is the kind of view that most would describe as "lovely" or "charming" rather than "stunning" or "inspiring." But lovely and charming it is. The largely unspoilt contours of steeply bluffed Salt Spring Island across Maple Bay itself, and then Sansum Narrows, are both gentle and reassuring. Even the far shore of Maple Bay, largely undeveloped, is refreshingly clean and uncluttered by human impact.

Winds, sun and shade Theoretically, this shore is completely protected from northwest winds and exposed to southeast winds. As at so many other places, however, convoluted geography can provide twists and turns in wind direction. Bring your sun-protection paraphernalia. Except in the first part of the morning and the last part of the afternoon, the beach is fully in the sun. And this, in part, makes it a great swimming beach in summer. Shade seekers can still enjoy the beach—if they move up 100 m to the Maple Bay Beach (see entry 81).

Beachcombing To the north, there is little scope to roam. To the south, however, it is possible to stroll unimpeded for a couple of kilometres until you run into Birds Eye Cove Marina. In fact, the adventure race called Mind Over Mountain has used the strip of shore between the launching ramp and the marina for part of its shore-running route. Emulate these gutsy athletes and you, too, can extend your shore walk to an assault on Mount Tzouhalem immediately to the south.

Seclusion This is a beach on which to see and be seen. Since, however, this is a family beach rather than an abs and/or bikini beach, you will not feel On Display so much as in the company of friendly folk—dotted along the shore, never cheek by jowl along it.

81

MAPLE BAY BEACH

A community park with a small grassy area, washrooms, picnic table and a protected pebbly beach

Location, signs and parking At the northernmost end of Beaumont Avenue—and the east-facing strip of beach—Maple Bay Beach is immediately identifiable by the gravelled parking strip and the chain-link fence. Don't expect a huge sign announcing the park's existence, even though the park is sizable for a village park. The signs declaring beach rules and closing times are located immediately above the beach rather than in the parking spot. Twenty or so cars can easily be accommodated here. Even better, the lot seems rarely to be full.

Path Although the path is well maintained and smooth, it is considerably longer and requires more huffing and puffing than does the boat ramp a short distance south. The 2 m wide asphalt path drops about 10 m over the course of about 50 m. Wheelchairs could be used on the path but only with a good set of emergency brakes for the approach to the beach and athletic assistance for the return journey. The solid metal handrail could well be useful for those with walking difficulties.

Beach The beach is backed by a grassy park area with a few big leafy trees, picnic tables, a litter bin, and—of great interest to some—a public washroom (of grimly functional concrete blocks). The beach itself is more or less the northern terminus of the strip that extends south through the entire bay. Look at the description of the Maple Bay Boat Ramp for more on the beach itself.

Suitability for children Those who want to get to the beach most quickly and easily will choose the boat ramp access to the south. Those who want not just the toilets and picnic tables but also early-day shade and a grassy area as an alternative to the sand-and-pebble beach will choose this spot. The grassy area is really a sequence of fairly steep tiers—great for rolling and romping, but not for Frisbee throwing or tag.

Suitability for groups This is probably one of the best spots to bring a small- to medium-sized group, not just because of the various amenities and easy parking, but also because the beach itself is never really busy. At the same time, the upper beach strip is quite narrow at high tide and doesn't provide the usual wide clutter of logs and pebbles that many a picnicking group might expect.

View Like the view from all points here, the one from this spot is quietly charming, particularly because of the graceful sweep of the bluffs on Salt Spring Island to the south.

Winds, sun and shade The spot is well protected from the northwest and exposed to the southeast. Because of the few large trees in the grassy area, it is possible to find sun or shade at any point of the day, if you are willing to move your beach blanket and lawn chair from spot to spot. By late afternoon, however, the sun will be behind you, and the concrete retaining wall backing the beach will cast a solid wall of shadow.

Beachcombing Look at the notes for the previous access spot, Maple Bay.

Seclusion Secluded this spot isn't: you're in the middle of a village. Quiet, however, it is. Come expecting to be far from the madding (or maddening) crowds.

✳ **Also nearby Spring Street.** Stairs provide another access to the north end of Maple Bay. Spring Street is a short street leading more or less directly to the shorefront top of a wooded bank. A steep flight of wooden stairs leads through arbutus to a shore composed largely of rock. This is a pleasantly secluded spot close to a busy village centre, but not the kind of shore that most would seek out for a very long visit.

82

PETER'S LANE
A tiny, quiet cove at the north
end of Maple Bay

Location, signs and parking Driving north out of Maple Bay on Arbutus, you will have to keep a sharp eye out for this obscure little street on your right, particularly since it doesn't appear on many maps of the area. Park at the end of the short, wooded street.

Path A dirt track leads directly ahead and down, dropping considerably as it passes through the woods toward the shore. Although the path itself presents no difficulties, getting onto the shore requires a little care over the jagged bits of rock and (usually) logs.

Beach The path emerges under overhanging oaks onto a tiny cove filled with sharp-angled basalt boulders. Most will not want to linger here, but will immediately make their way to the rocky bluff area projecting to the left. Here a series of large, natural steps allows you to find a pleasant spot to sit. Since the shore drops off quickly, it may be possible to cast a fishing rod from here. An assertive chain-link fence leaves no doubt about the edge of public land on this tiny promontory.

Suitability for children Patient (and sure-footed) children and/or those being lured with the promise of a snack will be cooperative with parents who decide to come here for a short stay. Most children, however, will be happier when they have a lot more scope than they will find here.

Suitability for groups The area is tiny and the access limited. Most groups of more than a cars' worth would be better off in Maple Bay itself.

View It is really the view framed by the high bluffs of Salt Spring Island and Mount Tzouhalem that gives this spot its charm. At the same time, though, don't expect more than a limited scan of the landscape to the south.

Peter's Lane

Winds, sun and shade Expect lots of protection from westerly winds, but none from those blowing up Sansum Narrows. The first part of the day floods the spot with sunlight. Later on, it is the rocky promontory that keeps sun the longest.

Beachcombing Few are the spots that offer less opportunity for walking!

Seclusion Although private property presses up against this narrow spot, the configuration of the shoreline, with the houses among the trees, is such that you might find this a great place to bring your diary or your beloved.

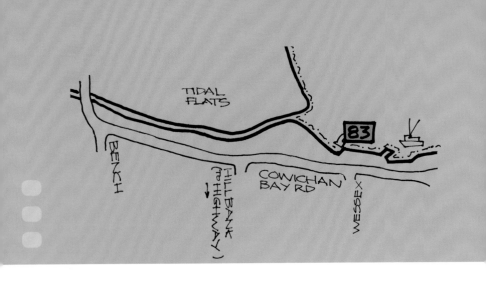

83

HECATE PARK COWICHAN BAY

A park maintained by Cowichan
Valley Parks, Recreation and
Culture, next to a boat ramp on
one side and a beach on the other

Location, signs and parking Once you have passed the estuary end of
Cowichan Bay and find yourself approaching the marina and village
along Cowichan Bay Road, watch for the large sign for Hecate Park
immediately opposite Wessex Road. You will find a substantial paved
parking area (mostly for the folks launching boats) and interpretative
signs about eelgrass and the purple martin, both distinctive features of
the area. On a fine summer's weekend, the parking lot can be full, so you
might be forced to park adjoining streets.

Path If it's the launching ramp for your eager kayak you're after, head
to the right-hand side of the parking area. If you have beach lounging
in mind, however, head to the left-hand end of the area. From here you
need only cross a narrow stretch of grass and step down onto the gently
sloping upper beach.

Beach The beach, about 75 m long, is set into a small bay facing roughly
northwest. The eelgrass interpretative sign is, unsurprisingly, there for a

reason. At low tide, these emerald green fronds drape thickly all over the shore. At high tide, they wave in the currents and provide the habitat for all sorts of creatures, including spider crabs and, in deep water, the highly edible Dungeness crab. If swimming, or even snorkelling, is paramount in your mind, choose high tide, when you can launch yourself from the beach well above the fronds of the eelgrass. Picnicking is comfortable on the upper beach, but some might prefer to take a Roman feast to the picnic tables.

Suitability for children Besides the easy proximity of the beach from the car, the park has many of those qualities that make beach-going life easy for the parent and giddy fun for the child. The picnic area, toilets, grassy spot, and above all, the gently sloping, safe beach all add up to the most child-friendly spot for many kilometres in either direction. Most children will be happiest at mid to high tide, when the eelgrass beds are out of sight.

Suitability for groups Bring your wedding party for a photo shoot or your extended family for a picnic, but do be aware that the beach area is not huge, particularly at high tide.

View Unlike any of the views north of here, this one is dominated by a large mass of rocky land rising directly in front: 500 m Mount Tzouhalem and its spectacular cliffs. The view otherwise is largely directed inland to the wooded shores (and industrial areas) at the estuary end of Cowichan Bay.

Winds, sun and shade Sometimes winds blow directly onto the shore from the northwest, but the beach is sheltered from the southeast. The only shade on the beach itself starts appearing well into the afternoon. The rest of the day, it's up to you and your beach umbrella. On the other hand, a few patches of shade are always to be had on the grassy area.

Beachcombing This is not a place to wander very far from the beach. To the left you will be cut off by private land and docks. To the right you will be struggling along a breakwater toward the marinas that line the whole next section of coast. Fortunately, at low tide, particularly for those interested in sand dollars, starfish and moon snails, there is a lot of exploring to be done in the immediate vicinity.

Seclusion The desire for seclusion is the last thing that could possibly bring you to this busy and bustling area.

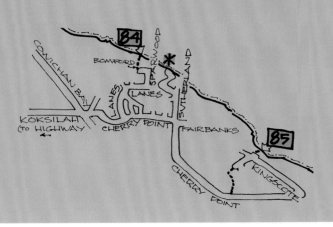

84

BOMFORD TRAIL

An obscure and quiet wooded path down a high bank to a level, pebbly shore

Location, signs and parking This spot just may win the prize as requiring the highest number of twists and turns from the inland highway to find. If, however, you decide to visit a few spots in the area and discover how pleasant it is to explore this land of rolling hills, farms and woods, then you can look forward to a wonderful day's outing. Probably the easiest route is to leave the highway on Koksilah Road and remain on it until you come across a little housing development. Turn left on Lanes Road until, after a surprisingly placed stop sign, you turn right, still on Lanes Road, then left onto Sparwood Road and finally left onto Bomford—whereupon you will be convinced that you have made a wrong turn. Before you will lie a private track—or so you might think. In fact, a few metres down this track and behind a screen of trees, you will find a welcoming parking area of crushed gravel.

Parking There is room for several cars in this well-groomed gravel area, but it is unlikely that you will find the spot crowded—and fairly likely that you will be alone.

Path This spot is identified as Bomford *Trail* rather than Bomford *Beach* for a fairly good reason. Though other spots will give you more of a trek to the shore than this one, you should come here willing to enjoy the pleasures of the walk itself. The trail begins, enticingly, as a clearly labelled, meadowy strip between rustic fences. Before long, you will find yourself turning toward the shore and walking a couple of hundred metres through dappled woods. In spring, keep an eye open for small patches of trillium. After a gradual descent, you will begin a much more considerable series of switchbacks down a forested bank of cedar and alder.

Beach Clearly this shore gets little wave action—the overhanging alders come right down to the few logs that tuck under them. The beach is probably at its best in the morning on a medium tide. The strip of soft dry sand and shells at the top of the beach is pleasant for perching, nestling or brooding. The gradually sloped mid-beach of small pebbles extends for some distance in either direction, but at low tide gives way to a 30 or 40 m strip of muddy, wet sand alternating with small rocks—fine to swim over, but not pleasant to walk on.

Suitability for children Few children would choose this as a favourite spot, given the average child's distaste for lengthy tromps and the relatively featureless beach. This is not to say, however, that many a child (witness the rope swing and treehouse down the shore) would hesitate to splash and explore. Be mindful that there are no facilities.

Suitability for groups Parking is fine for a small group, the walk pleasant and the picnic and strolling areas adequate.

View The view is intriguing, surprisingly varied and at its best during spring, when there is still some snow on the mountains to the north. The shore sweeps in a broad, heavily forested curve to the north and the end of Cowichan Bay. The striking contours of Mount Tzouhalem (more a rugged hill than a mountain) across Cowichan Bay give way to lower ground and, behind, the rising bluffs of Salt Spring. To the south, the view is more enclosed, framed by Cherry Point Marina at the end of the bay.

Winds, sun and shade Both northwest and southeast winds blow onto shore here, though indirectly. This is one of those north-facing, high-banked beaches common to the east coast of the Island, where the sun falls onto the upper beach only during the first few hours of the day.

Beachcombing The beach doesn't invite walking a great distance in either direction, though partway down the beach, the smooth surface of small pebbles makes it is easy to walk a few hundred metres.

Seclusion Except for a single beach house (actually jutting onto the beach), there is not much evidence of fellow humans nearby. Chances are you will be alone, unviewed and unviewing.

✳ **Also nearby** **Cherry Point Marina** is chiefly of interest to those who are looking for a place to launch a canoe or kayak to explore the shore between Cowichan Bay and Cherry Point. You may wish to phone 250-748-0453 for current launching rates. It is true that paddle-craft can be launched at points in either direction (Hecate Park or Cees and Miep Hof Park), but in the latter case, not so easily at low tide. It is possible to get onto the beach here at low tide for a bit of an amble, although the gravelly beach with its overhanging trees on the foreshore doesn't make for the most appealing beach walk. If you do come here, it would be courteous (and satisfying in other ways!) to treat yourself to a snack from the little shop.

To find the marina, turn onto Sutherland Road where Cherry Point takes a sharp turn and follow Sutherland to the end.

85
CEES AND MIEP HOF MEMORIAL PARK
Connected to a creek trail leading to a sand-and-pebble beach with views of nearby Salt Spring Island

Location, signs and parking Enjoy the meander through the pastoral scenery on your way from the highway along Koksilah Road. After a wiggle in the otherwise straight road, you will find that Koksilah has renamed itself Cherry Point Road, but it, too, has surprises—you will have to take a sharp right-hand turn at Fairbanks to stay on Cherry Point Road. Eventually you will see Kingscote Road on your left; follow this until you see a monumental sign telling you that you have arrived at Cees and Miep Hof Memorial Park.

Feeling spry? You can save two or three kilometres of driving by approaching the shore part of the park on foot through a lovely, streamside path. If you are up for this two-kilometre walk, keep alert for the park sign on Cherry Point Road and pull into the clearly marked parking area. There is plenty of parking for several cars in the gravel area off the side of the road and immediately in front of the estimable sign.

Path A crushed gravel path leads some 50 m toward the beach about 10 m below you—clearly visible through the lattice of small alders that line it on one side (and the lattice of a local resident's chain-link fence on the other.) Just before the shore, you will see a picnic table and, shortly thereafter, a park bench. If you have taken the path from Cherry Point Road more than a kilometre back, be aware that this path splits, allowing you to exit onto either of two short sections of approach road to the beach section of the park. You will almost certainly want to take the left fork from Cherry Point Road, since it will bring you to the cul-de-sac at the end of Kingscote Road, only a couple of hundred metres from the shore-bound trail. The alternative, right-branching trail will bring you out to Paradise Close, where you will have to walk about a kilometre down the roadway to the shore access.

Beach This is probably the beachiest beach in the entire area. Indeed, even before you step onto it, you will feel from the strip of tall beach grass and the logs among the sugary white dry sand that this is a Proper Beach. At low tide, the dry sand yields to a strip of pebbles (sprouting the odd barnacle) and, at the water's edge, a fine area of castle-worthy sand. While the gently shelving shore extends far in both directions, it is really only in the area of the park that you or your child's tender feet will find good sand.

Suitability for children This is almost the perfect park for children. The short, even path, the picnic table, the gentle, sandy beach, and even the mixture of sun and shade make this (almost) perfect for the classic afternoon at the beach. Just be aware that there is no toilet.

Suitability for groups Although you would not want to overwhelm the quiet neighbourhood with more than a few cars' worth of merry folk, you could certainly plan an outing here for a happy picnic of two or three families or—given the view—a group of artists.

View Although the view might seem a little enclosed for those expecting to see wide stretches of water or distant mountains, it is nevertheless very, very pretty. The lumps and bumps of the rugged hills around Cowichan Bay to the north and Salt Spring directly across, combined with the gentle curve of the treed shore, make for a lot of eye pleasure.

Winds, sun and shade Surprisingly, the southeast wind is a little fresher here than one might expect, given the angle of the shore. Still, if it is cooler than you want, you can escape most of its effects on the upper beach. In fact, neither northwest nor southeast wind strikes the shore directly, but both can be felt—for good or ill. Except when there are no leaves on the small alders above the shore, you will be able to find both sun and shade, due in large part to the gentle angle of the land behind the beach and the openings in the trees. Indeed, this beach is unusual along this section of coast in that regard—but do come prepared with sun protection for those determined to stay out of the shade.

Beachcombing Because of the pebbly, gently shelving mid-beach, it is possible to walk a considerable distance in either direction. You will probably want to wear sturdy water shoes, though, particularly at low tide, when you will be tempted to go close to the water's edge and are sure to find yourself squelching through tidal pools.

Seclusion Although there is a housing development immediately behind the park and a house close to the path to the beach, for the most part you will feel yourself well away from the public eye—not least of all because the park itself is unlikely to be crowded.

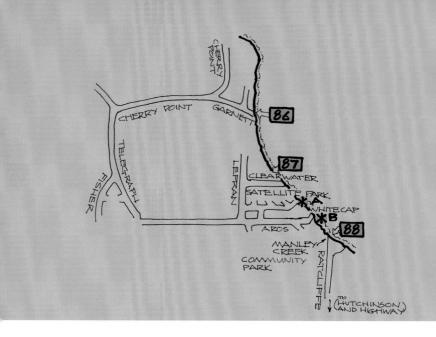

86

CHERRY POINT NATURE PARK

A few steps from car to an expansive sand and pebble beach with views of Mount Baker

Location, signs and parking Like many other spots in this area, Cherry Point requires a bit of a "scenic drive" from the highway. Getting there, you will have to remind yourself, is half the fun. In this case, the getting there can be most easily done from the north by following this sequence of roads: Koksilah, Telegraph, Cherry Point and Garnett to its end (though inventive map readers will try many other routes through the maze). Drivers from the south will have a much shorter backroads journey. They need only turn at Fisher Road (Cobble Hill traffic lights) until it turns into Telegraph Road, and from there onto Cherry Point to the end of Garnett Road. There is a lot of easy parking here in the large, area immediately adjoining the shore. A big sign in the corner of the parking lot includes a map of the beach and the immediate area.

Path The "path" could hardly be less a path. A few horizontal, level metres will take you, and whatever weighs you down, from your car to the beach. Kayakers, should, however, not get too excited by this information unless they really like carrying their kayaks a long distance to the water's edge: the tide goes out a long way here. A careful reading of tide tables, or using the spot in autumn and winter months, could nevertheless mean that you can launch and exit your kayak easily at high tides. Intrepid winter explorers will want to put this spot on the map as a perfect place to have their thermos-coffee and muffins while perched close to the water's edge.

Beach A languid little stream to the left of the parking area seems to be responsible for having made the large fan-shaped stretch of tidal flats. The upper beach, with its fine dry sand, logs and even clusters of beach grass, is the most typically beachy part of this spot. The extensive lower beach has some sandbars, often edged by "sea lettuce," but is mostly pebbles (and, of course, barnacles). Most picnickers will choose the upper beach—or picnic benches—to set up camp, but some families move farther out to one of the sandbars where, on a warm day, the sand becomes dry enough to allow comfortable roosting.

Suitability for children This is by far the most child-friendly beach in the immediate area—particularly if the beach-seeking child likes to have sand, warm water, lots of afternoon sun and play-logs, all on gently sloping shore. Add the conveniences of public toilets and the family car a few metres from the beach, and you have the recipe for a relaxing day at the beach. That relaxation will be maximized, however, if you bring water shoes and protection against the elements.

Suitability for groups This is a great place for a small- to medium-sized group. It is officially a nature park, though it is hard to see how it offers more nature than many other parks in the area that are not nature parks. Birders, however, are particularly aware of its suitability as a seabird viewing spot—and, indeed, use it as one of their officially designated spots for bird counts. Other nature lovers can use the spot as the beginning of a walk to one of the access spots to the south (Manley Creek, the last of three alternatives, being the most obvious destination). Frisbee throwers, kite fliers and picnickers will also find this a good spot for their group.

View Cherry Point is less a point than a slight bulge in the shoreline. In any case, this park isn't right on the "point," but rather partway into the shallow bay to the south. Thus your view both north and south is a little enclosed, however prettily, by heavily wooded, gently rising hills. To the east, however, the view is more immediately striking, with the rising bulk of Salt Spring Island to the north, the gentle undulations of the Saanich Peninsula directly ahead, and, rising magnificently above it all on a clear day, Mount Baker.

Winds, sun and shade If a northwest wind actually is blowing from the northwest, rather than curving down the channel, you will feel little such wind here. A southeast wind, though, is fresh enough that kite surfers sometimes use the beach, scudding back and forth decoratively under brightly coloured sails. On a sunny day, this is a full-on sunny beach, from early morning to late afternoon and into the evening. All of the protective creams, devices and clothing you can muster should be mustered in hot summer weather.

Beachcombing Though you are not likely to find many curiosities while walking along the shore, you can nevertheless make this the starting point for a good deal of stretching out. Do keep an eye open for (common) seals and (uncommon) harbour porpoises as you walk. The notes on nearby Manley Creek Park indicate how—at least when the tide is out—you can make this part of a walk of several kilometres.

Seclusion Although little known beyond the immediate area, the beach, particularly at low tide, is popular with families in warm weather, and with intrepid dog walkers in any weather!

87

CLEARWATER ROAD
A flight of stairs to a gravelly shore suitable for long-distance walks

Location, signs and parking If you are seeking out this spot from Highway 1, you might feel you're in something of a labyrinth of byways for a small prize at the end. If, however, you are exploring the area and would like an alternative to two more obvious access spots on either side, then it could be worthwhile making your way through the labyrinth. Leaving the highway at Fisher Road, angle back onto Telegraph Road on your right. From there, the sequence of Aros, Lefran (in the Douglas Hill Estates) and finally Clearwater Road will bring you to a small gravel area with that welcome BEACH ACCESS sign on a spanking new stairway post. The only other sign is one telling you to have no campfires. There is a small gravel turnaround area at the end of the narrow, shaded road. There is room for a few cars, but all will have to be careful not to block the driveway on the right.

Path The "path" is a skookum set of wooden stairs—38 in all, though relieved by a pair of landings, the last one with a pretty little built-in bench. The heavily wooded bank is attractively furnished with large firs, alders and swordferns. Those who have the lung capacity to cope with the long flight of stairs but are not sure of foot should be warned that the last 2 m or so is a bit of a scramble over roots and rocks.

Beach As you arrive on the beach, you might be a little put off by the concrete remains of what seems to have been a ramp or wharf. Otherwise, the beach is attractive enough in an enclosed kind of way. The tide does not go out here nearly as far as it does at Cherry Point, the much larger access spot immediately to the north. The shore here does, however, offer sandbars at low tide (the sand is firm but a little sticky), and lots of level, gravelly walking. Trees overhang much of the upper shore, creating a dampish feeling that doesn't encourage much nestling or picnicking.

Suitability for children If children are cheerful with counting out the steps down to and, more significantly, up from the beach, they will find themselves comfortable and amused here. The sandbar will be the magnet—at low tide for digging and romping, at high tide for swimming or paddling.

Suitability for groups Groups will find few reasons to come here, though a group with two vehicles might find it satisfying to leave one vehicle at the Cherry Point spot and one at this point, crossing paths mid-stroll, and thus avoid having to walk the beach twice.

View Because Clearwater Road brings you to the middle of a broad, sweeping bay, this access spot provides a framed view down the last stretch of Sansum Narrows and the characteristic sweep of the bluffs of Salt Spring Island. One of the more dramatic elements of the view is Mount Baker, rising elegantly above the Saanich Peninsula on the other side of Saanich Inlet. One of the less pleasant elements is an industrial wharf emerging from the point to your right.

Winds, sun and shade Because of the funnelling effect of the twisting geography here, winds can be a little fluky. In general, though, a northwest wind is not much felt here, while a southeast wind blows directly onshore. The high wooded bank and northeast exposure of the shore means that sun shines directly onto the upper beach only in the first part of the day.

Beachcombing Beach walking would be one of the main reasons for coming to this access spot, particularly if it can be combined with one of the shore walks either immediately north or south—Cherry Point to the north or Manley Creek Community Park to the south.

Seclusion Expect to see few, if any, others here. If, however, you walk toward Cherry Point, do expect to come across beach-strolling pooches with humans in tow.

✳ Also nearby
A. On the way to Clearwater Road, you can turn down **Satellite Park Drive** and follow it to its end. Here you will find a picnic table and many steps leading down to the pebbly shore. This is really just a continuation of the same piece of shore also accessible from Clearwater Road. Here,

however, the shore is slightly more north-facing and a little less sunny, so it might be a little less appealing.

B. One hundred metres farther south along the same pebbly shore is **Whitecap Road** beach access. Here, too, you descend a high wooded bank before beginning a stroll in either direction. In this case, follow Aros Road to its end and take a slight turn onto the very short Whitecap Road.

88 MANLEY CREEK COMMUNITY PARK

A network of trails beside a gurgling stream leading down a forested bank to the southern end of a pebbly beach

Location, signs and parking Access to this community park from Highway 1 is straightforward: simply turn off the highway at Hutchinson Road about 4 km north of Mill Bay. Arbutus Ridge, also down this road, is signposted off the highway. At the end of Hutchinson Road, turn left onto Ratcliffe Road to the very end (averting your eyes from the industrial site en route). Along with a large colourful sign announcing that you have, indeed, arrived at Manley Creek Community Park are two maps just off the parking area. One of these shows walking trails in the park. The other is a smaller-scale map of the whole area, with two walking routes (see Beachcombing). Additional signs beside a litter bin will remind you of the undesirability of lighting fires, unleashing your dog, partying at night and disrespecting your parks. A huge gravel turnaround provides lots of parking around the perimeter for about 20 cars, though, presumably, in a pinch, more could be parked in the centre.

Path For some, the paths, (there are more than one), will be less the means of getting to the beach than the end. As you look at the map, you might feel you need not just the map but also a GPS to get from your car to the shore. Once you start down the trails, you quickly discover that all the paths converge and reconverge in ways that keep taking you down, down, downward. Before you start your descent, you may want to note that the only toilet (of the portable chemical sort, behind a discreet wooden arrangement) is by the parking lot. You may also wish to note that the three picnic tables in the park are all en route to the shore rather than on the shore itself.

Do take some time to enjoy the paths, even if your goal is the beach. The creek that lends its name to the park is prettily dramatic at some points, running virtually all year, cascading through rocky clefts that approximate a miniature canyon at some points. Most of the way, the path is evenly surfaced with crushed gravel, at two points leading you across bridges over the stream. The final descent to the beach, however, is down 39 strong wooden steps over three flights, the steps in turn leading to another gravel-and-tie series of steps.

Beach The creek that is so decorative through the woods seems considerably less so on the gravel beach. However, it empties on your right, and all of the beach exploring you will want to do is on your left, so you can conveniently ignore the slimy bits of creek-on-shore. The beach itself is a little oddly surfaced, intermingling coarse sand, pebbles and golf-ball-sized stones with larger pieces of flat sandstone sprouting barnacles and rockweed. Low tide reveals a fairly wide stretch of shallowly sloping shore here, but note that if you are planning to make this the starting point of a beach walk, at high tide the beach narrows farther north before widening again toward Cherry Point, a couple of kilometres distant.

Suitability for children Unless you have slightly unusual children (read: enthusiastic about walking), you will probably find only older children would be happy coming here for an afternoon at the beach. For most children, you'll be better off heading for Cherry Point, geographically quite close—but not nearly so close via the tangle of roads. For those high-energy children who do like a good romp, the network of trails and bridges and the wide stretch of level shoreline could make for a good afternoon. If the tide is in, too, in summer the water is quite warm and the gently sloping beach is certainly safe—but do bring water shoes to fend off the barnacles at some points.

Suitability for groups The spot cries out as a starting point (or end point) for a walking group. In winter, when the tide is high for most of the day, such a walking group will probably want to undertake the inland circular route, the Granfield Footpath Loop clearly mapped on the sign at the park entrance (much of this 5.8 km path is on or by lanes and roads).

In summer, though, and particularly if you make arrangements with vehicle shuttles or exchanges, you can walk the two or so kilometres along the level, pebbly shore between this park and that at Cherry Point itself. Like-minded but less ambitious groups may wish to do something similar, but use the Clearwater Road or Champagne Drive access points for an abbreviated version of the shore walk.

View At this end of the bay, the viewer is led naturally to look back through the sweep of bay toward Cherry Point and Salt Spring Island in one direction. In the other direction, though Salt Spring and Mount Baker look pretty enough, they are largely framed by a long industrial wharf emerging from the shoreline only 100 m or so away.

Winds, sun and shade A southeast wind will be felt here; a northwest wind less so—though in this area, wind predictions that you hear on the radio won't necessarily be those you experience. Largely north-facing and backed by a high wooded bank, the upper shore is in sun only in the first part of the day. If you want to mingle sun and shade, though, and if the tide is out, you can expect the lower beach to be in sun most of the day.

Beachcombing This is a spot where beach walking is almost official! Wear water shoes if you want to walk near the water's edge at low tide, though; the various shallow tidal pools and wet areas of shore are guaranteed to soak even sturdy walking shoes.

Seclusion This is a popular spot—but it is a large park. While you will see others on the shore during peak times, they will be spread out. More important, you will not feel, as you do at many other access spots, under the scrutiny of local residents with telescopes!

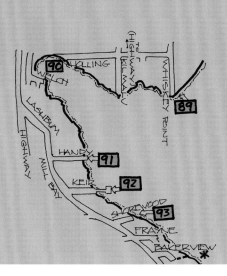

89

WHISKEY POINT ROAD
A well-marked trail to a rocky shore, chiefly of interest because there is no other access point in the area

Location, signs and parking If you have just visited Mill Bay Nature Park (see next entry), simply keep driving straight ahead until Holling turns into Whiskey Point Road, curves toward the shore and grinds to a halt. PUBLIC ACCESS and SHELLFISH WARNING signs will, implicitly, congratulate you on your navigation skills. Although there are driveways to be considered, this is not the kind of area that specializes in cheek-by-jowl houses, so there is plenty of room to pull over onto the shoulder.

Path You will have to put in a little effort to enjoy the beach at this access spot. Follow a gravel path about 100 m through a strip of firs and swordferns. The path crosses two little wooden bridges over a deeply rutted ditch, dry throughout most of the summer and fall. The path descends considerably, perhaps 20 m, and concludes in steps onto the shore.

Beach Not many will find the beach particularly attractive. There is little area on the upper shore that invites resting or munching or much else. The tide does not go out very far here, but when it does go out, it reveals some rough and slightly muddy-looking boulders.

Suitability for children Children in the right mood can enjoy themselves anywhere. If you have not told your brood that you are going to the beach but on an exploration, then they could well romp (a little awkwardly) over the rocks, splashing their way to good humour. If, however, they are expecting to build sandcastles, they will not be happy.

Suitability for groups The area is too confined and the attractions too limited to warrant bringing the rugby or primrose-fanciers' clubs here.

View The unusual view will please most collectors of Island views. This, in fact, is the best spot to see the steeply wooded hills behind Mill Bay and the village itself. It is possible to see a bit down toward Saanich Inlet, but the high shore behind prevents your seeing very far in this direction.

Winds, sun and shade There are almost no winds to be felt here, except for the odd blowy day. Since, unusually, the shore faces southwest, it is shady first thing in the morning and baking hot in the middle of a summer afternoon. Photographers or sketchers after unique perspectives on the landscape behind Mill Bay will probably want to come either first thing in the morning or late in the afternoon to avoid backlighting.

Beachcombing The rough shore does not invite strolling, though there will always be those who want to see what is around that corner or under that rock.

Seclusion Except for a beachfront cabin, there are few signs of habitation and few people who are likely to come here. Indeed, this spot could well be the most secluded public access in the whole district.

90

MILL BAY NATURE PARK

A sheltered and quiet forest park with access to tidal flats opposite the village of Mill Bay

Location, signs and parking A short distance from the highway, about a kilometre north of Mill Bay, this nature park is easily reached by turning first onto Kilmalu Road, then onto Holling Road. A beautifully crafted and impressively large sign clearly marks the park entrance. Once you turn down the gravel drive past the park sign, turn right into the oval parking lot, with its spots for a dozen or so cars.

Path Because this is a wooded nature park, it is threaded through with several forest trails. The path that takes you to the shore, however, leads directly ahead and to the left. A well-graded but significantly sloped forest path concludes with 23 very solid wooden steps onto the beach. Your eye will be first caught by an overhanging cedar tree. While you are here, be sure to explore some of the other forest trails, particularly the one that leads to a dramatically jutting platform from which, it seems, you are to view "nature"—including whatever is bobbing about on the water through the screen of trees.

Beach It is hard to find a more sheltered or enclosed beach anywhere. The result of its being so enclosed, however, is that waves have not exposed much upper beach, nor smoothed out stones. At low tide, considerable tidal flats are exposed, replete with all the creatures Islanders expect to encounter, and sometimes eat, on such flats. Again, because of the lack of wave action, the flats are best described as squelchy. When the tide is high (in summer, usually during the afternoon or evening), there is only enough shore left to squeak into a perching spot among the fine pebbles.

Suitability for children While this is not an obvious spot to seek out for an afternoon's water play, it does have features that make it suitable for certain kinds of outings with children. There is a (chemical) toilet; the paths are easy; the shore is level and easily trod; and, perhaps most important, unlike many other bits of shore in the area, on even a cool afternoon, this one is flooded with sun and devoid of wind.

Suitability for groups Small groups, and those whose chief interest is nature—photographing it, painting it, identifying it, or poking at it—would be happiest with this spot. Groups whose chief goals are social or gastronomic will be reasonably happy here, but probably happier elsewhere.

View At low tide, the view might seem a little dank unless you have a taste for this kind of tidal flat. At mid to high tide, however, you will find the close, deeply inset bay overhung by trees easy on the eyes. In addition, this is one of the few spots that allows a view back onto Vancouver Island and, in this case, the steep hills forming the beginning of the Malahat.

Winds, sun and shade You will be hard-pressed to find a spot more protected from winds—all winds. Because this bit of shore faces west, it is shady in the morning and sunny in the afternoon and evening. The lower beach, of course, is in full sun all day long.

Beachcombing Low tide makes lots of room to wander out to the water's edge. Keep eyes open for soft-shelled clams and moon snails. Be sure to bring water shoes, though. Avoid flip-flops, since the sometimes muddy sand can suck them from your feet.

Seclusion The park is nearly 3 hectares (over 7 acres) and heavily forested; it is also never crowded. Expect to see others of your ilk, but don't expect to feel crowded or conspicuous.

91

HANDY ROAD
A public boat launch ramp
in the centre of the village
beside a pebbly beach

Location, signs and parking From the centre of Mill Bay's commercial area, Handy Road leads from Mill Bay Road straight to the shore, a block's distance. Like other public accesses in Mill Bay, this one is marked from Mill Bay Road with a blue and white CVRD BEACH ACCESS sign. Straight ahead, you will see a concrete boat-launch ramp and a gravel strip on the left where more than a dozen cars can park. Don't be confused by the sign for Mill Bay Marina and its launching fee since this private facility is immediately beside the Handy Road public ramp. The sign relevant to the public ramp will tell you that you shouldn't launch at low tide—though this applies to cars launching boats from trailers, not those carrying a kayak or canoe.

Path A few concrete steps lead from the parking area, near two refuse bins, directly onto the pebble shore. Otherwise, you can easily get onto the shore from the concrete ramp, since it slopes at a shallow angle.

Beach Most beachgoers coming here will be primarily interested in launching a kayak or other small boat. Because the tide goes out well beyond the ramp, be prepared for a bit of a tromp to the waterline if you come at low tide. The gently shelving pebble beach is pleasant enough and easy walking, though a little stream near the ramp is not its prettiest feature. A fine pebble upper beach, dry at most tides, allows picnicking. Because the foliage presses close behind, however, and there are usually no logs, this isn't the best spot for sitting.

Suitability for children Children will be safe here and, with water shoes, can easily scamper over the pebbles—above or below the waterline. If your children like sand though—and most do—you would be better off going the short distance to Keir Road.

Suitability for groups While parking is plentiful here, there are few other attractions for a group planning anything other than paddling.

View Your view will be dominated by Mill Bay Marina on your right. Photographers and artists are often drawn to marinas, of course, but usually to ones with a higher proportion of commercial fishing boats than are common at this marina. Otherwise, you will see why Mill Bay is called a bay: a woody headland frames either side of your view across to the tip of the Saanich Peninsula.

Winds, sun and shade Neither wind nor sun is a major factor here, but you will be hard-pressed to find any shade.

Beachcombing This isn't the most obvious spot to choose for a beach walk, but it does make for an unusual bit of exploration. The gradually slanting pebbly shore extends a considerable distance in both directions, though you will be able to walk farther if you head south.

Seclusion You are likely to be alone on the beach—but you will be in a village, with houses and boats in all directions.

92
KEIR ROAD
An unusual and pretty public pier with a gazebo and access to a low-tide sandy beach

Location, signs and parking Look for not just the Keir Road sign off Mill Bay Road, but also a vertical blue and white BEACH ACCESS sign. A short block's distance down Keir Road brings you to a small parking area with a large covered sign identifying this tiny public wharf. Because of the unusual nature of this public access, you will see signs unique to this spot. Along with the predictable appeal to leash and clean up after your dog, you will be asked not to vandalize, and to understand that both swimming and use of the "wharfage" are done "at your own risk."

Path Those confined to wheelchairs will find this one of the most welcoming spots on the whole coast to come for some sea air and sea views. A meticulously kept concrete path curves smoothly down from the parking area onto a raised wooden wharf. Once onto the wharf, it is easy to go a few dozen metres to the pretty little gazebo (compliments of the CVRD) suspended over the water. Here, all visitors can sit under shelter on the benches and peer through the clear water at the various sea creatures performing or displaying themselves. The sure-footed may wish to descend the ramp onto the small floating dock. Those who want to get onto the shore itself can use the solid staircase of 14 wooden steps leading from the ramp at the beginning of the pier.

Beach Of the four similar beach access spots close by in Mill Bay, this one is most suited for those wanting sand between their toes. Although the upper shore is pebbly, low tide exposes a considerable stretch of soft sand and sandy tidal pools. Swimmers might be a little frustrated that the shore slopes so gradually. Those wanting a quick dip or easy access to deep water will be happiest either if they come at high tide or if they take their beach towel to the little dock at the end of the pier. Picnicking is possible on the upper shore, but probably more appealing in the gazebo-like sitting area at the end of pier.

Suitability for children Partly because of the sandy offerings of the beach and partly because of the little pier and dock, this is a great place for kids. Choose low tide for sand pies and wading; choose high or mid tide for swimming or splashing over a sandy bottom. In cold weather, bring play nets or fishing lines for sport on the floating dock.

Suitability for groups A couple of families or a small group of explorers might find this an appropriate spot for intermingling and enjoying the sea ambience. Even a small wedding party in search of an unusual setting for the official wedding photos might enjoy this spot—without having to worry overmuch about high heels snapping or twisting!

View Because you can get away from the shore itself, you will find a good deal of variety in the view as you stroll out onto the dock. You can also get a good sense of the geography of the bay, though the head of Mill Bay is not visible. Whiskey Point bounds the bay to your left, while the low land directly across is Patricia Bay (Pat Bay, as the locals call it) and, slightly to the right, the low hills of Saanich Inlet above Ardmore.

Winds, sun and shade A fresh westerly can blow across the considerable expanse of Saanich Inlet at this point and, of course, at the end of the pier you are exposed to all that the elements wish to treat you to. The roofed gazebo is the perfect sun shelter—and, on drizzly days, an equally perfect rain shelter.

Beachcombing This is not a beach that beckons you to explore, in large part because you are in the middle of a village. At the same time, the gently sloping—and easily traversable—pebbly upper shore extends a considerable distance, particularly toward the south.

Seclusion Seclusion should be last on your list of priorities if you choose to come here. That being said, you are unlikely to find more than the odd person strolling past you, either on the pier or on the shore. With a beachfront cabin actually overhanging the beach on one side, and several local residents storing their rowboats and canoes on the beach, you will feel very much as if you have entered a community bit of shoreline.

Shorewood Drive

93

SHOREWOOD DRIVE (MILL BAY)

A short, well-maintained flight of steps to the pebbly shore south of Mill Bay village centre

Location, signs and parking Shorewood Drive, a short and clearly signposted road, leaves Mill Bay Road about a kilometre south of the village centre. Access is a little strange, however; were it not that the CVRD has put so much effort into making the access so kempt and pretty, there would not be a strong argument for including it here. In any case, drive the short distance to the very end of the road and park in a narrow strip of grass and gravel wedged between a low wooden fence on one side and a bushy hedge on the other. One of the vertical blue and white BEACH ACCESS signs, along with a Rotary Club park bench and a natty refuse container, will welcome you. There is probably room for five or six cars, parallel parked—but their drivers will have to be prepared to back up several dozen metres before they can turn around easily.

Path Immediately in front of the bench, a solid wooden staircase leads down to a short flight of concrete steps. A grand total of 36 steps brings you directly onto the pebbly upper shore. Some will be comforted by the solid handrails, particularly useful on the return journey.

Beach Like the shore in the whole Mill Bay area, this one slopes gradually. Here, however, be prepared for more gravel and barnacles than you will find at the Keir Road access to the north. To the left of the shore, the otherwise unrelieved slope of gravel is given character by a small promontory of solid rock. Picnicking is possible at the high-tide line, but, because of the overhanging maples and alders, is not particularly appealing.

Suitability for children At first glance, this might not seem like a good spot to bring your children. Properly shod against barnacles, however, and predisposed to find fun in easily accessible, shallow water, children might enjoy playing here.

Suitability for groups There is no obvious reason for bringing a group here, particularly given the slightly awkward parking. A small group of shore explorers, however, might well enjoy using this as a starting point.

View The view from this Mill Bay spot is considerably less enclosed than that from the spots to the north. From here you can see the telltale hump of Mount Tuam on Salt Spring Island as well as the low-lying features of North Saanich. Make a point, in addition, of casting your eye along the shore immediately to your right and, in particular, to the low rocky point at the end of the curve of shore. This rocky point may well be a spot that you will choose to visit next.

Winds, sun and shade Winds from the south and east are fresh here, but otherwise the shore is fairly protected. The morning is the sunniest part of the day. In fact, this is generally the shadiest beach access in the immediate Mill Bay area, since the bank is high and heavily treed.

Beachcombing If you choose to do so, you can walk a considerable distance in either direction along the gently sloping pebble shore. In one direction you will reach Mill Bay Village, where you might wish to reward yourself with a latte. In the other direction, though, the attractions are mixed. On the negative side, you will find that Mill Road soon runs immediately above the shore. On the positive side, you will find, a couple of kilometres distant, a beautiful little rocky promontory where you might like to rest a while before making your return stroll.

Seclusion Don't be surprised if you are the only one on the shore when you visit, particularly given the more conventionally enticing access spots in either direction. The sense of seclusion is amplified by the fact that the adjoining houses are high on the thickly wooded bank.

✳ **Also nearby** **Bakerview Road** leaves Mill Bay Road south of the village and comes to an end in a small grassy turnaround. A well-maintained dirt track slopes fairly steeply down the bank to a gently sloping pebbly shore. From here it is possible to walk to Mill Bay Village for a sweet treat to punctuate your return trip, though a high tide restricts walking.

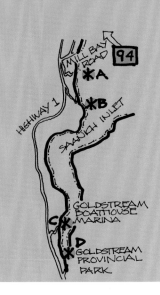

94
MILL BAY ROAD ROADSIDE
A beautiful bluffy area of arbutus, oaks and pebble beaches

Location, signs and parking South of the village of Mill Bay, Mill Bay Road runs immediately above the shore. There are many pretty places where you can stop by simply pulling off onto the shoulder. This means, of course, that you will find life easier if you are driving from south to north. You should know, however, that the road passes through First Nations land. If you choose to stop, respect this fact. Probably the most visited bit of shorefront between Cherry Point and Bamberton, in fact, is that around a little rocky promontory off this stretch of road. If you approach on a sunny day, you will almost certainly see a few cars parked on the shoulder or partway down bumpy dirt tracks leading into the firs, Garry oaks and arbutus. Don't expect any signs, since this is not a public beach access.

Path You will have only a short distance to walk on broad, bumpy dirt tracks that branch out to various spots on this rocky point.

Beach On the south side of the point, the rock bluff leads down to a gradually sloping pebbly beach backing the road. Small sections of pebbly beach on the upper shore of the point itself are interspersed with boulders and sections of solid rock. In contrast, the north side of the point comprises steep lumps of exposed bluffs. Some clusters of pilings offshore tell you something about the history of the spot and either embellish or scar the view, depending on your taste.

Suitability for children Visit the spot on a sunny day, and you will almost certainly see a family or two with children settled among the pebbly bits of beach, or in search of whales and pirate treasure off the steep bits of rock. Sure-footed children will probably be happier than those who are just getting the hang of bipedal movement.

Suitability for groups Although there is plenty of space here for two or three cars' worth of merry picnickers, this is not a public park and shouldn't be treated as such. In addition, of course, there are no facilities.

View Because this is a promontory, it is a great spot for viewing all the features around the northern end of Saanich Inlet. You will see some Island mountains to the north, the distinctive high profile of Salt Spring Island, the low undulations of Saanich Peninsula, and, to the south, the beginnings of the steeper shores of Saanich Inlet. A photographer or sketcher will find dozens of interesting angles and beautifully framed perspectives.

Winds, sun and shade Take your choice. No matter what the time of day or direction of wind, you will find places that expose you or shelter you. If you're nursing a bad sunburn from the previous day, however, you might have to find shelter under the trees rather than on the shore itself.

Beachcombing This is not the place to choose for a beach walk. Remember that, except at a few spots, Mill Bay Road runs close to the shore in either direction.

Seclusion You will be far from the suburban feeling of the other spots in the Mill Bay area; however, you will not find yourself alone.

✱ Also nearby

A. Bamberton Provincial Park is a full-facility park well signposted from the highway. From the pay parking lot (not open until 9 a.m.), stone steps and a broad asphalt track drop a considerable distance to a grassy area with washrooms and picnic benches. The 350 m of shoreline is mostly gently sloping pebbles with a few areas of low-tide sand.

B. The land around **Bamberton cement works** was sold in 2005 to Three Point Properties. These developers have proposed building an environmentally friendly community with a waterfront trail, though it is unclear whether the trail would be open to the general public. The proposal is posted at http://bamberton.com/.

C. Do you want a glimpse of deepest Saanich Inlet but don't have a boat? Do you have a kayak or canoe and would love to paddle in this dramatic wilderness landscape? **Goldstream Boathouse Marina** is a little tricky to get to, but worth keeping in mind for an unusual adventure, particularly because there is no other spot in the immediate area where you can gain access to this part of Saanich Inlet.

To reach it, you need to drive north (on the dangerously busy divided highway). A few minutes after passing Goldstream Park, look for a blue and white sign with the telltale anchor and the name of the marina. A narrow, winding road will bring you down the steep sides of the fjord to the marina. Here you can get a snack from the little shop or launch your craft from the huge concrete launching ramp, really designed for large powerboats. For small paddle-craft, the fees will seem high, but may well be worth paying for an unusual adventure. Keep in mind that the fee covers two kayaks and parking for a single car. Call 250-478-4407 for more information or check http://www.goldstreamboathousemarina.com/.

D. Goldstream Provincial Park is situated at the very end of Saanich Inlet, where the sides of the fjord close in tightly around Goldstream River and its estuary. Those who might expect to use the park as a way of gaining access to the inlet should be aware that the estuary has been closed to the public to encourage the return of wildlife to the area. The park and its visitor centre are well worth a visit, but not because they allow you access to the ocean.

BEST BETS

All beachgoers will find favourite spots, and for the most personal of reasons. Perhaps one beach will become a favourite because of a particular configuration of tidal pools. Another one might have a particularly cozy little nest among beach logs. Yet another might have much-needed public toilets! And so on. As a starting point, however, many will find the following recommendations handy.

PART 1 QUALICUM TO LANTZVILLE

1. Launching kayaks or canoes

14	Mariner Way C
19	Madrona Point Community Park
20	Madrona Point Road A
21	Madrona Point Road B
25	Higginson Road
26	The Jib
32	Seacrest Road
35	Blueback Community Park

2. Bringing small children

1	Judge's Row A, B and C
2	Hall Road
3	Seacrest Place A
11*	McMillan Street
14	Mariner Way C
15	Shorewood Drive
17	Arbutus Road
23	Wall Beach
33	Sunset Cove
40	Ainsley Place

3. Bringing adventurous children

8	Breakwater Road
19	Madrona Point Community Park
22	Craig Drive
23	Wall Beach
24	Seahaven Road
27	Beachcomber Community Park
39	Brickyard Community Park

4. Long beach walks or jogs

1	Judge's Row A, B and C
12–14	Mariner Way A–C
16	Juniper Road
21	Madrona Point Road B
23	Wall Beach
24	Seahaven Road
44	Nanoose Beach Road

5. Birdwatching

7	French Creek Estuary
11	Bay Avenue (brant season)
12*	Englishman River Estuary
23	Wall Beach (high tide)
25	Higginson Road (winter)
40	Ainsley Place
40*D	Nanoose Bay Wildlife Conservation Area

6. Kite flying or Frisbee throwing

4	Seacrest Place C
10	Doehle Avenue
15	Shorewood Drive
17	Arbutus Road
23	Wall Beach

7. Bringing groups

12	Mariner Way A
16	Juniper Road
18	Bay Road
19	Madrona Point Community Park
23	Wall Beach
27	Beachcomber Community Park
39	Brickyard Community Park

8. Afternoon sunbathing

1	Judge's Row A, B and C
13	Mariner Way B
27	Beachcomber Community Park
33	Sunset Cove
34	Park Place Community Park
39	Brickyard Community Park
40*E	Nanoose Beach Road

9. Seclusion

9	Sunray Road
24	Seahaven Road
34	Park Place Community Park
37	Outrigger Road
38	Mallard Place

10. Protection from northwest winds

1   Judge's Row A, B and C
20   Madrona Point Road A
23   Wall Beach
27   Beachcomber Community Park
        (south beach)
32   Seacrest Road
39   Brickyard Community Park
40   Ainsley Place

11. Protection from southeast winds

1   Judge's Row A, B and C
18   Bay Road
19   Madrona Point Community Park
23   Wall Beach
25   Higginson Road
26   The Jib
27   Beachcomber Community Park
        (north beach)
32   Seacrest Road
33   Sunset Cove
34   Park Place Community Park
35   Blueback Community Park

12. Wave watching

6   Admiral Tryon Boulevard
7*   French Creek Marina
        (southeast storms)
27   Beachcomber Community Park
        (northwest storms)
28   Seadog Road
37   Outrigger Road (southeast storms)

13. Foul-weather car picnicking

5   Mallard Road
6   Admiral Tryon Boulevard
14   Mariner Way C
28   Seadog Road

14. Combining with forest walking

12*   Englishman River Estuary
16   Juniper Road
39   Brickyard Community Park

15. Fishing from the rocks

19   Madrona Point Community Park
27   Beachcomber Community Park
38   Mallard Place

16. Snorkelling

24   Seahaven Road
28   Seadog Road
34   Park Place Community Park
39   Brickyard Community Park

17. A variety of shore types

8   Breakwater Road
19   Madrona Point Community Park
23   Wall Beach
33   Sunset Cove
39   Brickyard Community Park

18. A wedding or family photo shoot

12   Mariner Way A
19   Madrona Point Community Park
21   Madrona Point Road B (high tide)
24   Seahaven Road

19. A hilltop view

10   Doehle Avenue
26*   Whitecap Road

20. Those who have walking difficulties

3   Seacrest Place A and B
4   Seacrest Place C
12   Mariner Way A
17   Arbutus Road
23   Wall Beach
24   Seahaven Road

21. Viewing sunsets

1   Judge's Row
18   Bay Road
19   Madrona Point Community Park
25   Higginson Road
26   The Jib
27   Beachcomber Community Park
28   Seadog Road
33   Sunset Cove

PART 2   LANTZVILLE TO CHEMAINUS

1. Launching kayaks or canoes

42   Sebastion Road (high tide)
46   Jack Road
52   Fillinger Crescent A
57   Charlaine Boat Ramp
58   Wheatcroft Park
64   Nelson Road
69   Blue Heron Park
70   Elliott's Beach Park
75   Cook Park
75*B   Kin Park (Chemainus Rotary
        Boat Ramp)

2. Bringing small children
41	Benwaldun Road
45	Tweedhope Road
56	Morningside Beach Area
59	Pipers Lagoon Park
64	Nelson Road
69	Blue Heron Park
70	Elliott's Beach Park
74	Boulder Point
75*B	Kin Park

3. Bringing adventurous children
42	Sebastion Road
44	Huddlestone Road
48	Blueback Road
55	Neck Point Community Park
58	Wheatcroft Park
59	Pipers Lagoon Park
62	Biggs and Jack Point Park
68	Roberts Memorial Provincial Park

4. Long beach walks or jogs
41	Benwaldun Road
42	Sebastion Road
47	Seabold Road Parkette
48	Blueback Road
72	Holland Creek Park
73	Gourlay-Janes Park
74	Boulder Point

5. Birdwatching
55	Neck Point Community Park
56	Morningside Beach Area
58	Wheatcroft Park
59	Pipers Lagoon Park
62	Biggs and Jack Point Park
63	Cable Bay Trail
65	Swan Road
71	Raven Park (high tide)
72	Holland Creek Park

6. Kite flying or Frisbee throwing
41	Benwaldun Road
47	Seabold Road Parkette
49	Invermere Road
59	Pipers Lagoon Park
64	Nelson Road

7. Bringing groups
42	Sebastion Road
43	Harper Road
50	Sealand Park
53	Fillinger Crescent B
55	Neck Point Community Park
56	Morningside Beach Area
59	Pipers Lagoon Park
62	Biggs and Jack Point Park
68	Roberts Memorial Provincial Park
69	Blue Heron Park
74	Boulder Point

8. Afternoon sunbathing
43	Harper Road
44	Huddlestone Road
52	Fillinger Crescent A
55	Neck Point Community Park
56	Morningside Beach Area
59	Pipers Lagoon Park
62	Biggs and Jack Point Park
64	Nelson Road
67	Twin Oaks Drive
70	Elliott's Beach Park
75*B	Kin Park

9. Seclusion
48	Blueback Road
49	Invermere Road
50	Sealand Park
53	Fillinger Crescent B
60	Stephenson Point A
63	Cable Bay Trail
65	Swan Road
66	Slocum Road
67	Twin Oaks Drive
72	Holland Creek Park

10. Protection from northwest winds
55	Neck Point Community Park
56	Morningside Beach Area
59	Pipers Lagoon Park
61	Stephenson Point B
64	Nelson Road
65	Swan Road
70	Elliott's Beach Park
71	Raven Park

11. Protection from southeast winds
- 55 Neck Point Community Park
- 57 Charlaine Boat Ramp
- 59 Pipers Lagoon Park
- 62 Biggs and Jack Point Park
- 65 Swan Road

12. Wave watching
- 46 Jack and Oar roads (southeast storms)
- 51 Entwhistle Drive (all storms)
- 52 Fillinger Crescent A (all storms)
- 55 Neck Point Community Park

13. Foul-weather car picnicking
- 41 Benwaldun Road
- 46 Lavender, Jack, Myron, Oar roads
- 58 Wheatcroft Park

14. Combining with forest walking
- 50 Sealand Park
- 59 Pipers Lagoon Park
- 60 Stephenson Point A
- 62 Biggs and Jack Point Park
- 63 Cable Bay Trail
- 68 Roberts Memorial Provincial Park

15. Fishing from the rocks
- 51 Entwhistle Drive
- 52 Fillinger Crescent A
- 53 Fillinger Crescent B
- 54 Winchelsea Place
- 62 Biggs and Jack Point Park

16. Snorkelling
- 42 Sebastion Road
- 44 Huddlestone Road
- 53 Fillinger Crescent B
- 54 Winchelsea Place
- 68 Roberts Memorial Park

17. A variety of shore types
- 41 Sebastion Road
- 55 Neck Point Community Park
- 59 Pipers Lagoon Park
- 64 Nelson Road

18. A wedding or family photo shoot
- 42 Sebastion Road
- 44 Huddlestone Road
- 52 Fillinger Crescent A
- 58 Wheatcroft Park
- 59 Pipers Lagoon Park
- 69 Blue Heron Park

- 70 Elliott's Beach Park
- 75 Cook Park

19. A high viewpoint
- 47 Seabold Road Parkette
- 51 Entwhistle Drive
- 54 Winchelsea Place
- 55 Neck Point Community Park (McGuffie approach)
- 60 Stephenson Point A
- 60* Stephenson Point Road
- 75* Clifcoe Road

20. Those who have walking difficulties
- 41 Benwaldun Road
- 42 Sebastion Road
- 43 Harper Road
- 55 Neck Point Community Park (special handicapped approach)
- 59 Pipers Lagoon Park
- 64 Nelson Road
- 69 Blue Heron Park
- 70 Elliott's Beach Park
- 75 Cook Park

21. Viewing sunsets
- 51 Entwhistle Drive
- 62 Biggs and Jack Point Park

PART 3 CHEMAINUS TO THE MALAHAT

1. Launching kayaks or canoes
- 76* Crofton Community Seawalk— Town Centre (Crofton boat ramp)
- 80C Maple Bay Boat Ramp
- 83 Hecate Park
- 84* Cherry Point Marina
- 91 Handy Road
- 94*C Goldstream Boathouse Marina

2. Bringing small children
- 78 Crofton Beach Park
- 81 Maple Bay Beach
- 83 Hecate Park
- 85 Cees and Miep Hof Park
- 86 Cherry Point Park
- 94*A Bamberton Provincial Park

3. Bringing adventurous children
- 79 Osborne Bay Regional Park
- 88 Manley Creek Community Park
- 92 Keir Road
- 94 Mill Bay Road Roadside

4. Long beach walks or jogs
- 76   Crofton Community Seawalk— Town Centre (above the shore)
- 80   Maple Bay
- 86   Cherry Point Park
- 88   Manley Creek Community Park

5. Birdwatching
- 78   Crofton Beach Park
- 85   Cees and Miep Hof Park
- 86   Cherry Point Park
- 90   Mill Bay Nature Park

6. Kite flying or Frisbee throwing
- 78   Crofton Beach Park
- 85   Cees and Miep Hof Park
- 86   Cherry Point Park
- 87   Clearwater Road
- 94*A   Bamberton Provincial Park

7. Bringing groups
- 76   Crofton Community Seawalk— Town Centre
- 78   Crofton Beach Park
- 79   Osborne Bay Regional Park
- 81   Maple Bay Beach
- 85   Cees and Miep Hof Park
- 86   Cherry Point Park
- 94*A   Bamberton Provincial Park

8. Afternoon sunbathing
- 78   Crofton Beach Park
- 83   Hecate Park
- 86   Cherry Point Park
- 92   Keir Road
- 94   Mill Bay Road Roadside

9. Seclusion
- 79   Osborne Bay Regional Park
- 82   Peter's Lane
- 84   Bomford Trail
- 89   Whiskey Point Road

10. Protection from northwest winds
- 80A   Redcap Steps
- 81   Maple Bay Beach
- 86   Cherry Point Park

11. Protection from southeast winds
- 78   Crofton Beach Park
- 83   Hecate Park

12. Wave watching
see sections I and II

13. Foul-weather car picnicking
- 86   Cherry Point Park
- 92   Keir Road
- 94   Mill Bay Road Roadside

14. Combining with forest walking
- 79   Osborne Bay Regional Park
- 84   Bomford Trail
- 85   Cees and Miep Hof Park
- 88   Manley Creek Community Park

15. Fishing from the rocks
- 82   Peter's Lane

16. Snorkelling
- 81   Maple Bay Beach
- 94   Mill Bay Road Roadside

17. A variety of shore types
- 78   Crofton Beach Park
- 94   Mill Bay Road Roadside

18. A wedding or family photo shoot
- 78   Crofton Beach Park
- 85   Cees and Miep Hof Park
- 86   Cherry Point Park
- 92   Keir Road

19. A high-point view
- 81A   Redcap Steps

20. Those who have walking difficulties
- 76   Crofton Community Seawalk— Town Centre
- 78   Crofton Beach Park
- 81   Maple Bay Beach
- 83   Hecate Park
- 86   Cherry Point Park
- 92   Keir Road

21. Viewing sunsets
- 77   Crofton Community Seawalk— South
- 78   Crofton Beach Park
- 83   Hecate Park
- 92   Keir Road

INDEX TO ENTRIES

THEO DOMBROWSKI is a retired teacher who was involved for many years in international education, primarily at Lester B. Pearson College of the Pacific outside Victoria, BC. A writer, photographer and artist, he has a Ph.D. in English and spent many years teaching literature and writing. He studied drawing and painting at the Banff School of Fine Arts and the University of Victoria Fine Arts Department and has worked as a professional artist. Theo is donating his proceeds from sales of this book to local environmental group Georgia Strait Alliance and to international humanitarian support group Médecins Sans Frontières/Doctors Without Borders (MSF). He lives in Nanoose Bay, BC.

ACKNOWLEDGEMENTS Thanks to Eileen Dombrowski, Bruce Whittington, Anne Dombrowski, Bill Cavers, Joan Cavers, Louise Kadar, Vickie Jackson and Charlotte Gann for their help in many ways, including providing materials or information.